A Fragmented Continent

Politics, Science, and the Environment
Peter M. Haas and Sheila Jasanoff, series editors

For a complete list of books published in this series, please see the back of the book.

A Fragmented Continent

Latin America and the Global Politics of Climate Change

Guy Edwards and J. Timmons Roberts
Foreword by Ricardo Lagos, President of Chile (2000–2006)
and UN Special Envoy for Climate Change (2008–2010)

The MIT Press
Cambridge, Massachusetts
London, England

© 2015 Massachusetts Institute of Technology

This book was set in Stone by the MIT Press. Printed and bound in the United States of America.

Library of Congress Cataloging-in-Publication Data is available.

ISBN 978-0-262-02980-3

10 9 8 7 6 5 4 3 2 1

Contents

Series Foreword

As our understanding of environmental threats deepens and broadens, it is increasingly clear that many environmental issues cannot be simply understood, analyzed, or acted on. The multifaceted relationships between human beings, social and political institutions, and the physical environment in which they are situated extend across disciplinary and geopolitical confines and cannot be analyzed or resolved in isolation.

The purpose of this series is to address the complex questions of how societies come to understand, confront, and cope with both the sources and manifestations of present and potential environmental threats. Works in the series focus on matters political, scientific, technical, social, or economic. They all look at the intertwined roles that politics, science, and technology play in the recognizing, framing, analyzing, and managing of environment-related contemporary issues, and they all share a manifest relevance to the increasingly difficult problems of identifying and forging environmentally sound public policy.

Peter M. Haas
Sheila Jasanoff

Foreword

Ricardo Lagos, former President of Chile (2000–2006) and UN Special Envoy for Climate Change (2008–2010)

Good government stands on three legs. To achieve prosperity, a country needs democracy, economic growth, and social equity. Take away one of these components, and the tripod topples over. Fortunately, Chile has made excellent progress over the last two decades. Democracy flourishes, and poverty and social inequality have been drastically reduced. The Organisation for Economic Co-operation and Development holds up Chile as a leading global example in poverty reduction. Across Latin America, similar progress has also been made.

Chile's success lies partially in its exports and sound fiscal management. It is the world's largest producer of copper, which accounts for around a third of government revenue. During the 2008 financial crisis and its aftermath, Chile managed to ride the waves of the global meltdown due to a countercyclical policy and a fiscal stabilization fund that generated long-term savings from the copper boom. In 2005, we began to use some of the savings from the levy on mining and created the Competitiveness and Innovation Fund to invest in innovation, human capital, and science and technology. These policies allowed us to save for a rainy day and manage the systemic risk posed by the 2008 financial crisis by investing in our future without counting on natural resources such as copper indefinitely.

However, the threat of climate change presents a major challenge to Chile and the nations of Latin America and the world. If we fail to act now and prepare for the likely impacts, the rug could be pulled out from under the already fragile tripod.

Like the rest of Latin America, Chile is vulnerable to the impacts of climate change. Mean annual temperatures are predicted to increase by 1 to 4 degrees Celsius by the end of this century. Glacial melt, sea-level rise, droughts and desertification, natural disasters, and air pollution in urban areas could adversely affect key sectors of our region's economies. The impacts of global warming and the measures required to avoid its worst effects may undermine the region's fragile political, economic, and social balance—by rolling back years of progress while costing billions of dollars in loss and damages.

Chile's current share of global greenhouse gas emissions is considerably less than 1 percent, and Latin America as whole represents roughly 9.5 percent of global emissions, which is fairly insignificant compared to China or the United States. However, as with some other countries in the region, Chile's per capita emissions are higher than the global average. With economic growth and energy demand rising rapidly, Chile's projected emissions under business as usual are set to increase substantially in the coming decades—unless the government takes substantial action. Chile cannot sit back and do nothing. The accumulated emissions of middle-income countries in Latin America and worldwide represent a significant percentage of global emissions, and our contributions to global climate change cannot be ignored.

Latin American nations have an excellent opportunity to prove that prosperity and actions to mitigate climate change are not mutually exclusive. Rather, the right domestic policies and a strong global climate regime can help us prosper without exacerbating global warming. Latin America can show how countries can benefit from a low-carbon economy, reduce climate risks, and build long-term prosperity. One important indicator of progress will be whether governments can simultaneously increase per capita income and human-development indicators while reducing per capita carbon emissions.

Tackling climate change is also an imperative for the elimination of poverty and the reduction of inequality. We know that burying our heads in the sand and clinging to a business-as-usual approach through high-carbon growth will be a mirage that does not provide long-term prosperity or security. The only way to keep global average temperatures below the 2 degrees Celsius limit agreed to by the world's nations in Copenhagen in 2009 is a dramatic and rapid transition to low-carbon, resource-efficient growth. All countries—big and small—have a role to play based on their capacity to act.

Political leaders are aware that making difficult tradeoffs is an unavoidable and unenviable part of governing. Climate change is no different. In Chile, we are faced with grave energy shortages that will be exacerbated by spiraling demand. Hydropower was one possible option in the Patagonian region, but it was rejected following a strong campaign by Chilean environmental groups. To fill this void, the government is looking at other options, including attempts to boost energy efficiency and renewable energy with the aim of covering 20 percent of electricity with renewables such as solar and wind by 2025. Following substantial investments, Chile could meet this target by 2025 if not before.

A Fragmented Continent is an attempt to get to the heart of this wicked problem in Latin America, which may define the region's development prospects this century. Since the birth of the United Nations Framework Convention on Climate Change (UNFCCC) in 1992 in Rio de Janeiro, Latin American nations have witnessed major transformations in how governments perceive the climate issue. Initially, Latin American countries treated climate change as an external problem of the wealthy nations for which we held no responsibility. Aside from the unique case of Brazil, which hosted the Earth Summit in 1992 and contains the great Amazon rainforests, most nations were focusing on establishing democratic institutions and dealing with the latest financial crisis rather than on climate change. However, today, governments across Latin America are more conscious of the issue and better prepared. Most of them actively and constructively participate in the United Nations climate change negotiations. It is no coincidence that Christiana Figueres, the UNFCCC's current executive secretary, is from Costa Rica, a nation aiming to become carbon neutral by 2021. Across the region, most countries now have a range of different government institutions, strategies and policies committed to finding solutions.

Latin America represents a microcosm for the challenges facing the international climate change talks. We may be unified in acknowledging the severity of the issue but the divisions in our region's climate postures are shaped by the diversity of our countries and their economies, the disparities in annual emissions and vulnerability, ideology, competing foreign policy goals, and memberships in various regional and international fora. Our diversity on climate change may be a fact of life, but this does not mean progress is unachievable.

In fact, the opposite may be the case. The excellent leadership of the Mexican presidency at the UN climate talks in Cancun in 2010 and the strong Latin American support of that effort suggest increasing pragmatism by regional governments. Political will and effective climate diplomacy can be the vital ingredient needed to ensure the successful outcome of a contentious negotiation. This pragmatic approach is best demonstrated by those who are leading this endeavor. In 2008, at the Fourteenth Conference of the Parties (COP14) to the UNFCCC, Peru became the first developing country to offer a voluntary emissions-reduction target by reducing the net rate of deforestation of primary forests to zero by 2021. Brazil planned to curb Amazon deforestation by 80 percent by 2020, and in 2012, Mexico established a General Law on Climate Change, which includes targets to reduce greenhouse gas emissions by 30 percent by 2020, below a business-as-usual scenario. Peru's excellent effort to secure a new draft agreement on climate change at the UN climate negotiations in Lima in 2014 was a fitting example of how our region can be part of the solution.

In this multipolar world, our region is a staunch supporter of the UN and multilateralism. For middle-income countries, an international rules-based system is crucial to protect our sovereignty and ensure our best chance at dealing with international challenges such as climate change. This multi-polarity also presents new opportunities for small and medium-size countries to exercise their own diplomatic clout.

In April 2014, I chaired a Brown University conference on Latin American leadership on climate change and was joined by my friend and former president of Mexico, Felipe Calderón. We spoke about the essential role of presidential leadership in addressing climate change. We were joined by UNFCCC head Christiana Figueres; Manuel Pulgar-Vidal, minister of the environment of Peru and COP20 president; Luis Alfonso de Alba, formerly Mexican special representative for climate change, and others.

The conference paid special attention to the Independent Association of Latin American and Caribbean States (AILAC), which is made up of Chile, Peru, Colombia, Paraguay, Panama, Guatemala, and Costa Rica and is offering a new way forward at the UN climate negotiations. AILAC's role is especially important when considering the ongoing dispute between the global North and South in the negotiations, which has been a major sticking point for years. AILAC emphasizes the importance of the principle of "common but differentiated responsibilities and respective capabilities," yet it offers a flexible interpretation that it believes is required to encourage greater climate action by all countries rather than perpetuate a race to the bottom. We need to move beyond the finger pointing and the unhelpful North versus South approach to make progress in the negotiations. Latin American countries can be a linchpin for bridging the divide. AILAC members are designing emission-reduction offers as part of their national contributions to the 2015 climate agreement and are willing to make these offers legally binding as a demonstration of their commitment.

In May 2014, I visited Lima, Peru, to participate in a meeting of the Brazil-Chile Initiative. The initiative is an attempt to improve dialogue and build trust between Latin American and Caribbean countries on climate change to strengthen the region´s contribution to the UN climate negotiations. This timely diplomatic initiative led to the first-ever joint statement of the Community of Latin American and Caribbean States (CELAC), made by Costa Rica on behalf of the community at the Lima climate change talks last year.

In this groundbreaking book, Guy Edwards and J. Timmons Roberts provide a balanced picture of how Latin American countries have begun to play a major role at the UN climate change negotiations while also offering potential ways to tackle the problem back home. However, the authors question whether the impressive rhetoric that leaders espouse at international summits is met with credible domestic action. Governments should avoid seeing combating climate change and bolstering economic growth as contradictory goals. To ensure prosperity, they do not need to dismantle existing environmental legislation, weaken incipient climate policies, or favor fossil fuels over clean energy sources. The recent approval of a carbon tax in Chile suggests that politicians increasingly understand this.

Edwards and Roberts examine Latin American countries' participation at the UN climate change negotiations and address three of the principal Latin American groups of countries that often adopt distinctive and competing but also at times overlapping positions. They also look at questions of economic development, trade, the role of civil society and changing relations with the United States, Europe, and China. The authors present an argument that Latin America might hold some of the keys to resolving this seemingly intractable problem. However, the challenges that this leadership faces at the global and national levels are not ignored.

Despite the economic slowdown facing a number of countries in our region caused by a decelerating Chinese economy and lower commodity prices, Latin America exhibits a greater willingness and sense of responsibility to act on global warming. As we approach the Paris climate summit in December 2015, Latin American nations can play an invaluable role in securing a fair, equitable, and ambitious new global agreement. Latin American leaders can help set their countries—and the wider world—on a new course, giving rise to low-emission, prosperous, inclusive, and resilient societies. Edwards and Roberts soberly back this idea while addressing some of the obstacles that need to be overcome along the way. For this pivotal year and beyond, *A Fragmented Continent* provides insights to make sense of this complex issue in our often misunderstood region.

Preface and Acknowledgments

Very little scholarly literature covers the politics of climate change and Latin America. This is despite the fact that the region is a bellwether for how humanity will achieve economic growth and human development while staying within the limits of the planet's capacity. Without any explicit policies on climate change, some Latin American countries have emerged as among the few societies that have achieved high levels of human development (as measured by life expectancy and literacy, for example) while emitting low levels of greenhouse gases.

In fact, global diplomatic efforts to address the vexing issue of climate change began in 1992 in Latin America at the UN Earth Summit in Rio de Janeiro. Yet for nearly the next two decades, the region underperformed on the issue of climate change. At the 2010 UN climate talks in Cancun, Mexico (after the near meltdown of negotiations in Copenhagen in 2009), adept Mexican diplomacy resuscitated climate multilateralism. The 2014 round of negotiations concluded in Lima, Peru, and in December 2014, the Twentieth Conference of the Parties (COP20) gave the region another year in the spotlight. Although the results of the Lima COP were seen as modest, the Peruvian presidency of COP20 has been credited with performing the difficult diplomatic feat of setting the negotiations on a more constructive path for the final round of negotiations in 2015.

For decades now, academic think tanks and governments have acted as though high-speed economic growth would automatically solve the ills of developing nations. Years after the Earth Summit, the environmental time bombs that globalization and development are creating are still being widely ignored by politicians, planners and business leaders.

But something is shifting. There is growing concern among Latin American nations that climate change presents a fundamental risk to any development progress that has been achieved. Leading organizations in Latin America—such as the Inter-American Development Bank and the United Nations Economic Commission for Latin America and the Caribbean—have been calculating the economic impacts of unchecked climate change, and the results are sobering. If global emissions are not reduced and adaptation policies adopted, Latin America is at risk of losing billions of dollars in growth and facing the loss of decades of development gains.

Latin America and the Caribbean account for roughly 9.5 percent of global greenhouse gas emissions, with most of these emissions coming from deforestation. Recently, deforestation rates have fallen steeply, especially in Brazil. But sustained economic growth is driving an increase in Latin America's emissions. As the region grows and as its middle class expands, the ability to keep its emissions down presents a thorny challenge.

Simultaneously, there is increasing awareness that Latin America is a pioneer in low carbon development and has models that might be emulated elsewhere, including Brazil's success with reducing deforestation and biofuels; sustainable urban transport in Brazil, Colombia, and Mexico; forestry protection in Ecuador; and several nations with low-carbon electricity grids.

Latin American countries have recently emerged as leading voices and sources of innovation for possible paths forward in mitigating climate change and for breaking the impasse at the UN climate change negotiations. Several Latin American countries have taken important steps at home and put forward voluntary emission-reduction pledges to the UN climate negotiations. In 2008, Peru was the first developing country to announce a voluntary emission-reduction pledge, offering to reduce the net deforestation of primary forests to zero by 2021. Costa Rica pledged to become carbon neutral by 2021. Brazil has established a national emission-reduction target of roughly 36 percent below its projected emissions by 2020, largely based on reducing deforestation rates. Having drastically improved the protection of its Amazonian forests, Brazil is ahead of schedule to meet that goal. Mexico passed a climate change law in 2012, with targets to reduce greenhouse gas emissions by 30 percent by 2020 and 50 percent by 2050. Most countries now have national climate change strategies, clean energy plans, and even legislation to reduce emissions. But there are worrying examples that demonstrate both the difficulties in implementing these climate policies and the fact that Latin American governments (like all others around the world) have competing priorities that can result in climate policies being jettisoned, undermined, or simply ignored.

A Fragmented Continent brings together information about climate science and the region's political, economic, and social contexts. It attempts to explain how Latin America's countries are or are not dealing with climate change. Worldviews and material interests of nations shape societal responses to climate change. Competing visions of what roles governments should play and whether markets should be entirely free of tariffs and interventions have pitted leftist governments against centrist and conservative market liberals and free traders. The book draws on political economy, international relations, sociology, and geography to understand the region's efforts on climate change at the local, national, regional, and international levels. This kind of multidisciplinary approach is needed to understand a complex puzzle: How did some countries of this nearly neglected region come to be potential models for workable solutions on climate change and influence the United Nations climate change negotiations?

This book project has been seven years in the making. The authors met in September 2008, when Timmons Roberts visited the Overseas Development Institute (ODI) in London for the launch of his coauthored book *Greening Aid? Understanding the Environmental Impact of Development Assistance* (Oxford, 2008, with Robert L. Hicks, Bradley C. Parks, and Michael J. Tierney). Guy Edwards was a research assistant at ODI and had read Roberts's earlier coauthored book on Latin America and the environment, *Trouble in Paradise: Globalization and Environmental Crises in Latin America* (Routledge, 2003, with Nikki Thanos). This encounter led Roberts to hire Edwards as a research fellow at Brown University, and they began an ongoing research project on the politics of climate change in Latin America in Roberts's Climate and Development Lab. The seven year project's central aim has been to better understand the politics of climate change in Latin America.

Later in 2008, Edwards managed the Huaorani Ecolodge in the Ecuadorian Amazon and built a website on Latin America and climate change, Latino Cambio. A speech by James Painter, formerly of the BBC, pointed out the dearth of Latin American media coverage on climate change. Outside the corridors of the UN negotiations, the debate on climate change in Latin America was relatively new. There was a lack of quality information available on the Internet, even though coverage had been increasing in the region, the numbers of regional users of the Internet and social media tools were growing, and many Latin American citizens were concerned about climate change.

Edwards founded LatinoCambio.com, a website devoted to climate issues in the region, We later joined up with the Fundación Futuro Latinoamericano in Ecuador and the executive secretariat of the Latin American Platform on Climate, which consists of twenty civil society organizations from nine countries across the region and promotes dialogue on climate change in Latin America. In partnership with the Platform on Climate, we cofounded IntercambioClimático.com, Latin America's first multilingual website on climate change, which we launched in 2010. With thousands of monthly visitors, IntercambioClimático occupies a key space in the region for debating and sharing information and knowledge on climate change.

An essential part of our work takes place each year at the annual negotiations of the UN climate change negotiations. Roberts attended the Tenth Conference of the Parties (COP10) in Buenos Aires in 2003; Edwards and Roberts have attended many UN climate conferences together, beginning with the Cancun 2010 talks and continuing with the Durban, Doha, Warsaw, and Lima talks, the period on which this book focuses. At these conferences, we have met with Latin American country negotiators and civil society representatives, and teams of our students have conducted research before and at the negotiations.

We have attended some highly relevant events in the region. In October 2012, Edwards participated in a regional forum organized by the Latin American Platform on Climate in Lima to debate the importance of public policies on climate change in Latin America. At the meeting, a hard reality was displayed as incipient climate policies encountered the imperative of economic growth and entrenched discourses of unsustainable development. In January 2013, Roberts attended an event on climate change and public finances in Mexico City that was cohosted by the United Nations Economic Commission for Latin America and the Caribbean (ECLAC) and was attended by Latin American government experts. In May 2013, Roberts also traveled to Brazil to give talks at the Federal University of Fluminense in Niteroi and at the State University of Rio de Janeiro and to conduct interviews in Brasília. At the COP20 in Lima, we coorganized an official side event with the think tank Nivela and the Natural Resources Defense Council about Latin American national and international climate policies, bringing together twelve experts from civil society and government from across Latin America.

In 2011, 2012, and 2014, we organized three conferences at Brown University on Latin America and climate change to learn directly from the region's experts and political actors and to get their input while we developed our thinking. These workshops were organized with the former Chilean president, Ricardo Lagos, previously a professor at large at the Watson Institute for International and Public Affairs at Brown, which hosted the events. The workshops allowed us to conduct interviews and have informal conversations with Felipe Calderón, former president of Mexico (who pushed for that country's initiatives on climate change and led the 2014 New Climate Economy report); Christiana Figueres, executive secretary of the UNFCCC; Manuel Pulgar-Vidal, Peru's minister of the environment and president of the 2014 UN negotiations; Marina Silva, former Brazilian minister of the environment; Luis Alfonso de Alba, former Mexican special representative for climate change; and various other experts we acknowledge below. These events were made possible by generous support from Brown University's Watson Institute for International and Public Affairs, Office of International Affairs, Institute at Brown for the Environment and Society, and the Office of President Christina Paxson.

Ongoing engagement with Latin American universities, civil societies, and governments has provided many opportunities that shaped the rationale behind this book. Working beside our Latin American partners has provided us with extraordinary access to those working on climate change. We do not just write about the leading characters in this book, we have been fortunate enough to get to know them and work with many of them to advance and understand the region's efforts on climate change. We have conducted over sixty formal and informal interviews with negotiators from nearly every Latin American nation and many of its leading civil society groups. Our method could be summed up as participant observation or participatory action research: we built the opinions that shaped this book by researching and writing articles and papers encouraging action in the region, attending COPs and attempting to make strategic interventions with quality policy research, organizing conferences, conducting interviews, and developing connections across the region. So although we are outsiders who are looking in on the region, we attempt to offer new perspectives on the politics of climate change in Latin America based on significant interactions with the people and institutions of the region.

At Brown University, we would like to thank President Christina Paxson, Richard Snyder, Michael Kennedy, Matthew Gutmann, Peter Andreas, Carolyn Dean, Rick Locke, Bonnie Horta, Dov Sax, Amanda Lynch, Kate

Goldman, Patti Caton, Jeanne Loewenstein, Leah VanWey, Jeanne Medeiros, Dave Ciplet, Laura Sadovnikoff, Susan Hirsh, Anne Noyes and the members of Brown's Climate and Development Lab whose work contributed to this project: Keith Madden, Adam Kotin, Suzy Mage, Olivia Santiago, Arielle Balbus, Spencer Fields, Spencer Lawrence, Graciela Kincaid, Michelle Levinson, Alex Durand, Olivia Santiago, Bryna Cofrin-Shaw, Cecila Pineda, Linlang He, Brianna Craft, Michael Murphy, Paola Eisner, Ximena Carranza, Jeff Baum, Sophie Purdom, Zihao Jiang, Camila Bustos, Cassidy Bennett, Allison Reilly, Alison Kirsch, Maris Jones, Marguerite Suozzo-Gole, and Tory Hoffmeister.

We would like to thank the team at the MIT Press who helped enormously with the production and editing of the manuscript including Beth Clevenger, Clay Morgan, Miranda Martin, Rosemary Winfield, Deborah Cantor-Adams, and Susan Clark.

Guy would like to thank Victoria Edwards, Geoffrey Edwards, Chloe Edwards and Charlie Edwards for their support and encouragement. Timmons would like to thank Holly Flood, and Phoebe and Quinn Roberts and Gann and Jim Roberts for all their support and patience over these years.

We are indebted and very grateful to our colleagues, friends, and other contacts who generously gave us much of their time: Marcela Jaramillo, Pablo Larco, Gilberto Arias, Ramiro Fernández, Mónica Araya, José Alberto Garibaldi, Andrew Hurrell, Laurence Allan, Graham Woodgate, Jakob Skovgaard, Antonio Hill, Rebecca Hollender, Anthony Bebbington, Alain Muñoz, Daniel Ryan, Enrique Maurtua, Carlos Henrique Fioravanti, Sarah Vellozzi, Milo Wallace, Virgilio Viana, Eduardo Viola, Ana Flavia Barros, Selene Herculano, Carlos Milani, João Paulo Gomes, José Miguez, Carlos Henrique Tome, Cristovam Buarque, Marcio Pontual, Alba Simon, Yolanda Kakabadse, Carola Borja, Tarsicio Granizo, Pippa Heylings, Mónica Andrade, Marianela Curi, Isabel Cavelier, Paula Caballero, Andrea García, Manuel Rodríguez Becerra, Mariana Castillo, Andrés Flores, Fernando Tudela, Sandra Guzmán, Hughie Wallace, Luis Miguel Galindo, Jose Luis Samaniego, Rodolfo Godínez, Alejando Rivera, Gerardo Honty, Eduardo Gudynas, Alicia Villamizar, María del Pilar García-Guadilla, Waldemar Coutts, Andrés Pirazzoli, Andrea Rudnick, John Ashton, Jeremy Hobbs, Liz Gallagher, Carlos Rittl, Úrsula Oswald Spring, Hans Günter Brauch, David Waskow, Mónica López, Walter Vergara, James Wallace, Luis Miguel Galindo, Amal-Lee Amin, Claire Langley, Erica Downs, Harold Trinkunas, Nathan Hultman, Kathryn Hochstetler,

Jaime Dipple, Kevin P. Gallagher, David Barkin, Gabriela Pérez, Ana Toni, Natalie Unterstell, Fernando Farías, Giovanna Valverde, Manfred Kopper, Daniel Ortega, Carolina Zambrano, Silvia Garza Galván, Gabriela Niño, Pedro Gamio, José Luis Capella, David King, Carol Franco, Luis Alfonso de Alba, Alejandro Rivera, Manuel Pulgar-Vidal, Vanessa Morales, Jorge Voto-Bernales, Osver Polo, Lisa Friedman, Christiana Figueres, Leo Peskett, José Carlos Orihuela, María Laura Rojas, Juan Pablo Bonilla, Dan Reifsnyder, and Enrique Mendizabal. There are many others, and we thank them as well. Any errors remain our own.

1 Paradoxes of a Neglected Region

The New Engineers of Consensus

The brilliant sun and sparkling white sand of Cancun, Mexico, belied the dismally low hopes of over eleven thousand climate change delegates who traveled from around the world in November 2010 to the Caribbean resort. This was the sixteenth year in a row that 194 countries were trying to advance the UN climate change negotiations. Following the chaos and acrimony at the previous year's talks in Copenhagen, the Sixteenth Conference of the Parties (COP16) in Cancun sought to pick up the pieces and restart the effort to negotiate a new global agreement on climate change.

Before the Cancun meetings, Nigel Purvis from the German Marshall Fund of the United States lamented that "global climate talks have begun to resemble a bad soap opera—they seem to never end, yet never really change and at times bear little resemblance to reality."[1] Many saw the talks as desperately needing to rescue the viability of the international community's approach to resolving global warming. Was the UN able to address one of humanity's greatest threats?

For two weeks, among the rumbling air conditioners of the hotels lining the strip of shimmering sand, the efforts of the host nation Mexico seemed unable to move multilateralism forward. But as president of the negotiations for the year, Mexico was committed to keeping the UN climate talks alive by bridging the fractious negotiating blocs and resuscitating the process. On the final day, photographers scrambled to the western windows of the conference center to capture one of the most poignant images of the meeting—an orange and red sun setting behind a lone wind turbine.

On the final night and to nearly everyone's surprise, a carefully crafted "Cancun Agreement" was pulled together under the leadership of two remarkable Latin American women. Costa Rican Christiana Figueres, executive secretary of the UNFCCC, proclaimed the conference a "success," stating that "Cancun has done its job. The beacon of hope has been reignited and faith in the multilateral climate change process to deliver results has been restored."[2] Patricia Espinosa, former Mexican secretary of foreign affairs and president of the COP16, called the conference a "victory for multilateralism."

The praise was nearly universal. The Brazilian minister for the environment, Izabella Teixeira, called the meeting a success, saying that the Mexicans "had been absolutely spectacular in their running of the conversations."[3] Out of 194 countries participating, Bolivia was the only country to oppose the final agreement, which it regarded as woefully inadequate to stem global warming. Many countries expressed frustration about the weak outcome and the overruling of Bolivia but went along with the nearly unanimous agreement to keep the multilateral process alive.

Although there are broadly divergent opinions about the substantive meaning of what was decided in Cancun and plenty of reasons to support Bolivia's claim that it was inadequate in terms of trying to solve the problem of climate change, everyone agreed that the Mexican diplomatic team emerged as the new engineers of consensus on the issue.[4] Christiana Figueres, Patricia Espinosa, and the diplomatic team led by the Mexican ambassador Luis Alfonso de Alba's adept management of complex and delicate negotiations raised the prospect of Latin America emerging as a significant, potentially game-changing player in the UN climate change negotiations.[5]

The region is not a significant source of global greenhouse gas emissions and real leadership on climate change will have to be exerted by those countries with a central position in the global carbon cycle (China, the EU and the United States) and the willingness and ability to decarbonize the global economy.[6] Some Latin American countries, such as Brazil and Mexico, could exert coleadership functions as major emitters and representatives of large middle-income countries. Other nations, such as Costa Rica, Colombia and Chile, could be considered coleaders due to their pathbreaking efforts to reduce their own emissions through domestic policies and their strong support of an internationally ambitious agreement on climate.[7]

A handful of Latin American countries such as Brazil, Costa Rica, Mexico and Peru have been ambitious in their pledges of emissions reductions. Their ability to deliver on those pledges is uncertain, and what countries are saying internationally often appears detached from the reality at home. Even more revolutionary, several nations pledged to give climate-assistance finance to the Green Climate Fund in late 2014. Colombia, Mexico, Panama, and Peru stepped away from the doctrine that this problem was created by the global North and should be dealt with solely by the historically rich countries. Although aware of historical responsibilities for the problem, these countries have argued that all countries need to lend a hand to address a global crisis. These international and national efforts and discourses on climate change by countries in the region are not well documented or understood: elucidating them is a key goal of this book.

Latin America is a sharply fragmented region in many regards. Countries vary in proactiveness and contributions to the UN climate negotiations and in their policies and actions at home. Several countries are outliers by sharply reducing deforestation. Some Latin American nations have among the most efficient economies in the world in terms of how much human development they generate per unit of energy consumed and greenhouse gases emitted.[8] In some cases, Latin American countries are challenging the conventional wisdom that confronting climate change undermines economic growth, arguing instead that climate action provides an opportunity to leapfrog traditional development while delivering affordable and positive low-carbon, sustainable development.[9]

Another set of nations are pioneers in adapting to the impacts of climate change. Caribbean nations are among the world's most advanced in hurricane preparedness, others in South America are dealing with severe droughts and water-supply destabilization from the loss of mountain glaciers, and still others are pioneers in financing mechanisms to prevent future climate disasters. The piloting of these solutions put some Latin American cities and nations as examples to follow for other countries and regions in both the developing and industrialized worlds. Meanwhile, other countries in the region play an important role in promoting discourses of climate justice at the UN climate negotiations and offering unique proposals to counter global warming that are shaking up climate-development debates.

These efforts have received little serious discussion internationally and remain largely absent in the scholarly literature. This book explores a poorly understood but crucial dimension of global responses to climate change—the political economy and comparative national and international climate change politics of Latin America.

Our questions fall into three main groups. First, we take up questions about the roots of climate policies in Latin America and why the region and its fractious subgroups are such compelling cases. What are the roots of Latin American positions on climate change? What does climate change mean for Latin American countries' economies, societies, and foreign policies? What is it about Latin America that makes some of its nations willing to attempt to take bold action, and what will it take for other nations in the region to follow suit? How does that bold action manifest itself, and what forces are working against it? In short, what drives Latin American countries to act or not to act on climate change?

A second group of questions focuses on the negotiations. How did Latin American countries rise quickly from being largely unnoticed in the UN climate negotiations to positions of influence, and in some cases leadership? What in the positions or experiences of these nations explains their rise? Third, what can we learn from the region about the future of global climate politics and action? Finally, can any Latin American countries be considered coleaders on climate change, or is this a case of successful rhetoric with little realized action? This first chapter seeks to lay out the direction for our inquiry, beginning with a brief look at what is at stake for the region in terms of the grave impacts it faces from climate change.

An Acutely Vulnerable Region

Latin American leaders and citizens are increasingly voicing their concerns about the dire impacts of climate change. At the podium before the Cancun plenary hall, the former Guatemalan president, Álvaro Colom, beseeched the nations of the world:

How many deaths do we have to report? How many bridges have to be destroyed … and how many kilometers of roads ruined need to be reported before some parts of the [UN] Convention recognize that Guatemala is a developing country and highly vulnerable to the changes and variability of the climate?[10]

Presidents and foreign ministers have often highlighted the pressing nature of tackling climate change and the dramatic effects being felt across their countries and around the world. Climate change is now considered a problem that could determine the future development of the region.

The projected impacts that are set to intensify this century make for a somber tour of Latin America's future. These impacts include the potential collapse of the Caribbean coral biome, rising sea levels, intensification of weather patterns and storms leading to increased flooding and droughts, warming of the high Andean ecosystems, increased exposure to tropical diseases, and risk of dieback of the vast Amazon rainforest ecosystem.[11]

According to different climate models cited in the Intergovernmental Panel on Climate Change (IPCC), the projected mean warming for Latin America to the end of the century ranges from 1 to 6 degrees Celsius. This suggests sharp uncertainties, but some patterns emerge in the different forecasts. Climate change impacts on biodiversity and forests will be severe. The replacement of tropical forest by savannas is expected to take place in eastern Amazonia and also central and southern Mexico and Central America.[12] The expected increases in sea-level rise and extreme climatic events are likely to ravage coastal areas. Adverse impacts would be observed in mangroves, in the availability of drinking water on the Pacific coast and the Rio de la Plata estuary.

By the 2050s, 50 percent of agricultural lands will likely be subjected to desertification, and salinization is expected in some areas. But the picture in agriculture is likely to be mixed: overall, there may be increased soybean yields but decreases in rice yields, maize yields, and coffee production.[13] A report published by the Brazilian Panel on Climate Change in 2013 predicts that agricultural losses will be severe, with estimates that the Brazilian sector will suffer around US$3.1 billion a year in losses after 2020. Eduardo Assad, a researcher with Embrapa, the Brazilian Agricultural Research Corporation, and one of the report's authors, told the Inter Press Service News Agency that "we will have strong waves of heat and cold and losses in agricultural productivity."[14]

Glacial melt throughout the Andes is likely to affect water supplies across the subregion and take its toll on power production from hydroelectricity. Water shortages have serious consequences for millions of people. According to a study, glaciers in the tropical Andes have shrunk by 30 to 50 percent since the 1970s. The glaciers are retreating at their fastest rate in the past three hundred years, due to an average temperature rise of 0.7 degree Celsius from 1950 to 1994.[15] Colombia expects to lose all its glaciers this century, and Peru projects that glaciers lower than five thousand meters above sea level may disappear between 2015 and 2020.[16] In Peru, glacial retreat is likely to affect the availability of water for urban areas and the power sector, where there will be an estimated annual incremental cost ranging from $212 million to $1.5 billion for the generation of energy.[17]

Glacial retreat is projected to decrease the availability of water for human consumption, agriculture, and energy generation through hydropower. This renewable source of energy accounts for roughly 60 percent of the region's installed capacity and 70 percent of power generation.[18] Ironically, this renewable source of energy is threatened because of disappearing glaciers and drought, which in some cases has forced countries to look for alternative energy supplies such as oil- and gas-fired power plants.[19]

In 2009, during Ecuador's worst drought in decades, water levels at the Paute River Dam, the Andean nation's largest, were extremely low. The government was forced to declare a state of electrical emergency nationwide and implement daily rationing of electricity, which led to blackouts for hours at a time. Ecuador had little choice but to buy 700,000 barrels of diesel from Colombia and Venezuela to fuel its thermoelectric plants to provide electricity to an increasingly weary population.[20] Businesses, industry, and private homes suffered severe financial losses due to the blackouts.[21]

The potential risk of dieback of the Amazon rainforest ecosystem is of grave concern. The Amazon basin is a key component of the global carbon cycle, with old-growth rainforests representing a stock of approximately 120 billion tons of carbon dioxide in their biomass. Annually, these tropical forests, through respiration and photosynthesis, process approximately 18 billion tons of CO_2, which is more than double the rate of global fossil fuel emissions.[22] Disturbingly, major droughts in 2005 and 2010 in Brazil's Amazon region threaten to undermine its role as the planet's most important carbon sink, potentially turning it into a CO_2 source from forest fires and a source of methane emissions from rotting forests and drying soils. The carbon impact of the 2010 drought may exceed the 5 billion tons of CO_2 released following the 2005 event. This compares to the estimated 5.4 billion tons of CO_2 emitted through fossil fuel use in the United States in 2009.[23]

The small island developing states of the Caribbean are particularly threatened by rising sea levels and stronger hurricanes, both of which will disrupt their natural resource base and core economic activities, including tourism and agriculture.[24] Heat stress, malaria, dengue, cholera, and other water-borne diseases are areas of grave concern across the region.[25]

Latin America and the Caribbean have seen a recent increase in extreme climatic events and with it a rise in the number of people affected. Available data show that such disasters are increasing: a total of 2,555 events in the past forty years caused 512,481 fatalities and affected more than 232 million people.[26] The Caribbean recorded the highest death toll from natural disasters in the Western Hemisphere, highlighting it as an especially vulnerable area. Natural disasters in the Americas in the past decade are estimated to have cost more than US$446 billion.[27]

As Guatemala's former President Colom plaintively cried, Latin American leaders are linking the frequency and intensity of these natural disasters to climate change. In the wake of Tropical Depression 12E, which ravaged Central America in October 2011, the leaders of Belize, Costa Rica, El Salvador, Guatemala, Honduras, Nicaragua, and Panama met in El Salvador's international airport Comalapa for an extraordinary summit to evaluate the damage. The summit led to the signing of the Declaration of Comalapa, which urged industrialized countries to make significant reductions of greenhouse gases and recognize Central America as a region that is vulnerable to climate change.[28] In his speech at the COP17 in Durban, two months later, El Salvador's former minister of the environment, Herman Rosa Chávez, said,

Our climate system has been severely disrupted and many countries are paying a high and only growing price because of it.... The Tropical Depression 12E that struck El Salvador ... was the last in this terrible and destructive sequence. We experienced ... huge losses of infrastructure and agriculture.... We could not avoid the economic losses that totaled $840 million—4% of our GDP.[29]

The United Nations Economic Commission for Latin America and the Caribbean (ECLAC) and the Inter-American Development Bank (IDB) have published numerous studies on the economics of climate change in Bolivia, Central America, Chile, Mexico, Paraguay, Peru, and Mexico, each showing the grave costs the region faces if humanity does not address this issue urgently. In 2013, the IDB stated that damages in the region caused by the impacts associated with a rise of two degrees Celsius over preindustrial temperatures will likely approach US$100 billion a year by 2050.[30] In the Caribbean, natural hazards already represent a significant risk to inhabitants and economies of the region. Annual expected losses from wind, storm surges, and inland flooding amount to up to 6 percent of gross domestic product in some countries. Climate change has the potential to exacerbate these risks and could increase expected loss by 1 to 3 percent of GDP by 2030.[31]

The United Nations Development Program (UNDP) said in 2007 that climate change presents a serious challenge to hard-won development gains, is deepening the divide between rich and poor across Latin America, and threatens to halt and then reverse advances in health and education for the most vulnerable.[32] Researchers say climate change threatens the progress made in recent decades in development and in the achievement of the Millennium Development Goals.[33] For Latin American leaders and citizens, climate change is no longer considered a distant problem in the future but an existential threat today.

A Low-Carbon Continent?

It is unfair that Latin American countries—which are responsible for a minor percentage of historical greenhouse gas emissions—are far more vulnerable to climate impacts than those countries that have reaped the benefits of cheap fossil fuels for their development. Despite being responsible for only around 9.5 percent of global emissions, Latin American countries still need to support efforts to reduce their emissions in order to stabilize the earth's climate. Given the level of risk and the global nature of the problem, the region does not have a free pass to avoid taking on emission cuts.

Latin America has been an important innovator in developing new economic measures that matter for addressing climate change. These include policies to improve macroeconomic stability and undertake major programs of economic reform, investments in social welfare and social protections, and new approaches to compensating those providing environmental goods and services.[34] Flagship programs such as Brazil's Bolsa Familia, Chile's Solidario, and Mexico's Oportunidades have attracted international attention, while the Bolivian and Ecuadorian models of development centered around Buen Vivir (the good life) have also received growing attention.[35] Innovative social protection and poverty-reduction programs have now been implemented across the region, reaching nearly 100 million people.[36] The Latin American and Caribbean middle class is projected to grow to 42 percent of the population by 2030. However, a sense of insecurity pervades many within this new class who are increasingly vocal about threats to their standard of living, leading to an increase in political protests in some countries.[37] Levels of poverty may have been reduced across the region, but Latin America remains the most unequal region in the world.[38] With expanding middle classes come middle-class emissions, so the region's emissions are expected to increase considerably.

Further, climate impacts risk reversing some of these important social and economic gains and, in some cases, returning those in the middle class to poverty. The recent economic slowdown in Latin America follows a ten-year boom in economic growth across the region, which also presents challenges for policymakers. The puzzle is to increase the region's per capita income without increasing it emissions. In this section, we briefly outline the state of Latin America's emissions from different sectors and lay out some possible future scenarios, based on the region's enormous endowment of energy reserves and vast agricultural potential. Although the region overall has a relatively low-carbon economy to begin with (and has achieved major advances in reducing emissions from deforestation), emissions from power generation, transport, and agriculture could push the region's emissions upward quickly.

Latin America and the Caribbean account for approximately 9 percent of the world's total population, roughly 9 percent of global GDP,[39] and 9.5 percent of global greenhouse gas emissions. There is a wide range of emissions across Latin America in per capita terms. Emissions per capita fall in widely different groups. The high group produces over ten tons of CO_2 per capita (Argentina, Bolivia, Venezuela, and some Caribbean nations), the middle group produces around five to seven tons (Brazil, Chile, Honduras, Mexico, Panama, and Peru), and the lowest countries produce under three tons (Costa Rica, the Dominican Republic, El Salvador, and Haiti).[40] The region is the second-lowest total emitter in the world after Africa, placing it above the low-income countries and below the high-income countries.[41]

The region has historically made a substantial contribution to keeping down levels of emissions. The region is home to about one-third of the world's forest biomass and two-thirds of the biomass existing in tropical forests.[42] Latin America has also achieved a large part of its development with cleaner sources of power. Due to its low use of coal-fired power plants and its high use of hydroelectricity, the region's power sector generates 40 percent fewer CO_2 emissions per unit of energy than the world as a whole and 74 percent fewer than China and India.[43] Latin America is therefore described as an outlier in terms of its emissions. In contrast to the global picture, most of the emissions in the region are generated not from energy use but from land use, land-use change, and forestry (LULUCF) and agriculture. In 2005, the breakdown of total greenhouse emissions in the region consisted of 47 percent from LULUCF and 20 percent from agriculture.[44]

This ratio is shifting in important ways, but data and analysis are lagging the state of current trends as deforestation drops and the burning of fossil fuel rises (table 1.1).

Although the region's emissions from energy production have been rising substantially in the past two decades, per capita energy emissions were about 5.5 tons of CO_2 equivalent per person in 2011, well below the world average. With relatively large areas to traverse, transportation creates a greater proportion of energy emissions in Latin America than globally.[45] There are some important projects in the region, but it still has only small shares of geothermal, solar, and wind power.[46]

Latin America is an important player on the world fossil fuel energy map, with potentially serious consequences for global carbon emissions. The region has the second largest reserves of oil outside of the Middle East. Latin American governments are interested in opening up unconventional deposits that previously were deemed too expensive or difficult to exploit. Brazil's offshore presalt (*pré-sal*) layer oil discoveries have the potential to establish

Table 1.1
Emissions of greenhouse gases in Latin America and case study nations, with and without land-use emissions: Total emissions and emissions per capita

Country	Total greenhouse gas emissions (MtCO$_2$e)		Greenhouse emissions per capita (tCO$_2$e per capita)	
	Excluding land-use change and forestry per capita	Including land-use change and forestry	Excluding land-use change and forestry	Including land-use change and forestry
Latin America	3311	4207	5.5	7.0
Brazil	1131	1419	5.7	7.2
Mexico	699	723	5.9	6.1
Venezuela	267	381	9.1	12.9
Peru	83	154	2.8	5.2
Bolivia	62	150	6.0	14.5
Ecuador	53	136	3.5	8.9
Costa Rica	15	7	3.1	1.5

Source: World Resources Institute (WRI), Climate Analysis Indicators Tool (CAIT) 2.0, © 2014; Food and Agriculture Organization of the United Nations Corporate Statistical Database (FAOSTAT), "Emissions—Land Use," http://faostat3.fao.org/faostat-gateway/go/to/browse/G2/*/E.

it as one of the world's largest oil producers. Argentina has one of the three largest reserves of shale gas in the world, and Mexico's reforms to its energy sector could see oil and gas production increase substantially. Venezuela sits atop the world's largest known oil reserves.[47]

Although much of these fossil fuels will be exported rather than used domestically, their exploitation nonetheless creates additional emissions that are pumped into the atmosphere. It remains an open question whether Latin America can keep its own emissions down, lead the world in transitioning to renewables, and continue to develop economically. New directions need to be taken. The executive secretary of the UNFCCC, Christiana Figueres, put it plainly:

If the opportunities for renewable energies are not taken advantage of and supported, the developing countries of the American continent will intensify their capacities for energy production based on fossil fuels as they quickly develop their infrastructure [and] seal the permanency of infrastructure with a high level of carbon emissions and the natural endowments of renewable energies would be wasted.[48]

Because most Latin American countries are still low-carbon economies that are based on hydropower, a unique challenge facing Latin America is not solely to decarbonize but also to achieve long-term prosperity without continuing to increase emissions. The region still offers a vital perspective on developing economies that want to avoid locking into growth models that render climate protection incompatible with development.[49] There appears to be a correlation between strong domestic climate change legislation and high international ambition at the UNFCCC.[50]

The region is a major supplier of food and other natural resources,[51] whose growth may also expand its carbon footprint. The IDB makes the case for why Latin America can be the next global breadbasket: the region has both a third of the world's freshwater resources and a third of global arable land. To feed the 9 billion global population expected by 2050, agricultural output needs to double from current production levels, but increasing farm exports creates new risks.[52] Greater production needs to be achieved even as climate change creates new challenges. Latin America has the second-largest remaining rain-fed crop-production potential area,[53] which is more immediately vulnerable to drought and other more intense weather events.[54] The problem is made yet more complex by the degradation of the region's natural resources and the growing competition for land and water.[55]

Agriculture, forestry, and land use (AFOLU) accounted for nearly two-thirds of all greenhouse gas emissions from Latin America's emissions in 2005[56] but was down to about 21 percent by 2011.[57] Although the causes driving deforestation are complex, the expansion of maize and soybean is linked to a decrease in forest area in Latin America from 1990 to 2006.[58] But this picture is changing, as is explored in more detail in chapter 3 on Brazil. In fact, the decrease in land-use emissions and improvements in energy efficiency caused total Latin American emissions per capita to fall from 10.4 tons in 1990 to 7 tons in 2011. This recent trend could be reversed by rising rates of deforestation or energy-related emissions. The region's per capita emissions from burning fossil fuels rose from 2.3 tons in 1990 to 2.8 tons in 2005 and 5.5 tons in 2011; according to some projections, they are likely to continue to increase.[59]

Brazil is currently the dominant source of the region's emissions followed by Mexico, Argentina, and Venezuela. Latin America is relevant globally in terms of greenhouse gas emissions only because of Brazil and Mexico. These nations are critical for achieving the global emissions reductions that are needed to avoid dangerous climate change, but all countries are required to play their part to reduce the risk of catastrophic change.[60]

Although land-use emissions have fallen, sustained economic growth is driving an increase in Latin America's energy emissions, particularly from power generation and transport. Reductions in land-use emissions will soon be overshadowed by increased emissions from agriculture, energy generation, and transport.[61] The International Energy Agency (IEA) predicts that Latin America's per capita energy-related emissions will grow by 10 percent between 2005 and 2015 and by 33 percent from 2005 to 2030. These projections are much lower than those made for other developing countries such as China and India.[62]

So the big picture is that Latin America's emissions from deforestation will likely continue to diminish and its energy-induced fossil fuel emissions will continue to increase, with the fastest growth expected from transport and power generation. Although Latin America's energy sector is the world's cleanest, economic growth and drought have increased electricity demand, placed a strain on existing hydroelectric dams due to changing rain patterns, and driven demand for a greater share of fossil fuels in the region's power matrix.[63] To satisfy rising demand for energy, more fossil fuels are being incorporated into the electricity generation mix, which is projected to grow nearly 5 percent annually over the coming decade.[64] Rapid urbanization and motorization rates are increasing transport-sector demand for fossil fuels. The substantial growth of food exports has driven higher emissions from the agricultural sector.[65] This presents political leaders with a difficult situation as the low-hanging fruit of emission reductions from reducing deforestation tapers off (see chapter 3). Tough decisions need to be made about how to avoid increases in emissions from energy, transport, and agriculture, which have a strong connection to economic growth and the expectations of the expanding middle class. Fossil fuel companies are also some of the largest enterprises in the world and wield their persuasive powers aggressively in national and state capitals around the region, both directly and through their local agents and interests.

Four Factors for Understanding Climate Politics in Latin America

We set out to explain the two-way relationship between global climate negotiations and Latin American nations' efforts at home to confront global warming. How do domestic climate change politics and policies influence Latin American countries' positions at the UN climate negotiations? How do international pressures and foreign policy goals influence national policies? Have Latin American countries adopted notable positions on climate change, and if so, why? When and how do national politics and the need to advance economic growth constrain both domestic and international policies on climate in Latin America?

The following chapters present a mixed picture of how some countries in the region have taken up ambitious positions or highly critical discourses at the UNFCCC but then have sometimes struggled or failed to back them up with action at home. Why has this been the case? Other countries, meanwhile, have taken up some aggressive climate policies at home but resisted international commitments for fear of losing sovereign control over their territories and economies. What has led them to do so?

This mixed picture raises questions about how much Latin American countries are changing because they perceive worsening physical climate impacts and shifting global governance on climate change. Can Latin American countries successfully confront climate change, given some of their past experiences with low-carbon development, or will the imperative of economic growth and the constraints of domestic and global political economy undermine that effort?

Development is a priority for the region and constrains and shapes national climate policy in different ways in different nations. Overlapping groups of Latin American countries are fragmented into eight different negotiating blocs at the UN climate talks, which is discussed in chapter 2. A common focus in our country case studies are the constraints imposed on them by domestic constituents (such as national business interests and political elites) and powerful global forces (such as markets and foreign powers that play geopolitics inside and outside the UN climate talks). Although some Latin American countries are important for global climate governance and can be regarded in some cases as agents for progressive policy, they are still strongly constrained by these outside and internal forces.

There has been a tendency to look at climate change politics predominantly from an international relations perspective, with a focus on explaining multilateral agreements based on the interests or ideational orientations of states as unitary actors. This is an important perspective, but too often authors do not open the "black box" of domestic politics that drive countries' positions at the negotiations.[66] A focus on how Latin American countries act at the UNFCCC provides vital insights into how the region engages with the international climate change regime, but country negotiation teams do not operate in a UN bubble, cut off from their national institutional and social dynamics. They operate under strict instructions from their capitals and are in constant contact with their ministers and occasionally presidents before, during, and after the talks.

We take a political economy approach, which focuses on the comparative politics of climate change in Latin America. As Thomas Tanner and Jeremy Allouche point out, a political economy approach helps to take apart technocentric and managerial approaches to tackling climate change by looking at these processes in apolitical terms.[67] The diverse range of ideological worldviews—for example, in Latin America between the leftist countries of the Bolivarian Alliance for the Peoples of Our America (ALBA, Alianza Bolivariana para los Pueblos de Nuestra América) and the more pro-market countries of the Independent Association of Latin America and the Caribbean (AILAC, Asociación Independiente de América Latina y el Caribe)— also influence responses to climate change. Some AILAC voices are calling for market-based approaches to drive action on climate change, while most ALBA nations and some civil society organizations reject outright carbon trading as part of a commodification of environmental services and instead call for the rights of Mother Earth to be respected.[68] These starkly different approaches to the current reality are based in nations' colonial and neocolonial history—which we have argued elsewhere are critical in preshaping climate debates.[69] Latin America was violently brought into the global economy in the role of dependent supplier of natural resources and cheap labor, much of its population enslaved and oppressed through evolving systems of racism and oppression based on economic class, race, and ethnicity.[70]

In a global study, Christopher Rootes, Anthony Zito, and John Barry remark on the considerable cross-national variations in the adoption and implementation of climate change policies.[71] They explain those variations by pointing to four factors that often interact with one another—international relations, economic structures, national cultures, and domestic political competition. Focusing on these key factors is a useful approach to understanding climate politics in Latin American countries, but a broader set of causal factors is at work, as we lay out shortly in this section. Subnational actors may be significant in driving national positions:[72] for example, grassroots activism from outside the formal political process has sometimes been decisive in sharpening the focus of formal political actors, increasing their willingness to act internationally on climate change. That is, strategic protestors plus a sympathetic media can quickly raise the salience of environmental issues, as we will see especially in the cases of Bolivia and Ecuador. In some other cases, the lack of a strong environmental or indigenous social movement, and the inability of government to pay heed to these movements, has left national positions focused nearly entirely on economic development. Some of the key actors driving climate change action or inaction are coalitions at the global level, international institutions, national political networks, political parties, and social movement organizations.[73] We utilize and build on this literature to situate Latin American countries' engagement at the UNFCCC and their national climate efforts in a broader context by examining the role of specific structural trends, actors, ideas, and institutions.

Throughout the book, we attempt to explain the relationship between Latin America and climate change issues through the following four factors—nature, development, foreign policy, and civil society. Nature refers to natural resources and differing vulnerability to climate impacts in the region as an incentive for nations to take action on climate change. Development refers to the unrelenting pressure on government officials to generate economic growth and jobs under competing models of how to improve society. Until recently, jobs were associated almost exclusively with environmentally destructive actions, such as mining and the expansion of polluting factories. Foreign policy refers to how issues of regional integration, international alliances, and trade have proven formative in the climate change postures and coalitions of Latin American countries. In some cases, external influences have had dramatic impacts on national postures on climate. There are cases of action being taken on climate and of resistance to action. Finally, civil society refers to the major gap between climate concern and actual action taken by society on the issue. Some segments of Latin American civil society have focused on the UN climate change negotiations but have made somewhat less effort on climate change as an issue of economic development at the national level. Chapters 3 to 5 consider the cases of Brazil, the left-wing countries in the ALBA group, and the AILAC group of more open-trade countries. Although these case studies stand alone as compelling examples of the complexity of the global climate change politics in Latin America, focusing on these four factors allow us to connect and make sense of these crucial case studies, and each requires an explanation.

Nature: Natural Resources and Vulnerability to Climate Impacts

Latin America has a stunning endowment of natural resources that have complex and foundational relationships with its economic growth and development, its trade and foreign policy, and ultimately the role of civil society. Latin America's history has been shaped by the extraction of these natural resources for export to colonial and neocolonial powers, for internal consumption, and increasingly for export to world markets, including China.[74] There are also domestic drivers such as a lack of skills and low productivity that put pressure on its ecosystems. Innovation and diversification of economies lag, extending reliance on exploiting natural resources to bring in tax revenue and secure growth. Natural resource dependence creates contradictory pressures on Latin American states in terms of climate change policy. The focus on delivering projects and benefits to potential voters often drives short-term thinking about exploiting natural resources and deters setting and meeting strong climate targets. But dependence on natural resources, including the production of agricultural and forest products for export, increases the region's vulnerability to climate impacts, which has created some climate champions in the region's political class.

In this section, we set the stage with an accounting of the region's natural wealth and its possible significance for climate politics going forward.

Latin America's natural resources include 25 percent of the planet's arable land, 22 percent of the world's forest area, 10 percent of its oil reserves, 5 percent of natural gas reserves, and 40 percent of its copper and silver reserves.[75] The region has been described as a "biodiversity superpower" containing a wealth of species and accounts for key environmental services.[76] Of the world's seventeen megadiverse countries, six (Brazil, Colombia, Ecuador, Mexico, Peru, and Venezuela) are in the region. The region is estimated to have 31 percent of the earth's freshwater resources.[77] Unfortunately, in the current global political economy, there is little leverage for countries with biodiversity dominance globally, and a lack of awareness about it locally leads to its undervaluation. Except for garnering some foreign assistance funding,[78] these nations are geopolitically underpowered.

Fossil fuel extraction and burning cut two ways, bringing some economic wealth but placing Latin American exporting economies at risk when prices fall or if the world seriously begins to reduce emissions (and fossil fuel imports). To "avoid dangerous climate change," as was agreed in 1992 in the UNFCCC, the global economy will have to stay within a proposed carbon budget, which amounts in some estimates to about 500 gigatons in carbon dioxide emissions to 2050.[79] The Grantham Research Institute on Climate Change at the London School of Economics estimates that only 20 to 40 percent of oil, gas, and coal reserves on the books of the two hundred largest energy companies can be exploited if we are to stay within the two-degree limit,[80] A study by Christopher McGlade and Paul Ekins shows that about 40 percent of Latin America's oil, about 55 percent of its gas, and 75 percent of its coal reserves, when combined with other fossil fuel reserves in other regions, would have to stay in the ground if we hope to stay below two degrees of warming.[81] Latin American countries such as Argentina, Brazil, Colombia, Ecuador, Mexico, and Venezuela (which have large reserves of fossil fuels) and countries such as Chile and Costa Rica (which are dependent on fossil fuel imports) are potentially exposed to this systemic risk.[82] Venezuela and Argentina have considerable fossil fuels reserves but they would have to leave nearly all of them in the ground under such a scenario. Whether and how these countries might be compensated for doing so is a highly complicated issue unlikely to be resolved soon.

On the other hand, Latin America could be a leader on clean energy. The Inter-American Development Bank says that Latin America can meet its future energy needs through renewable energy sources, including solar, wind, marine, geothermal, and biomass energy, which are sufficient to cover its projected 2050 electricity needs twenty-two times over.[83] According to the Climatescope report in 2014, which ranks countries on the level of attractiveness for clean energy investment, Latin America and the Caribbean is regarded as one of the great frontiers for clean energy investment. From 2006 to 2013, it attracted a cumulative $132 billion for biofuels, biomass, geothermal, solar, small hydro (up to 50 megawatts), and wind.[84] However, some countries are lagging, and the region needs to act decisively in order to realize its potential. Progress is being held back by vested interests in the status quo, fossil fuel subsidies, difficult investment climates, and a lack of capital.[85]

The region's status as a biodiversity heavyweight is both a blessing and a hindrance. One of the greatest challenges facing Latin America is the sustainable management of its rich and (socially and economically) important natural resources.[86] The development model focusing on commodity-led economic growth has put Latin American natural resources under serious pressure. The model leads to increased land clearing for agroexports and deforestation, forced migration and displacement of peoples and increased pollution. Further impacts include desertification, fisheries under stress, and mineral resources extracted causing air pollution.[87] The current production structure, type of infrastructure, inadequate levels of innovation, and other elements all feed into an unsustainable and unequal growth path.[88]

Latin American countries, especially in South America, have been relying heavily on their extractive sectors, such as mining and fossil fuels. This creates more vulnerability to climate-related risks in the short term (such as water scarcity and local contamination) and the long term (such as those risks coming from a lack of diversification of the economy). This situation exacerbates vulnerability in the region, which also is facing the climate impacts raised above from glacial melt, extreme climatic events, among others.

It remains to be seen whether a growing vulnerability and awareness of the fragility of the region's ecosystems and economic systems will drive action at the national and international levels on climate change by Latin American countries. In previous work, we used the term *ecofunctionalist* to describe decision making that was based on ecological imperatives, and we uncovered some modest support for this explanation of national actions.[89] As we examine various cases, we reflect on whether these factors are playing a role in shaping negotiating positions of nations. We turn now to resource extraction and exports within national development strategies.

Development: Economic Growth and Competing Development Models

Natural resources and energy reserves have played an instrumental role in determining Latin American countries' economic performance, and they will play a crucial role on how Latin American countries tackle climate change. The growing body of literature on the perils of extractivism illustrates concerns about exploiting natural resources to the detriment of the environment, social development, and technological innovation and the government's appetite for action on climate change.[90]

Latin America's bountiful natural resources have played a fundamental role in its integration into the global economy for half a millennium. Beginning with Christopher Columbus's landing in the New World in 1492, when he asked for gold with his first utterance, and including today's transnational corporations and traders who seek soy, copper, and oil, natural wealth has been exploited to build prosperity for those who can control it.[91] Despite the efforts of some countries to diversify their economies, commodity production and exports continue to be an essential revenue source for many Latin American countries, especially in South America.[92] The prior confidence in the region about its development trajectory stems in part from its resource revenues and adept handling of the global financial crisis of 2008, which left it relatively unscathed.[93] The recovery was driven by strong economic growth, careful macroeconomic and monetary policies, higher commodity prices, very high levels of foreign direct investment, and the insatiable demand from Asia for the region's raw materials.[94] Latin American countries' overreliance on natural resources has been revealed during the recent economic slowdown, which is partly a result of dropping Chinese demand for commodities, along with a fall in prices (especially for oil).

Before, China and India's demand for raw materials drove up world prices for commodities to unprecedented levels. This played an important role in accelerating Latin America's rate of economic growth to an average of 5.5 percent from mid-2003 to mid-2008.[95] Since 2003, the boom in global demand for minerals, hydrocarbons, and agricultural commodities has been crucial in strengthening Latin America's economic growth. These natural resources contribute to these countries' development, but they also bring risks, sometimes summed up as "the resource curse."[96] These include the problem known as Dutch disease, where local currency appreciates in value, lowering the price of imported goods to the detriment of national industry. Locally produced goods end up being overpriced and noncompetitive in foreign markets. Second, when a national government reaps huge revenues from resource sales, it discourages the implementation of difficult industrial policies to expand the country's productive and technological base. The intensive exploitation of natural resources also has led to corruption, weakened democratic institutions, and triggered environmental and social conflicts.[97]

The United Nations Economic Commission for Latin America and the Caribbean (ECLAC) suggests that Latin America is at a crossroads. The Commission has argued that progress has been made in reducing poverty and inequality, greater macroeconomic stability has been achieved, but sustaining these advances will be difficult given climate change, slowing international trade, fluctuating commodity prices, and a failure to diversify their economies and improve productivity.[98]

China's interests in Latin America focus on securing access to natural resources and energy reserves.[99] The relation is surging ahead: Latin American exports to China grew by 370 percent between 2000 and 2007, primarily in oil, soy, copper, iron ore, and forest products, while manufacturing imports from China grew by 420 percent.[100] In South America, China is not creating a new problem for certain Latin American countries of "resource dependency" but is extending, transforming, and increasing an old resource dependency. China's presence in Latin America is not uniformly dispersed, and the benefits of China–Latin American trade are highly concentrated in a few countries and sectors, such as soy in Argentina and Brazil, copper and other minerals in Chile and Peru, and oil in Ecuador and Venezuela.

Beyond trade, Chinese investments in the region have also focused principally on natural resources. Since 2005, China has provided loan commitments upward of $75 billion to Latin America. For some Latin American countries, Chinese finance represents a lifeline. China's loan commitments of US$37 billion in 2010 were more than those of the World Bank, Inter-American Development Bank, and US Export-Import Bank combined for that year.[101]

The renewed focus on exporting primary goods and on traditional development models focusing on the heavy use of fossil fuels has significant environmental consequences, accentuating a development model that puts great pressure on natural resources. The increases in raw material prices over the last decade and the expectations of sustained or even increasing demand create ever-greater pressure to extract more natural resources. The exploitation of some exported resources—including coal, hydrocarbons, steel, copper, cement, and other energy raw materials —causes serious environmental impacts.[102]

In the chapters that follow, we look at cases where pursuing economic growth through utilizing natural resources has clashed with a country's climate policy. Ecuador's efforts to be compensated by the international community to "keep the oil in the soil" in the Yasuní-ITT Initiative are especially revealing (chapter 4), and the building of a new oil refinery in Costa Rica has confounded that country's flagship climate policy and spilled into national politics (chapter 5). Several other cases reveal the living and evolving impact of the colonial legacy of dependence on exports of raw materials, and these, in turn, affect either directly or indirectly national positions in the climate negotiations and domestic climate change and environmental policy. These ideas are not entirely new ones, based as they are on Latin American Marxian political economy power perspectives of how states seek to create the conditions of capital accumulation to remain in power.[103]

Foreign Policy: Regional Integration, International Alliances, and Trade

At the international level, equally old ideas are realist theories of international relations, which begin with the assumption that states act in their self-interest and achieve their goals in an anarchic world according to their military and economic might.[104] We observe Latin American nation's foreign policies and attempt to understand whether they are driven more by the material interests of states or by idealist views of the public or state actors on the correct ways for humans to behave. This latter view, constructivism, describes norms and values that are spreading around the world, including norms of human rights and environmental protection. In postcolonial Latin America, significant soft power is gained by countries that can claim to be leaders in South-South cooperation—in diplomacy and trade. As is shown in chapter 3 on Brazil, things have changed sharply since the bad old days of major dominance by colonial and neocolonial powers—this is a transformed arena for state interaction.

Latin American countries are demonstrating independent and assertive foreign policies,[105] and the region's diverse positions on climate change reflect this. As Andrew Hurrell and Sandeep Sengupta argue, power is shifting in global politics, and emerging powers such as Brazil are assuming an important role.[106] Power is diffusing through the global system, and more voices demand to be heard in both domestic and international spaces. Rising states are challenging the status quo and questioning the dominant norms of the global geopolitical system to reflect their own interests and values.[107] For example, Lau Øfjord Blaxekjær and Tobias Dan Nielsen argue that "practices and narratives shape how we respond to climate change, which can be set up against mainstream analyses of climate negotiations based on (fixed) interests and power."[108] At the United Nations or the Group of Twenty various interests, concerns, values, and historical memories are on display as rising nations seek to influence the proceedings and outcomes.[109]

We observe a connection between Latin American countries' greater assertiveness on the international stage and their increasing presence and influence at the global climate talks. Brazil has worked hard to secure a permanent seat on the United Nations Security Council. Leaders there are using the climate change issue to bolster their case for its promotion to the groups that are tasked with caring for the global commons. At the very least, by joining with China, India, and South Africa in the BASIC negotiating bloc, Brazil has shown that decisions cannot readily be taken without them. The ALBA countries, including Bolivia, Cuba, Ecuador, and Venezuela, appear to be using the climate negotiations as an important outlet for rejecting different forms of exclusion and for criticizing the injustice of the existing but weakening US-centered international order. The UNFCCC is an ideal forum for the ALBA countries to expose the failure of US leadership and the liberal democratic models of rich nations and to promote their own notion of global equality, justice, and development.

For Latin America as whole, a rules-based international system based on respect for multilateralism and cooperation is a central element of just international relations. Being excluded by the world's main powers in key decisions remains a sore point, requiring a broader-based model of decision making.[110] Latin American countries' commitment to the UNFCCC becomes clearer from this perspective and explains their objection to ad hoc "minilateral" agreements that exclude them at critical points in the decision making.

Latin American governments are forming their own regional institutions that sometimes reinforce but also compete with traditional inter-American organizations like the US-led Organization of American States.[111] The Union of South American Nations (Union de Naciónes Suramericanas, UNASUR) and the Community of Latin American and Caribbean States (Comunidad de Estados Latinoamericanos y Caribeños, CELAC) demonstrate this new willingness to formulate and create new foreign policies and spaces for regional integration and cooperation. Our observation, however, is that these regional integration efforts rarely and inadequately attend to climate change.[112]

Latin America has been keen to step out from under the US's shadow and is increasing its relations with China, India, and others to do so. An especially revealing part of that shift has been the sharp increase in trade and diplomatic visits and agreements with China since 2004. In 2011, China became the top destination for the exports of Brazil, Chile, and Peru and the second for others, including Venezuela.[113]

Chinese policy toward Latin America focuses on trade and commercial ties that are designed to promote economic growth in China. China's 2008 Policy Paper on Latin America and the Caribbean explains the logic behind China's interest in Latin America and the region's strategic importance, primarily for encouraging trade and commerce and the purchase of natural resources.[114] China also seeks to isolate its long-time runaway province of Taiwan diplomatically by focusing on those countries in Latin America and the Caribbean that still recognize it as the Republic of China. A number of Caribbean and Central American republics fall into the latter group, representing a significant bank of Taiwan's support in the UN. Chinese investment in renewable energy is the most tangible exchange related to climate change outside of the UN climate negotiations. In January 2015, the China-CELAC ministerial forum took place in Beijing and was seen as an important indication of the growing partnership between China and Latin America. We look at the role of China in Latin America in chapters 3, 4, and 5.

Finally, to understand how the distinct qualities of foreign affairs ministries across the region drive the peculiar behavior of Latin American nations in climate negotiations, we recall Robert Putnam's 1988 study on "two-level games."[115] Discussing other issues besides climate, Putnam describes how negotiators must balance the benefits of pleasing domestic constituencies (and infuriating others) while "minimizing the adverse consequences of foreign developments." Administrations that face difficult domestic politics come to the negotiations with very small "win sets" of possible positive outcomes. The ironclad demands of their local constituents often exclude the demands of foreign states with their own domestic interest groups. Some Latin American countries have more difficult domestic politics on environmental issues because of their more or less organized agricultural and industrial elites. These "polluting elites" constrain some negotiating delegations far more than others. Well-organized and vocal environmental nongovernmental organizations (NGOs) could theoretically have the same impacts on the behaviors of delegations but have not yet widely done so. Much of the remainder of this book considers the domestic pressures that are driving the climate-related foreign policies of Latin American nations.

 ## Civil Society: The Gap between Climate Concerns and Action

It is a paradox (not limited to this region) that when asked, people in Latin America say they are very concerned about climate change. However, Latin American civil society has not been able to assert itself strongly on the issue of climate change at the national level due to a small number of groups focused on the issue, sometimes ineffectual strategies, and sometimes overbearing states that stifle, coopt or repress nonstate actors. Instead, we can witness a strong concentration of groups from the region focused instead on the UN climate change negotiations, where they hope to have a greater impact and provide specialized and technical expertise to countries.

Surveys illustrate that Latin American citizens are concerned about climate change. A 2011 survey carried out by Gallup in a hundred countries indicated that Colombia, Ecuador, Mexico, and Venezuela are among the countries that are most concerned about global warming. Another poll, conducted by Nielsen among 25,000 Internet users in fifty-one countries, concluded that in Latin America concerns about climate change were expressed by 90 percent of those consulted, far above the global average of 69 percent.[116]

Latin American civil society organizations are diverse, vibrant, and active. They include volunteers and staffers in non-governmental organizations, think tanks, national and local chapters of native-born Latin American NGOs, and branches of foreign NGOs like Greenpeace and the World Wildlife Fund. During the 1980s, citizen movements were limited in number, but in some countries they began to gain public support to address environmental consequences of development.[117] We look at the role played by civil society on climate change and explore to what extent there is an emerging social movement on the issue in the region. Our observation is that although it is stronger on some traditional and local environmental issues, Latin American civil society has come quite late to the climate change issue.[118] This delay has meant that these organizations have had only a limited impact and have made few significant contributions to shaping their governments' directions in international negotiations and only inconsistent impact at the domestic level. The region is not alone in this regard: climate movements are relatively weak in the United States, Asia, Africa, and Europe. However, a few times their role has been instrumental and highly influential in creating the conditions where governments have become more likely to act on the issue, both at home and at the UN negotiations.

Apart from the Latin American branch of the Climate Action Network (CAN-LA), which was established in 1992, the majority of Latin American civil society groups that work on climate change have only recently emerged. For example, the Latin American Platform on Climate was formed in 2009. Several groups and networks are focused on climate change (as well as other environmental issues) in the region, including the AVINA Foundation, Coordinator of Indigenous Organizations of the Amazon River Basin, Interamerican Association for Environmental Defense (AIDA). The activities of these NGOs are diverse, frequently overlap, and are not easily categorized. Groups like the AVINA Foundation and COICA work on capacity-building measures with governments, indigenous peoples and rural communities, other NGOs, and businesses and also hold workshops and other events to increase climate-change awareness and expertise. Others generate and facilitate dialogue and advocacy by lobbying for specific issues, writing declarations, and launching campaigns. These groups all work on online platforms, research outputs, media events, and conferences, but they also occasionally organize protests against government and business actions, which is the focus of organizations such as Acción Ecológica and La Via Campesina. Finally, some NGOs (including the Mexican Center for Environmental Law) research climate change, while others (such as the

Latin American Platform on Climate) build communications tools to assist policymakers and practitioners.

The Latin American NGOs that are working on climate change share some general characteristics. They have been highly effective in bringing together national and regional nonstate actors for workshops and conferences, epitomized by the First World People's Conference on Climate Change and the Rights of Mother Earth in 2010 in Cochabamba, Bolivia. A number of these NGOs have good working relations with Latin American governments, which have proved successful in gaining access to events and generating space for dialogue. Some are fully government supported, providing research or outreach services for national, state, or local agencies. There are also important cases of NGO members moving into governmental roles and vice versa. Former executive director of the Sociedad Peruana de Derecho Ambiental (Peruvian Society for Environmental Law), Manuel Pulgar-Vidal, for example, is Peru's minister for the environment and was president for the COP20 negotiations in 2014 in Lima.

We offer in the chapters ahead examples of the key influences on civil society in Bolivia, Brazil, and Ecuador. Sometimes NGOs meet with country delegations to the UNFCCC delegations, and sometimes they are included on the diplomatic team. Being included in delegations can be a double-edged sword because it can defuse the most informed critics of administrations and sometimes erodes their groups' capacity. Sometimes it coopts and stifles civil society voices. In some cases, however, there appears to be an improvement in partnerships and capacity between both sides, and government seems more willing to listen and be inclusive. At the same time, however, interactions between government and civil society on climate change can be weak, due to eroded civil liberties and narrow space for dialogue. As will be shown, this is the case in Ecuador, where government reaction to ongoing criticism of its decision to exploit oil in the Yasuní national park has led to arbitrary closures of a civil society office in an attempt to silence critics.

Four of Many Factors

These four factors provide the conceptual framework for this book and the themes that frame the analysis—nature, development, foreign policy, and civil society. Each theme contains critical sets of issues for explaining national positions at the UN climate negotiations and at home on reducing emissions and preparing for climate impacts. They arise repeatedly in the following chapters. These four are an abbreviated list: other themes behind our study include the desire of politicians to secure reelection, their varying levels of scientific knowledge on climate change, their principled values, parliamentary rules and voting systems within countries, centralized or federalist systems, the weight that international actors have within each country, public opinion, and the nuanced and complex relationships that occur between competing and cooperating nations at the UN climate negotiations.[119]

A brilliant cross-national study by Kathryn Harrison and Lisa Sundstrom examines the power that these factors have to explain the participation of the top wealthy nations in the Kyoto Protocol and their levels of ambition in reducing emissions.[120] They found that the costs that a nation would incur to meet its pledges mattered significantly, and that ideational commitments can be fragile if leaders fail to hold views strongly supported by their publics and if their local polluting elites are strong and well organized. One key to the difficulty of convincing players like the US lies in the decentralized power given to provinces and states, where powerful players become aware of the costs of implementation and fight ratification or implementation of a climate treaty. A mix of moral suasion and direct material incentives brought many key countries onboard with Kyoto, and hopes for funding have been seen as important for the acceptance by developing countries of the Kyoto Protocol and the Copenhagen Accord.[121]

Also useful is Elizabeth DeSombre's attempt to understand why the United States often acts unilaterally on environmental treaties and fails to sign and ratify many key agreements, like Kyoto Protocol.[122] DeSombre raises and refutes a series of arguments that are based mostly on the US domestic political system. The contrary cases—like the Montreal Protocol on Ozone-Depleting Chemicals and the CITES treaty on endangered species (Convention on International Trade in Endangered Species of Wild Fauna and Flora)—show times when the country accepted science, took a precautionary approach, allowed redistributary funding to developing countries, did not act selfishly because it was especially vulnerable, and so on. Even the institutional rules of the US Senate that require a two-thirds vote to ratify treaties explains only some nonratifications but not those that were approved. She concludes that the United States accepts only treaties where it is ahead of other nations or at least has its own domestic regulation before it will accept external agreements on controlling them. DeSombre's study raises another crucial set of potential explanations for national behaviors in negotiations and observations, including in Latin America.

These factors can be considered among those driving Latin American countries' behaviors at the UN climate talks and at home. A set of other external concerns of countries is long, including such issues as competitiveness, relations with peers and negotiating groups, their international reputation, and their conceptualization of the "cobenefits" of action on climate change.[123] So there are many variables, but given that nature, development, foreign policy, and civil society factor in shaping a nation's political economy, we believe that they have the most explanatory power and focus on them in this book. We can present strong support for these factors in past studies, but our goal here is to tell the story of how Latin American nations have treated the UNFCCC process and acted at home on climate change and what appears to be driving those behaviors.

The Shape of the Book

One of our goals is to decipher the competing visions on climate change in Latin America, so its core is case studies of the three main blocs of countries. Chapter 3 focuses on Brazil; chapter 4 looks at the ALBA group, with cases of Bolivia, Ecuador, and Venezuela; and chapter 5 examines Mexico and the AILAC countries, with case studies of Costa Rica and Peru. Space and limited time led us to leave to future research other important Latin American regions and countries, such as the Caribbean, Central America, and Argentina. Looking at them would have uncovered yet more competing visions of the problem of climate change and the right way to address it, but these visions have been expressed less boldly in the UN negotiations compared to the case studies presented here. We chose to use this space on what we believe are the region's three main actors on the global stage.

Chapter 3 focuses on Brazil, which officially accepts the imperative of dealing with climate change but has taken the position that developing countries should have to act only after the wealthy developed countries have first addressed this problem they created. In 2009, the former Brazilian president, Luiz Inácio Lula da Silva pledged to reduce the country's emissions, and the nation has reduced deforestation (and its emissions) sharply since 2005. But it will be shown how Brazil has backpedaled in the negotiations, at some points to an uncompromising position that led other countries to call it a spoiler. Brazil is a developmentalist state, and the current administration of President Dilma Rousseff is more concerned with economic development than with climate change. To the exclusion of its neighbors, Brazil has aligned itself with BASIC, a group of other large emerging economies (China, India, and South Africa) that are seeking to protect their right to develop, and that with the US effectively took over the UNFCCC negotiations in Copenhagen. In the 2014 Lima round of negotiations, Brazil seemed to adopt a different (and some said more constructive) tone, but uncertainty and worrying signs persist on its forest policy and its climate policies more generally.

The ALBA countries can be described as populist, largely state-run economies. The late Venezuelan President Hugo Chávez created the new bloc to provide an alternative to the United States' free-trade initiatives in the region, supported by his charisma and generous oil diplomacy. At the UNFCCC negotiations, the group made strong arguments about the injustice of climate change for poorer countries and the need for a fair and inclusive process. The group is important to understand because on more than one occasion it has threatened to shut down the UNFCCC process. After Bolivia, Ecuador and Venezuela are the other case studies in that chapter. We describe how the economic foundation of ALBA is based on the export of oil and other raw materials, a worrisome and contradictory situation in the case of climate change that could be driving some obstructionist negotiating partially wrapped in justice arguments. With Venezuela currently in political and economic free-fall, ALBA as a group is quieter and less assertive than at its peak in 2009. Its members continue to advance climate justice arguments, and have joined forces with the Like-Minded Developing Countries group in asserting the obligations of rich nations to act first (see chapter 4).[124]

Our third set of countries is the AILAC Group (Chile, Colombia, Costa Rica, Guatemala, Panama, Paraguay, and Peru), which formed in 2012. They are attempting to look at development though a climate change lens, and have declared that they are assessing ways to make the transformation into low or zero net carbon economies. These countries have decided to take action now to avoid the increased costs further down the line that climate change will bring, and they hope to motivate other countries to follow. In chapter 4, we also examine Mexico's leadership at the Cancun negotiations in 2010, and the ways that it led to an underappreciated achievement—major climate legislation at home. Yet this legislation has to be viewed in the broader national context, which has witnessed the passing of energy reforms to Mexico's energy sector, which could clash with the climate change law. We then follow Costa Rica's bold pledge to be carbon neutral by 2021. The country may have difficulty achieving this goal due to a decision to proceed with plans to upgrade an oil refinery. Finally, we review Peru's early pledge to slash its emissions and its successful bid for hosting the COP20 meeting in 2014. We show how revisions to environmental protection laws at home partially undermined the credibility of the Peruvian government to host the COP20 in December 2014, and how that process unfolded in the context of Peru's national and foreign policies and development objectives.

This book focuses on Latin America, but the region's domestic and international climate politics matter deeply for shaping global conversations around low-carbon growth and the future of the UN climate change negotiations. Our case studies also reveal relevant and timely lessons on the relationship between domestic economies and politics and the international posturings of nations. The examples inform larger theories of international development, international relations, comparative politics, political geography and political economy. They address an important gap in the existing research and inform key questions about the global politics of climate change by developing explanations for an entirely undiscussed set of climate-focused policies and positions.

As just described, we seek to explain the diverse positions of Latin American countries in the climate change negotiations and at the national level partly by using our four factors—nature, development, foreign policy, and civil society. An overarching line of inquiry explores whether and why Latin American countries have become important in breaking the Gordian knot of climate change negotiations. We wish to avoid a romanticized and simplistic view of the region as a set of leaders, which is an inaccurate portrayal of the region's significance. The complex reality of climate change politics in Latin America suggests a fragile basis for action by those countries that are willing to take up the torch and try innovative and ambitious actions for the developing world. Latin American countries have adopted important roles at the domestic and international levels on climate change. They have been active and at times controversial.

We take up a fuller assessment of the countries' positions on climate change in the concluding chapter, but for now we provide two of our main conclusions. They matter for policy and for the advancement of social theory. For climate policy, our review of these cases shows some grounds for hope and some serious cause for concern. Our hope is based on some of the extraordinarily bold steps that some Latin American countries are taking on climate change. As foreshadowed above, we also are concerned that economic pragmatism has led to increased extraction and sales of natural resources, which in turn is driving some nations away from more progressive emissions reduction policies at home. One countervailing force that needs more observation is whether growing awareness of vulnerability to climate change (in civil society and among local and national government ministries) is potentially moving countries to address the issue and the kinds of actions it inspires. The region is unified in demanding increased funding from the wealthy countries to pay for these efforts, but the ALBA countries and to a lesser extent Brazil have taken a stand that they will not undertake further mitigation efforts until these funds materialize.[125]

The book comes back repeatedly to two observations. First, the division and fragmentation in Latin America that are demonstrated by the region's numerous regional integration projects are also manifested at the UN climate negotiations. We also conclude that civil society organizations in the region need significant support to push their governments' feet closer to the fire of climate change—forcing emissions reductions and rapid action to reduce vulnerability to climate risks like flooding and droughts. Our concerns are based on years of working with civil society in the region: we see a substantial gap between climate concerns in the population and actions taken by the state, business, and citizens.

To arrive at these case studies and conclusions, in the next chapter we outline some history of the region's role in the negotiations; its fragmentation into a series of economic, trade, and negotiating blocs; and some reasons that countries there emerged as pioneers and innovators on tackling climate change. That chapter sets up the case studies and moves us closer to answering our core questions: why are Latin American countries emerging now as a set of crucial actors on climate change, and what can we learn from the region about the future of global climate politics and action?

2   Latin America's Emerging Leadership on Climate Change

Looking beyond Latin America's Decade

Rising to speak at the United Nations General Assembly in 2010, Colombian President Juan Manuel Santos announced that Latin American nations are beginning to take a global leadership role in economic, environmental, and development issues and declared that "This is Latin America's decade!"[1]

The region's fate has indeed turned. This chapter attempts to paint the big picture of how Latin America got where it is in the climate negotiations today and in national actions on climate change. First, we look at where its confidence is coming from—the economy—and examine some of Latin America's important achievements and some of its ongoing challenges.

At the May 27, 2011, launch of his book *The Decade of Latin America and the Caribbean: A Real Opportunity*, Luis Alberto Moreno, president of the Inter-American Development Bank, summarized some of the important changes underway in the region. In 1990, he said, half of the population of Latin America was poor, and by 2010, that figure had fallen to a third.[2] Dependence on one trading partner has become much more diversified with increased levels of South-South trade. In 1990, the United States accounted for 60 percent of Latin America's and the Caribbean's foreign trade, and Asia accounted for 10 percent. By 2010, trade with the United States had dropped to 40 percent of the total, and trade with Asia doubled to 20 percent.[3]

The confidence demonstrated by Presidents Santos and Moreno stems from the region's high degree of resilience and adept handling of the 2008 financial crisis, which left it relatively unharmed.[4] The recovery was driven by strong economic growth, sound macroeconomic and monetary policies, record levels of foreign investment, high commodity prices, and demand from Asia for the region's raw materials.[5] Latin America's favorable terms of trade resulted from expanded international trade and increased world growth rates, particularly those of India and China. These factors partly explain the strong growth rates observed in Latin America between 2003 and 2008 and a relatively rapid recovery after the 2008 financial crisis.[6] Recently, economic growth in the region has slowed due to a cooling off of the Chinese economy and lower demand for the region's natural resources.

From 2003 to 2010, Latin America's economies grew at an annual average rate of close to 5 percent, which bought good times for many.[7] Since 2012, the region's economic growth has slowed, reaching about 1.1 percent in 2014, which was the lowest since 2009. There are considerable differences between countries in the region. Argentina and Venezuela both posted negative growth in 2014, while Bolivia, the Dominican Republic, and Panama were the region's fastest-growing economies.[8]

As renowned Colombian economist José Antonio Ocampo commented, "The time has come to bury the concept of 'the decade of Latin America.'"[9] The main culprit has been the end of the commodity boom. According to *The Economist*, as China's growth slows, commodity prices have returned to their lowest levels since the 2009 global recession. The drop in oil prices has hurt the oil-exporting economies of South America, although some are benefitting from cheaper oil.[10] The World Bank suggests that in the absence of vigorous productivity reforms, a new normal of around 3 percent growth would be a reasonable estimate for the region as a whole.[11]

The most recent resource boom supported Latin American countries in their push for more assertive foreign policies.[12] This assertiveness extends to the UN climate negotiations, where some Latin American nations began to put forward emission-reduction pledges and adopt more radical positions. As Latin America is a middle-income region, foreign aid is less of a necessity just as less is offered, so governments are less likely to self-censor in fear of losing support from rich donor countries. China's surging presence in the region appears to provide some countries with the leverage to be bolder.

The consolidation of democracy in the region is mixed, but from 2005 to 2009, the region saw thirty-five reasonably free and fair elections.[13] Recent protests in Brazil, Chile, Ecuador, and Venezuela, however, show the ongoing challenges facing citizens as they oppose powerful vested interests, corruption, and government shortcomings on a raft of issues.[14]

The 2014 presidential elections in Latin America saw new administrations take office in Bolivia, Brazil, Colombia, Costa Rica, and Uruguay.

In a number of cases, existing leaders were reelected, albeit with slimmer margins, often forcing them to strike deals with the opposition. In Brazil, President Dilma Rousseff had a rough start to her second term in office in early 2015. Scores of politicians close to the president faced corruption allegations for accepting bribes from the state oil company Petrobras. Corruption charges in Brazil and discontent with the ruling parties and elites were the main reasons that Marina Silva, a senator and former minister of the environment, was able to obtain millions of votes in the first round of the 2014 presidential election. According to Brazilian Ana Toni, the Petrobras scandal demonstrates the proximity of this fossil fuel company to the administration and represents a major barrier for Brazil's transition to cleaner sources of energy.[15]

Argentinian journalist Andres Oppenheimer suggests that at the start of 2015 Latin America was a leaderless region, with its major players in Mexico, Brazil, and Argentina for example, significantly weakened by domestic troubles such as corruption scandals, weak economic performance, and internal violence. These issues appear to be forcing these countries' leaders to focus on the domestic agenda rather than engage fully with foreign policy issues like climate change.[16]

This book examines some of these domestic and international issues in our attempt to explain the region's climate change positions. We believe that Latin America is a bellwether for the future of international climate change negotiations because its countries are diverse, constructive, and a controversial group of actors at the UN climate talks, reflecting some key fragments of the new multipolar world order.[17] As former Chilean president, Ricardo Lagos, suggests in the foreword, Latin America is a microcosm for the difficulties confronting the global climate change talks. Disparities in its economies, in various nations' greenhouse gas emissions, in ideological positions, and in foreign policies reflect a highly fragmented region. Latin American countries are geographically and climatologically diverse, with very different shares of land and natural resources. There also are striking differences in national income, with the region's richest country having a per capita GDP that is twenty-four times larger than that of the poorest one.[18]

Since the birth of the UNFCCC in 1992, little academic literature has looked at Latin America and climate change. The region's media still provides only limited analysis of domestic and international climate change policies. Scholarly attention has tended to focus on China, Europe, and the United States and on the divergent and often contentious perspectives of the global North and South, largely excluding Latin America. Pieces on Latin America and climate change tend to be scientific studies addressing the impacts of climate change in the region and technical and policy-oriented reports by intergovernmental organizations. Latin American countries' own perspectives, interests, positions, approaches on climate change have remained largely enshrouded in obscurity.

The roots of the region's inconsistent and unpredictable climate policies lie in its economic structure, which is in turn a product of its colonial heritage. One legacy of its heritage is that the region's economies are still highly dependent on exploiting and exporting natural resources. Although they benefited from a strong Asian demand for commodities in the first decade of the 2000s, this export structure has resulted in insufficient value added, weak links with the rest of the economy, and vulnerability to sudden declines in commodity prices. These extractive industries are capital-intensive, create few permanent jobs, and pose important social and environmental challenges. They also do little to address the region's severe income inequality. Despite some recent improvements, Latin America and the Caribbean still languish in last place as the world's most unequal region.[19]

This chapter briefly reviews the evolution of Latin American countries' role within the international environmental negotiations and climate treaties and provides some other relevant background information. We begin at the 1972 United Nations Conference on Human Environment in Stockholm and work toward the present day. By providing some historical perspective, we illustrate how Latin American countries have gone from being passive to playing central roles in global climate change governance. We describe how in the early 2000s, some Latin American countries began to adopt positions that were independent from those taken by the Group of 77 and China, which contributed to weakening that group. We assess Latin America's emergence as a low-carbon region and review the role played by its relatively low-carbon electricity-producing system, which is built predominantly on hydropower, itself a controversial and uncertain energy source for the future. Finally, we look at how Latin American countries became inadvertent pioneers on policy issues such as forestry protection and sustainable urban transport. These solutions often were developed for reasons other than addressing climate change, but after developing them, the region was predisposed to accept solutions that put them in a position to profit from their codification in international agreements.[20] But first, we begin the chapter with a look at the level of fragmentation in the region, with its multiple regional integration groups which extends into the UN climate change negotiations.

A Continent of Blocs

Lumping together Latin America´s diverse countries into one monolithic region is unhelpful. In over twenty years of international climate negotiations, Latin American countries have rarely spoken with one voice but rather have expressed their positions through various formal and informal groups and sometimes as individual countries. After an accretion of new collaborations, different Latin American and Caribbean countries are now part of a number of negotiating groups in the climate talks. Some groups consist of only Latin American countries, while others include countries from other regions.

All Latin American and Caribbean countries have long been part of the Group of 77 and China (the G77), which consists of 134 countries.[21] Mexico was a founding member but left the group in 1994 after joining the Organisation for Economic Co-operation and Development (OECD). Within the G77, Latin American and Caribbean countries participate in various groups (see table 2.1), such as the Alliance of Small Island States (AOSIS), the BASIC bloc, Bolivarian Alliance for the Peoples of Our America (ALBA), Independent Association of Latin America and the Caribbean (AILAC), Cartagena Dialogue for Progressive Action, Environmental Integrity Group, Central American Integration System, and Coalition of Rainforest Nations. The story of each of these groups is worth knowing, but given space constraints we focus below on Brazil in BASIC, ALBA, and AILAC.

On the substantive issues under negotiation, Latin America has yet to show a unified perspective and rarely adopts common goals. Occasionally, Latin American countries do share some common goals, as demonstrated at the COP17 in Durban in 2011, when they agreed on the need for a second commitment period of the Kyoto Protocol. [22] The United Nations' Latin America and the Caribbean Group (GRULAC) is the only official mechanism on climate change that brings the whole region into a formal setting. However, GRULAC focuses on nominations and candidacies, such as selecting board members for global institutions or bodies like the Green Climate

Table 2.1

Latin America and Caribbean participation in UNFCCC groups, 2014

Grouping	Latin American and Caribbean (LAC) members
Alliance of Small Island States*	Antigua and Barbuda, Bahamas, Barbados, Belize, Cuba, Dominica, Dominican Republic, Grenada, Guyana, Haiti, Jamaica, St. Kitts and Nevis, St. Lucia, St. Vincent and the Grenadines, Suriname, Trinidad and Tobago
Central American Integration System	Belize, Costa Rica, El Salvador, Guatemala, Honduras, Nicaragua, Panama
Bolivarian Alliance for the Peoples of Our America (ALBA)	Antigua and Barbuda, Bolivia, Cuba, Dominica, Ecuador, Grenada, Saint Kitts and Nevis, Nicaragua, Saint Lucia, Saint Vincent and the Grenadines, Venezuela
BASIC*	Brazil (with China, India, and South Africa)
Environmental Integrity Group*	Mexico (with Liechtenstein, Monaco, South Korea, and Switzerland)
Organization of the Petroleum Exporting Countries (OPEC)*	Ecuador, Venezuela
Group of Highly Vulnerable Countries*	Chile, Colombia, El Salvador, Guatemala, and Peru
Independent Association of Latin America and the Caribbean (AILAC)	Chile, Colombia, Costa Rica, Guatemala, Panama, Paraguay, and Peru
Like-Minded Developing Countries*	Bolivia, Cuba, Dominica, Ecuador, El Salvador, Nicaragua, and Venezuela
Coalition of Rainforest Nations*	Argentina, Belize, Chile, Costa Rica, Dominica, Dominican Republic, Ecuador, El Salvador, Guatemala, Guyana, Honduras, Nicaragua, Panama, Paraguay, Surinam, and Uruguay
The Cartagena Dialogue*	Antigua and Barbuda, Chile, Colombia, Costa Rica, Dominican Republic, Guatemala, Mexico, Panama, Peru, and Uruguay
G77 and China*	All LAC countries except Mexico are members of this group.

Note: *Includes countries from other regions.

Fund (designed to channel money to developing countries to support their efforts to tackle climate change), rather than the climate negotiations.

The roots of Latin American countries' conflicting negotiating positions offer important insights into what is driving them to act both at home and at the UNFCCC. Due to their intense vulnerability to rising sea levels and hurricanes, sixteen Caribbean nations have joined together with other islands in the Alliance of Small Island States (AOSIS) to call for drastic reductions in the emissions of greenhouse gas emissions by all nations and to push for adaptation funding and even reparations. Brazil is a member of BASIC, the club of rapidly emerging economies that includes China, India, and South Africa. Economic growth is a top priority for these countries, so they find the aggressive agenda of AOSIS threatening because it might curtail their development plans. They push for the developed countries to act according to their historical responsibilities for having put greenhouse gases in the atmosphere first—because carbon dioxide remains in the atmosphere over a hundred years. Bolivia and Venezuela have delivered impassioned statements for the ALBA group on the rights of Mother Earth and climate justice, and they have repeatedly questioned carbon trading, which most other Latin American countries have accepted. Some countries have relatively advanced experience with carbon markets and consider them to be important opportunities for business and investment. Open economies in the region make up the Independent Association of Latin America and the Caribbean (AILAC), which includes Chile, Colombia, Costa Rica, Guatemala, Panama, Paraguay, and Peru. Along with the Dominican Republic and Mexico, AILAC countries were decisive in creating the Cartagena Dialogue's eclectic mixture of developed and developing countries. Mexico is also part of the Environmental Integrity Group (along with Korea and Switzerland). In 2012, the Like-Minded Developing Countries group emerged, which combines some ALBA countries but also China, Egypt, India, and Saudi Arabia, among others. Between and within these groups and blocs, countries can take different positions from their fellows and make separate statements at the negotiations. Within the ALBA group, for example, Ecuador has been more open to market mechanisms than Bolivia or Venezuela and sometimes makes statements to that effect.

In the following chapters, we focus on Brazil as part of BASIC, ALBA, and AILAC to understand what the origins of these important groups are and what drives them together or apart. We are interested in linking domestic politics with the UNFCCC and internal dynamics within the groups. The effort reveals a fragmented and divided region, reflecting some of the forces pulling the G77 apart globally.

Away from the UNFCCC, Latin American countries are members of various regional institutions. All countries in the hemisphere (excluding Canada and the United States) are members of the Community of Latin American and Caribbean States (CELAC). There is also the Organization of American States (OAS), which includes Canada and the United States and also Cuba which had its suspension lifted in 2009.[23] Further groups include the Union of South American Nations, the Pacific Alliance, the Bolivarian Alliance for the Peoples of Our America (ALBA), and a number of subregional integration bodies. These include the Central American Integration System (SICA), Caribbean Community (CARICOM), Southern Common Market (MERCOSUR), and the Andean Community. Of these, only ALBA, SICA, the Pacific Alliance, and CELAC have spoken in the climate negotiations.

Outside of Europe, Latin America has enjoyed the longest tradition of regionalism. Although meant to be an expression of unity and solidarity, it has become a reflection of Latin American diversity and division. Latin American regionalism is characterized by a number of competing projects whose rationales and agendas are often divergent and even incompatible.[24] Michael Shifter at the Inter-American Dialogue says some groups have a more ideological identity, but most are products of distinct strategic priorities and national interests, which reflect economic agendas and geographical positions.[25] In addition, simple rivalries and old grudges divide the group.

Gian Luca Gardini argues that looking at Latin American regional integration reveals three tensions.[26] The first is between change and continuity. As new projects for regional integration multiply, attaining the goal of integration is less likely, and continuing ineffective regionalism is more probable. The second tension is between unity and diversity. The many regional institutions and norms are meant to signal a unity of regional intent but in fact reflect the plurality and incompatibility of agendas and interests. Finally, there is a tension between ideology and pragmatism. Declarations and principles are required to balance the reality of diplomatic practice and structural constraints. With finite resources, accommodation can be a more generally rewarding option than confrontation.

This regional diversity extends to climate change governance and explains why Latin American countries do not tend to speak with one voice on climate change at the UN climate negotiations. For example, as is shown in chapter 4, ALBA rejected the Copenhagen Accords, which was drafted by a group that included Brazil, whereas Mexico and others voted for it.

Latin American regional integration bodies approach climate change governance in different ways. ALBA negotiates as a group at the UN climate negotiations, and UNASUR, MERCOSUR, and CELAC do not. Except for the recent case of CELAC, these groups have yet to begin working on climate change in any meaningful way. Brazil, which has played a defining role in creating both UNASUR and MERCOSUR, coordinates mostly as part of the BASIC group with countries outside the region. Regional integration bodies made up of smaller states—such as the Central American Integration System (SICA)—have been more willing to make joint statements at the climate negotiations. ALBA and the Pacific Alliance have competing visions on regional integration, which extends into the climate negotiations. In the Pacific Alliance—which is a free-trade pact made up of some countries in AILAC and Mexico—countries' positions differ on some key issues from the ALBA group.

The difficulties facing regional integration projects and competition between them helps to explain why the achievement of one regional voice on climate change is slow to materialize. The region is fragmented, and its diverse negotiating positions and perspectives are complex. Coalitions and memberships of different blocs are in a constant state of flux. But now we step back briefly to the origins of global environmental negotiations.

A Rift Emerges in Stockholm

The postures that Latin American countries have taken in the UN climate negotiations fit into positions that they have taken in global environmental political battles in past decades, geopolitical struggles shaped by colonization, and attempts to break free of dependence on the world's rich nations. The modern environmental movement usually is said to date from the late 1960s and early 1970s in North America and Europe. Some US-centric observers date it to the founding of the Environmental Defense Fund in 1968, the Santa Monica oil spill and the burning of the Cuyahoga River in 1968, and the first Earth Day on April 22, 1970, which remains the largest public protest in US history. In 1968, astronaut William Anders took a photograph of the moon when he was on the way back to earth, and it provided the iconic view of "Earthrise," the vision of a fragile oasis in space that still flies on earth flags. As a result of massive public mobilization, sweeping environmental laws were put into effect in a number of countries in the early 1970s.

Environmentalists quickly realized that the issues they were fighting locally—like air, water, and soil pollution—were linked to each other and that they could not be solved only in their own countries or even in just the global North's wealthy nations. Stanford University biologist Paul Ehrlich published his shocking book, *The Population Bomb* in 1970, warning that we were headed off a collective cliff as booming human populations consumed more resources and polluted the ecosystem. The emerging "spaceship earth" perspective sought to muster the attention and efforts of people from all countries, and the wave of environmental protests drove the UN to respond. In 1968, Sweden submitted a proposal to the UN, declaring an "urgent need for intensified action at the national and international level, to limit and, where possible, to eliminate the impairment of the human environment." The United Nations Economic and Social Council (ECOSOC) approved Sweden's proposal and sent it on to the General Assembly, which endorsed it and agreed to hold a Conference on the Human Environment in June 1972, to be hosted by Sweden in Stockholm.

Even before the meeting, a rift between North and South was opening at the preparatory meetings, which the delegates from 113 nations sought to bridge in Stockholm. Northern environmentalists were worried about the world's shrinking resource base, spreading pollution, and ever-expanding populations.[27] In Stockholm, wealthy nations' activists and governments railed on the importance for all nations to prioritize environmental protection. Developing nations pointed out that they had not caused the global problems of industrialization and did not have the resources to pay for addressing them. A Brazilian negotiator pointedly remarked that it was a "happy coincidence" that the rich countries that were the source of the problem were precisely the ones that had the capacity (money) to pay to clean it up.

Developing nations feared that the nascent effort to gain foreign aid funding from the developed nations for their basic needs—education, health, and infrastructure projects to pull their economies out of the mire— would be cut down by the new wave of environmentalism that was pointing out the "limits to growth"[28] and "carrying capacity" of the planet.[29] The Sri Lankan ambassador put the fear of derailing development clearly: "we must not, generally speaking, allow our concern for the environment to develop into a hysteria." The role of the developing world therefore was to put the brakes on environmental "hysteria."

Brazil emerged in Stockholm as an important player and leader but was seen by some as an "anti-environmental pariah."[30] Brazil made five strong arguments that continue to reverberate today. First, it needed to develop first to be able to clean up later. "No growth" was unacceptable. The Brazilian delegation argued that environmental problems in poor countries are due not to overuse of natural resources but to poverty and insufficient use of resources. Second, that they alone would control the growth of their own population. Third, richer countries should pay for the cleanup. Fourth, international environmental treaties should not be used to limit sovereignty or alter development paths, reduce aid, or slow investments or lending. And fifth, no one should claim that all nations have a share of the earth's resources that forms a "common pool" or "world trust." This "beautiful assumption" also requires the sharing of economic and political power, industry, and financial control, which wealthy nations find unthinkable. Brazil's position struck a chord with most other developing nations.

The broader geopolitics of those days was critical in forming the shape and tone of the dialogue between the global North and South. Latin American countries gained formal independence from their Spanish and Portuguese colonial masters in the early 1800s but then fell into exploitative relationships with other colonial and neocolonial countries that were eager to exploit their resources.[31] Only the Great Depression of the 1930s and World War II distracted those powers, allowing Latin American nations some limited success in developing their own industries for local consumption.[32] Some economists and sociologists proclaimed that the region needed to extricate itself from the global economy, where rich countries already dominated the markets for manufactured goods and manipulated the prices of the only things the region had to sell—minerals, coffee, sugar, lumber, and cheap labor.[33]

Realizing the imperative to negotiate on economic treaties and to unite to demand better terms in getting their needs met, developing countries formed the Group of 77 countries in 1964. The bloc grew rapidly and today has 134 countries, including China. The UN climate negotiations cannot be understood in isolation from the demands of developing countries for a New International Economic Order and how the world economy has evolved. Some countries (especially in East Asia) have advanced substantially, while others remain in poverty. The cold war ended, eliminating the main alternative to the dominant paradigm of liberal democracies and free trade.

This history explains in part the attitude of both politicians and publics that climate change was a problem created in the world's richest nations, which by rights should address it there. In a forcefully written piece entitled *Úselo y tírelo*, the late Uruguayan writer Eduardo Galeano wrote that calling climate change "everyone's problem" distracted from the fact of who caused it and would only succeed in making it "no one's problem."[34]

Yet some nations, especially Brazil, faced pressure to act. The burning of the Amazon brought pressure on the nation to "save the rainforest." In 1985, the US space shuttle photographed over five thousand fires in the Brazilian Amazon. The legendary Brazilian social and environmental activist and leader Chico Mendes was murdered in 1988 by assassins hired by cattle ranchers. Before being inaugurated as the first democratically elected president after nearly twenty years of military dictatorship, Brazil's newly elected president, Fernando Collor de Mello, toured the capitals of the developed world in early 1990, only to be relentlessly asked what he was doing about "the Amazon problem." He learned that to secure the loans, grants, and investments needed to develop the country, he would need to convince the world that Brazil cared about the environment. For this reason, he offered to host the twenty-year follow-up conference to Stockholm in Rio de Janeiro in 1992.

Blame It on Rio

The 1992 United Nations Conference on Environment and Development (UNCED) or "Earth Summit" in Rio de Janeiro, was reported to be the largest gathering of world leaders in human history, with 168 countries represented, including 117 heads of state. There was also a huge parallel NGO People's Forum that adopted thirty-three peoples' treaties, and by acting inside and outside the official plenary rooms, the NGOs had a substantial impact on the negotiations. The importance of Brazil's civil society cannot be underestimated in understanding the outcomes of Rio: thousands of social movement organizations had spent two years in meetings to develop their positions in preparation for the Earth Summit.[35]

Andrew Hurrell and Sandeep Sengupta of the University of Oxford argue that the weakness of Brazil and other developing countries at Rio exactly at the time when Europe and the United States had overcome the Soviet Union meant that more ground was given by the North at Rio than normally would have been the case at such affairs. They argue that with the United States uncontested in hegemonic power, "The very weakness of such developing countries as India and Brazil in the late 1980s ... may have contributed to their success at Rio, resulting as it did in their underestimation by the North.... Concessions to weaker states, on this account, are easier to make in times of predominance."[36] The gap between what was agreed at Rio and what has happened in the following two decades of frustrating diplomacy is an important puzzle.

Among the five major documents finalized at Rio in 1992 was the United Nations Framework Convention on Climate Change (the UNFCCC). In 1993, Ecuador became the first developing country to ratify the climate convention. The text of the treaty includes foundational language, including that Parties (eventually 194 nations, nearly every one on earth) should act to "avoid dangerous climate change," protect vulnerable countries and ecosystems, and act "according to their common but differentiated responsibility and respective capabilities." This last phrase, referred to as "CBDR+RC," was the kind of phrase everyone could agree on because everyone had something different in mind. That simple phrase contains three parts. The word "common" expresses the idea that we all live on one spaceship Earth, which everyone needs to protect. This wording was agreed on to satisfy developed world environmentalists. The phrase "differentiated responsibilities" was chosen to satisfy developing country representatives, who saw that the rich countries had contributed much more than others to the problem. This suggested that nations would act according to their historical responsibilities for the problem. Finally, "respective capabilities" was selected to place the burden of payments and emissions reductions on the nations that have the most resources, especially Gross National Product (GNP).

As the UNFCCC began to be "operationalized" over the next few years into a binding treaty that aspired to "avoid dangerous climate change," Brazil again stepped in with a proposal to force those with the most "differentiated responsibilities" to take on the greatest commitments of reductions of greenhouse gas. At the 1997 Kyoto Protocol negotiations, Brazil pushed hard for nations to have to reduce their emissions according to their "historical responsibility" for polluting. The idea is logical: polluters should have to pay for the damage they have done, as is the case in a number of national laws, including in developed nations. The "Brazilian Proposal" was that all emissions since the industrial revolution should be included in the calculus of how to "share the burden" of reducing emissions. It was even more radical for the wealthy and powerful high emitters like Australia and the United States than was the proposal that emissions should be decided on an equal "per capita" basis, an approach popular with China and India.[37] The Brazilian Proposal would force the early industrializing nations in the North to reduce their emissions rapidly and to pay for damages in the South. In this and several other issues of intense and long-lasting negotiation, Brazil fought hard, arguing that it was fighting for the "environmental integrity" of the treaty.

Beyond Brazil, however, most other nations in Latin America scarcely had their voices heard in Rio or Kyoto and were considerably less active in the process than they are today.[38] Rather, the region was largely "towing the line" or "acting in solidarity" with the G77, which spoke for all developing nations and took largely defensive positions.

Kyoto was a success for the region in one sense: no Latin American country had any binding commitments to reduce their emissions of greenhouse gases under the Kyoto Protocol. Their hopes for a new wave of funding were pinned to a new carbon-trading exchange. In a 2001, Colombia and Costa Rica were described as "Emissions Entrepreneurs" after Kyoto, seeking to gain international funding for development projects through the "Clean Development Mechanism," known as the CDM. Brazil originally proposed the idea of the CDM, but it was reshaped in the negotiations, especially with the influence of the United States, which threatened not to sign the treaty without it. The idea was to allow rich nations that could not meet their own emissions-reduction targets to buy "credits" from developing countries that took on projects to reduce emissions that would have occurred if they did not take such a "clean" approach. For example, if chemical plants took expensive steps to avoid emitting harmful greenhouse gases such as fluorocarbons that would have increased global warming substantially, then that chemical company and its host country would have credits to sell. If a planned coal-fired power plant were replaced by a solar- or wind-powered one, then credits would be certified by the UNFCCC to be sold by the host nation. Installing a hydroelectric plant instead of connecting diesel genera-tors would allow lucrative CDM permit sales.[39]

Argentina hosted the 1998 and 2004 UN climate change negotiations (COP4 and COP10), both at a huge livestock auction hall in Buenos Aires in midsummer. As president of the Conference of the Parties for the year, the host nation is expected to organize, facilitate, and chair the negotiations. Argentina has never defined a clear position in the talks, however, and the Buenos Aires meetings did not produce any breakthroughs in the negotia-tions.[40] In fact, COP4 and COP10 rarely are mentioned in histories of the negotiations or in discussions of the tasks to be completed, unlike some other important meetings—no major work programs were agreed there.

A group of Latin American nations did show up at the Buenos Aires COP10 in 2004 with a joint message at an official event ("Central America Is Open for Business") and with CDM projects and permits ready to be purchased. Fliers for the event proclaimed "CDM in Latin America: A way already paved for investments." Panama's slick brochure declared that it was "a country engaged with the environment" with a "well-defined pro-cess for the evaluation and approval of CDM projects" and where "English is widely spoken particularly for business relationships." The brochure was the first ever to list projects in the forestry, energy, and waste sectors with estimated costs and the number of estimated permits that a Northern coun-try could get from investing in them. Three million emission credits went on the block in thirty-three projects, with over US$1 billion as their overall price tag. These were among the first national efforts anywhere to attempt to make money from the climate change treaty, and some observers we spoke to were in shock that "the talks are now all about money."

With Russia's hesitant accession, in 2005 the Kyoto Protocol finally came into effect. But besides trying to promote the CDM, Latin American coun-tries were still largely inactive in the talks. One notable exception involved Costa Rica. In 2005, Costa Rica and Papua New Guinea, supported by a number of countries, proposed a mechanism for reducing emissions from deforestation. This later evolved into REDD+ (Reducing Emissions from Deforestation and Forest Degradation), which is likely to be an important part of a new global agreement. In 2006, Papua New Guinea created the Coalition of Rainforest Nations, which pointed out that developing coun-tries could sell CDM credits for replanting deforested areas but that there was no way for them to receive funding for protecting standing forests. This

idea of having a market for permits to fund nations for protecting standing forests was linked to their conception of REDD+. Eventually, a long
list of Latin American countries joined Papua New Guinea in the Coalition of Rainforest Nations (either temporarily or for the long haul) such
as Argentina, Belize, Chile, Costa Rica, Dominica, El Salvador, Guatemala,
Guyana, Honduras, Nicaragua, Panama, and Paraguay. All were hoping to
profit from keeping standing forests standing.

From the start, however, Brazil's official position was discomfort with
earlier versions of the REDD+ proposal because it feared a loss of its sovereignty and control over its national territory if it sold off the ability to
change land-use in the future. An alternate Brazilian deforestation proposal
asked for funding to be supplied to nations only after they reduced their
deforestation and in the form of grants with fixed prices, not the sale of
permits in a marketplace with uncertain price. Thus, even the rainforest-
covered nations in the region remained split on the issue. REDD+ reflects
Brazil's unique positions and its steadfast protection of its sovereignty over
its resources and future, which was the core of the bargaining position it
took in Rio in 1992, when it had tremendous sway over the world's most
important environmental conference ever.

Is the G77 Disintegrating?

For two decades, the climate negotiations were dominated by the battle
between the Group of 77 and China, on the one hand, and the global
North, on the other. The two worlds were enshrined in the Kyoto Protocol
as the Annex 1 list of countries for the wealthy North and "non-Annex 1"
for the rest of the world. The core principle of the UNFCCC Common but
Differentiated Responsibilities and Respective Capabilities (CBDR+RC) in
1992 meant that rich countries were to go first in making emissions-reductions. The G77's main position was always that there should be no binding
commitments for any non-Annex 1 country.

Quietly, however, a few nations in Latin America and the Caribbean were
making noises that differed from their G77 partners. The Alliance of Small
Island States (AOSIS) had for a long time been demanding action by emerging economies like China and Brazil, but in the mid-2000s, Colombia and
Ecuador suggested that they would be willing to make emissions-reduction
pledges. Even as the negotiations were coalescing around declaring 2 degrees

Celsius of warming as a threshold that could not be crossed if we were to avoid dangerous climate change (associated with 450 parts per million of CO_2 equivalents in the atmosphere), AOSIS was pushing for 1.5 degrees Celsius and lining up with the 350.org campaigning group to support the level of greenhouse gases seen as required to stay under that level of warming. The ambition (and difficulty) of hitting a "350 parts per million pathway" to keep the world under 1.5 degrees Celsius is clear from the fact that in 2014 global concentrations crossed over 400 parts per million of carbon dioxide in the atmosphere.

Around the year 2000, an Ecuadorean NGO named Acción Ecológica proposed the idea of "the ecological debt." Spanish economist Joan Martínez-Alier joined with the group to argue that national debts of poor countries paled in comparison with the debt they were owed from the ecological damage and energy drain created when their natural resources were extracted over the past several centuries by wealthy countries.[41] The terms "carbon debt" and "climate debt" began to be used around the world, starting in a conference in Cuba in 2000 and quickly picked up by developing country governments and NGOs around the world. By the end of the decade, the terms "climate debt," "climate justice," and "climate apartheid" were frequently seen in pamphlets, briefing papers, academic articles, and protest signs at the UN climate talks.

Beyond AOSIS, traditionally Latin American countries followed the common G77 line of demanding that developed countries drastically reduce their greenhouse gas emissions first. They also requested specific advances on forestry under the UNFCCC and Kyoto's Clean Development Mechanism. After a largely nondescript first half of the decade for the region in the negotiations, in 2005 Mexico began taking stronger positions. First, in 2005 it announced an intersecretariat commission on climate change and adopted an ambitious position at the G8+5 meetings that same year.[42]

Latin American countries began to demonstrate leadership at the UN climate negotiations with voluntary emissions-reduction targets. Peru led the way with its voluntary emission-reduction pledge in 2008, followed by Brazil and Costa Rica. Still, it was not until the Copenhagen meeting in 2009 that the fragmentation of the G77 really took shape with the emergence of BASIC, the Cartagena Dialogue, and ALBA. In the Bonn midyear meetings in May 2008, Mexico made a major proposal for a World Climate Fund, an idea that was transformed into the Green Climate Fund, which was officially signed in Cancun in 2010. ALBA emerged as a more radical player than other G77 members (see chapter 4) and sought to become a champion of the core G77 positions and of climate justice social movements in 2009. Chile, Colombia, Costa Rica, the Dominican Republic, Mexico, Panama, and Peru pushed a more moderate yet ambitious stance at the UNFCCC, before some of them formed AILAC in 2012 (see chapter 5). In 2007, Ecuador announced its flagship Yasuní-ITT Initiative, which sought international financial compensation for its offer to leave 20 percent of its known oil reserves underneath a national park, which we describe in chapter 4.

As is shown in the next chapter, Brazil's climate change policy has shifted significantly since 2007 due to the impact of domestic and transnational factors.[43] Brazil joined up just before Copenhagen with the leaders of China, India, and South Africa in a new group called BASIC. All four countries wished to avoid limits on their rapid economic growth and sought to pressure the wealthy nations to act first, and they capitalized on G77 solidarity to support this claim by invoking the universal injustice of climate emissions and impacts for all developing countries.

At the UN climate negotiations in Poznan in Poland in 2008, Peru positioned itself proactively by offering mitigation action in forestry in exchange for further action by developed countries. These announcements by Mexico, Peru, and others came earlier than those made by other larger developing countries. Peru's decision reflected a growing awareness of the advantages and disadvantages of what it could gain or lose by adopting a more or less ambitious position in a high-ambition international coalition. Peru's 2010 national mitigation guidelines explicitly argued that the country would be better off contributing positively toward a high-ambition regime than to supporting one of low-ambition in which it committed to little or no mitigation action.[44]

In 2008, the pace of commitments quickened in advance of the 2009 deadline to create a new climate change treaty in Copenhagen. The hope was that making ambitious pledges would foster a bidding war that would eventually shame the richest countries (like Australia, Canada, and the US) into cooperating. Costa Rica pledged to become carbon neutral by the year 2021. It planned to go to zero net emissions by offsetting greenhouse gas through reforestation and through reducing emissions in the waste, transport, and agricultural sectors.[45] At COP14 in 2008, Brazil announced its National Plan on Climate Change, which included a target of reducing deforestation by 70 percent by the year 2017, drastically improving energy efficiency, and increasing the use of renewable energy.[46] Mexico also stated its aim to cut greenhouse gas emissions by 50 percent of 2002 levels by 2050.[47] On announcing Mexico's voluntary emission-reduction targets in 2008, the country's former environment secretary, Juan Rafael Elvira, stated that he hoped Mexico's target would challenge other countries to do the same.[48] Brazil's former minister of environment, Carlos Minc, was more blunt when he announced Brazil's National Plan on Climate Change, by stating that Brazil has the moral authority to demand immediate action from developed countries.[49]

There are more examples that are discussed in other chapters, but these flagship examples illustrate the way that Latin American countries broke with the G77 orthodoxy of emissions-reduction limits only for rich countries. At the same time, we can see some of the different approaches behind these decisions. Costa Rica, Mexico, and Peru have felt compelled to act due to a growing awareness of their own vulnerability to climate impacts and a hope to bring along the richer and larger countries. Brazil has also felt obliged to act on climate change, given its role as a major economy, and its aspiration to become a world power while responding to growing international and domestic pressures from civil society and business groups to reduce deforestation in the Amazon and associated emissions.

Much of this book attempts to understand the roots of these positions and their future. We examine through case studies whether national economies support these climate policies or undermine them. Before getting to the case study chapters, we briefly turn to Latin America's unique electricity matrix, which is the cleanest in the world due to the dominance of hydropower. In our estimation, hydropower has been one of the principal reasons behind Latin America's ability to lead on climate change by promoting its status as a low-carbon region. It is often overlooked that Latin America is already relatively low-carbon, which means that the challenge for the region is not solely to decarbonize but to achieve long-term prosperity while not increasing emissions.[50] On top of this, the longevity and sustainability of big hydropower is questionable and under increasing scrutiny.

The Double Edge of Big Hydro

The energy matrix of various nations makes it either easier or harder for them to shun or accept the kinds of carbon-emission reductions that are needed to avoid dangerous climate change. A distinguishing feature of Latin America's electricity supply is its reliance on large hydroelectric facilities, which has facilitated the bold stances taken by some countries in the region. This section describes those stances, the reasons they came to be important in the region, and the environmental double edge that they create.

Latin America has the cleanest supply of electricity in the world, which is largely the result of the Organization of the Petroleum Exporting Countries (OPEC) oil embargo of the 1970s, when crude oil prices soared, and shortages struck nations across the region. For countries with no local oil or few quality coal reserves, big hydro was an attractive option for breaking their dependency on world markets. It was generally reliable and cleaner and often created a new natural feature (a giant reservoir) that delivered reliable water to nearby farms and cities and attracted regional development. Hydroelectric power can deliver electricity and also open up (or close down) transport options in a region. Building on earlier hydroelectric projects, Brazil began building huge dams as part of great regional development initiatives and in the 1970s and 1980s took the next step of developing a massive sugar cane–based ethanol program to power its growing fleet of private automobiles.

According to 2012 data from the International Energy Agency, around 23 million Latin Americans still lack access to electricity, and 68 million still cook with traditional biomass (mostly wood).[51] Although Latin America's energy sector is cleaner than that of any other world region, economic growth has increased electricity demand, strained installed capacity, and driven demand for a greater share of fossil fuels in the region's power matrix. To satisfy a rapidly rising demand for energy, the generation mix is incorporating a growing share of fossil fuels.[52] Sustained economic growth is driving an increase in Latin America's energy-related carbon emissions, particularly from power generation and transport. In sectors such as these, which are vulnerable to infrastructure and technological lock-ins (where initial decisions shape decades of later ones), transitions to a low-carbon future would need to start now to allow emissions to peak soon and then drop drastically, as climate scientists argue is necessary to avoid danger-ous climate change.[53] The International Energy Agency forecasts that the region's energy needs will be 75 percent higher in 2030, requiring as much as $1.8 trillion in new energy infrastructure.

Climate change threatens the future reliability of hydropower in a num-ber of Latin American countries, such as Brazil, Colombia, and Honduras. Global circulation models indicate that global warming will bring both more intense rainfall events and longer dry periods to Latin America, which could adversely affect hydropower capacity in a region where hydropower accounts for about 60 percent of installed capacity and 70 percent of power generation.[54]

In March 2014, Sebastian Vicuña of Pontificial Catholic University in Chile said that hydropower's dependency on water could suffer from the potential impacts of climate change. He reports that many hydro project managers still assume a nonchanging climate, based on climate data from averages that stretch back fifty or a hundred years. But he stresses that cli-mate change has made such assumptions less reliable, and this has impli-cations for how hydroelectric systems are operated or developed.[55] In the Andean Community of Nations (Bolivia, Colombia, Ecuador, and Peru), which generate a little over 70 percent of their electricity from hydropower, the melting of glaciers caused by climate change could undermine their principal source of electricity.[56]

In a curious twist of fate, research highlighted by the IPCC's Fifth Assess-ment Report suggests that Ecuador could face an *increase* in hydropower generation capacity, which is associated with high levels of precipitation above its largest hydroelectric generation plant on the Paute River.[57] In this scenario, Ecuador could be in a position to become an exporter of electricity. The eight hydroelectric projects under construction scheduled for completion in 2016 have the potential to transform Ecuador's energy matrix. According to the Electric Corporation of Ecuador, the percentage of electricity from hydropower could increase from the current 62 percent to 93 percent from 2016. By avoiding other sources and exporting electricity, Ecuador could save more than US$100 million per year on fossil fuels used to power its thermoelectric plants. Ecuador's minister for electricity and renewable energy, Esteban Albornoz, has said that Ecuador could become a pioneer in exporting clean energy to Bolivia, Chile, Colombia, and Peru—all of which suffer problems of supply due to their dependency on rain for their hydropower.[58] Even though Ecuador may see an increase in stream flow and associated generation capacity, it has had difficulties in managing deforestation, erosion, and sedimentation, which can limit the useful life of reservoirs.[59]

✦ Wind and solar are increasing slowly in Latin America, so a clean alternative to hydropower is not immediately available, making it likely that a gap may be filled by natural gas or fuel oil. As Giulio Boccaletti points out, the development of hydropower has a troubled history because concerns surrounding the relocation of communities for reservoirs and flooding and downstream environmental impacts create serious problems for planners and policymakers. Hydropower can be considered a renewable source of energy, which brings essential base-load supply, energy storage capacity, and flood control.[60] But the large-scale hydroelectric plants that have been built in the region in recent years or that are in the process of being built have resulted in many arduous disputes with local communities—especially indigenous peoples—and with environmental groups.[61] In Brazil, indigenous and environmental groups persistently protested against the Belo Monte dam project, slowing it down by decades and forcing the reconceptualization and downscaling of the project.[62]

Researchers such as Philip Fearnside argue that big hydroelectric dams are not necessarily sources of clean energy because they can produce substantial amounts of greenhouse gas emissions. Fearnside suggests that methane is emitted by above-water decay of trees and roots left in the reservoir and initially by below-water decay. CO_2 emissions also come from the massive amounts of materials and energy used during dam construction.[63] These emissions from major hydroelectric dams are often portrayed as nonexistent by the hydropower industry and have been largely ignored in global calculations of emissions from land-use change.

Brazil's Tucuruí Dam provides an example with important lessons for policy debates on Amazonian development and on ways to assess the global warming impact of different energy options. As part of a regional "growth pole" development plan, Tucuruí was built on the Araguaia river in Pará state to provide cheap and plentiful electricity to aluminum smelters that were processing bauxite from the vast Trombetas mine, which was run by the state-owned mining company Albras. The reservoir was filled so quickly that thousands of trees were left in parts of its reservoir area to rot. After two dozen pages and nine tables of calculations of methane emissions from Tucuruí's open water, from areas where trees were left to decay, from its turbines, and from its spillway, Fearnside estimates that Tucuruí's emission of greenhouse gases in 1990 was equivalent to 7.0 to 10.1×10^6 tons of CO_2-equivalent carbon. That amount is substantially greater than the fossil fuel emissions of Brazil's largest city, São Paulo.[64]

Again, these kinds of emissions have been underestimated or entirely ignored in many global and national greenhouse gas accounts.[65] The Brazilian ministry of mines and energy's ten-year plan for the period from 2011 to 2020 calls for the construction of an additional forty-eight large dams in the country, thirty of which would be in the country's Legal Amazon region. Amazonian dams are being promoted, in part, on the basis of a supposed benefit in mitigating global warming. The time frame is critical in dealing with climate change: dams produce large emissions in the first few years and lower emissions that are sustained indefinitely for the useful life of the reservoir, whereas fossil fuels produce emissions at a more constant rate. Unfortunately, these dams may have cumulative warming effects that exceed those of fossil fuel generation for periods of up to several decades, making them incompatible with solutions to global warming. The greenhouse gas debt created by the dam in the first years when emissions are much higher than those from fossil fuel generation can take decades to pay off after the dam emissions stabilize at a level below those of fossil fuels.[66]

Due to rising energy demands and abundant untapped potential, regional governments in the Andean Amazon of Colombia, Ecuador, and Peru are prioritizing new hydroelectric dams as the centerpieces of long-term energy plans. There are plans for 151 new dams greater than 2 megawatts over the next twenty years, a more than 300 percent increase in Bolivia, Colombia, Ecuador, and Peru. The current planning for hydropower lacks adequate regional and basin-scale assessments of potential ecological impacts. An ecological impact analysis by Matt Finer and Clinton N. Jenkins classifies 47 percent of the potential new dams as high impact and just 19 percent as low impact. Sixty percent of the dams would cause the first major break in connectivity between protected Andean headwaters and the lowland Amazon, a major problem for migratory fish and for riverine human transport. More than 80 percent would drive deforestation due to new roads, transmission lines, and inundation. The authors suggest that hydropower dams of over 2 MW need to be reconsidered as an energy source in this region and that they may no longer merit the label "low-impact."[67]

In 2014, the Chilean government bowed to public pressure and canceled the HidroAysén project, which included plans to build five dams in the south of the country in Patagonia. They did so following an eight-year battle between developers and environmentalists opposing the plan. The plan was approved in 2011, but strong pressure by national and international civil society forced a rethink. The HidroAysén project would have provided 15 to 20 percent of Chile's energy needs. According to Chilean environmentalists, this episode is a major victory for civil society. As Patricio Rodrigo from the Patagonia Defense Council said in a statement: "The government's definitive rejection of the HidroAysén project is not only the greatest triumph of the environmental movement in Chile, but marks a turning point, where an empowered public demands to be heard and to participate in the decisions that affect their environment and lives."[68] However, Hugh Rudnick, an expert in energy at the Catholic University in Santiago, Chile, questioned the validity of the campaign against HidroAysén, exposing the deep-seated skepticism that abounds about big hydro. He told the BBC that "Compared to many hydro-electric schemes in the world, HidroAysen would have actually been very efficient…. The area to be flooded was very small for the amount of electricity it would have generated. But it's been defeated by a well-organized campaign by NGOs who've managed to convince the country that it would mean that the whole of Aysen would be flooded."[69]

Chile has an impressive potential for solar, geothermal, and wave and tidal power,[70] but it is still an energy-poor nation that relies heavily on imported natural gas to meet its growing demand, especially from its booming mining sector as the world's largest copper producer. To plug the gap from the rejected dam project, Chile's government plans to build new terminals to receive liquid natural gas from abroad and will invest heavily in energy efficiency. The government set a target of cutting energy consumption by 20 percent from the level that it would otherwise reach by 2025. Chile's Non-Conventional Renewable Energy Law aims to produce 20 percent of the country's electricity from renewable sources by 2025. To date, Chile has made some impressive advances and is an outlier in the region on renewable energy. In 2014, Bloomberg reported that Chile is attracting US$7 billion of renewable investments.[71] In that year, it also opened the largest photovoltaic solar power plant in Latin America and one of the largest in the world to date, with a total installed capacity of 100 MW.

Lastly, Chile established a carbon tax, making it the first country in South America to tax carbon dioxide emissions. The carbon tax targets the power sector and is meant to force power producers to shift to cleaner sources to help reduce the country's emissions and boost renewable energy. However, according to analysis by the Climate Action Tracker, Chile is still not close to achieving its emission-reduction pledge of 20 percent below business as usual in 2020 (as projected from 2007), but it has various emissions-reduction proposals, which may lead the way to further emissions reductions in the future.[72]

The situation in Chile is emblematic of broader energy challenges in Latin America and the double edge of big hydro. Energy demand is soaring, and governments are under immense pressure to fill the gap to keep economic growth ticking over and keep the lights on. The potential of major hydroelectric plants and other renewable energy options including wind, solar, and geothermal are among the principal options. China is capitalizing on this potential, and its interest in Latin American hydropower has recently increased dramatically, expanding from a small number of dams to multiple projects in Argentina, Belize, Colombia, Costa Rica, Ecuador, Guyana, Honduras, and Peru. Chinese hydro corporations have faced resistance and scrutiny over the environmental and social impacts of their projects due to poor implementation of environmental regulations and prickly relations with affected communities.[73]

Major hydropower projects will continue to feature as a central pillar of the region's energy supply, but the controversy surrounding their construction in terms of environmental and social impacts and their disputed reputation as low-carbon will increase. In the absence of hydropower, there is a worrying tendency to reach for fossil fuel alternatives that are sharply increasing Latin America's energy-related greenhouse gas emissions. New renewable energy targets across the region focusing on solar, wind, small hydropower, and geothermal are promising, and as in the case of Chile, some progress is being made but will need considerable government backing and private investment. We return to this issue shortly.

Inadvertent Pioneers

Latin America has a large number of the world's top-performing nations in terms of human development outcomes (such as life expectancy, literacy, and health) per unit of CO_2 and other greenhouse gases emitted.[74] The World Bank suggests that Latin America offers examples of how it has served as the world's laboratory for inclusive green growth through innovations in areas such as the world's most extensive use of bus rapid transit in urban areas and payments for environmental services.[75] However, this high performance is largely not the result of actions taken to address climate change. Rather, pioneering efforts have been made on a range of issues that, like the advent of big hydropower, originated not from decisions related to climate change but from other factors, such as concerns about energy security and dependence on imported oil, urban congestion, and air pollution in cities prone to terrible smog inversions. Another example is Brazil's use of efficient liquid propane gas cookstoves, which eventually replaced charcoal, wood, coal, and kerosene stoves. This began in 1937 after an Austrian-origin Brazilian was looking for a use for excess dirigible (blimp) fuel after the explosion of the Hindenburg collapsed that market.[76] These were inadvertent pioneers but pioneers nonetheless.

In this section, we look at policy areas where Latin American countries have made important contributions that recently have become highly relevant for our response to climate change. These include sustainable urban transport, disaster risk reduction, market mechanisms to protect forests, and the promotion of the rights of Mother Earth. In each case, when their relevance to climate became clear, the issues were "climatized," which often meant reframing and adjusting the approach taken. Advocates for issues like biodiversity or public health have recently seen funding decline as climate change captures attention from donors and campaigners. Reframing these issues with climate change allows them to argue for renewed attention to their concerns. In the end, though, Latin American domestic action on climate change and sustainable development is critical to informing the UN climate change negotiations and strengthening comprehension of climate-compatible social development. The region has first mover advantages.

 In cities, Latin America has been a clear innovator. Curitiba, Brazil, is globally renowned for the restructuring of urban space during the administration of mayor and then governor Jaime Lerner. During a period of exceptional autonomy, Lerner modified key shopping districts into pedestrian-only malls and reorganized boulevards and zoning to create a bus rapid transit system and city design that are among the most efficient in the world.[77]

In 1996, Brazil's megacity, São Paulo, adopted every-other-day car privileges (*rodízio veicular*) to address seasonal local air pollution, and it was regularized in 1997 to address serious traffic congestion.[78] This policy was, in fact, counterproductive from an emission-reduction point of view: some citizens increased car sales by purchasing an additional car to drive on the day in which their other car was not permitted to circulate. These "spare cars" were mostly older, more heavily polluting models, which resulted in increased emissions. São Paulo has taken steps to correct this loophole over the last couple of years with the implementation of bus corridors.[79] Santiago de Chile instituted restrictions on driving a decade earlier and extended them in 2001.[80] Bogotá, Colombia, has held car-free days on key axes, pushing auto commuters onto bicycles, public transport, and other means of commuting. Building on this success, Bogotá staged its first car-free week in February 2014 and closed specific routes completely to cars. To address air pollution and congestion, Mexico City was the first city to adopt every-other-day car privileges based on the final digit on license plates.[81] More recently, Mexico City has organized and upgraded its fleet of small buses, which are now a promising example of sustainable urban transport. A number of other cases of local leadership focus on addressing air pollution, congestion, and sprawl, but generally not climate change. But climate change is increasingly included in the list of reasons to take on such initiatives.

In the area of disaster risk reduction, several countries in the region have become world leaders. Hurricanes routinely pound Caribbean countries, and some have developed administrative and infrastructural systems that are highly resilient to the worsening disasters being seen and predicted with climate change.[82] Cuba is perhaps the most dramatic example, as its entire population undertakes two-day hurricane-preparedness drills each year before the storm season. Their preparations result in exceptionally low numbers of deaths and injuries, even in the face of fearsome storms. Other countries continue to have terrible mudslides and deaths in both urban and rural areas when hurricanes or exceptionally strong seasonal storms bring intense levels of rain. In the case of Colombia, the 2010 to 2011 La Niña phenomenon affected 4 million Colombians and caused over US$7 billion in damages related to the destruction of infrastructure and flooding of agricultural lands.[83] This has driven the creation of a national fund for climate-adaptation projects (one of the first in the world) and the development of a world-leading national disaster planning effort.[84]

Forestry is another area of Latin American innovation. In the 1980s, Latin America was a pioneer in the adoption of market mechanisms to bolster forestry protection with programs such as debt-for-nature swaps, which were pioneered in Bolivia, Costa Rica, and Panama. These have become relevant for climate change mitigation and adaptation efforts, laying the groundwork for later programs where individuals, firms, and others can offset their own carbon emissions by paying for reforestation or forest protection in the region.[85] As is discussed in chapter 3, Brazil has reduced deforestation (although deforestation has begun to creep up again), and in chapter 5, we describe how Costa Rica became a leader in payments for environmental services, which has helped drive reforestation there. Ecuador has implemented forestry protection through its Plan Socio Bosque, which pays landowners to protect their forests. Chile, Costa Rica, Uruguay, and Venezuela have made important advances on reforesting their territory. In 2011, Bolivia presented its "Sustainable Life of Forests" proposal in response to its questioning of REDD+ market-based schemes. The joint mechanism for mitigation and adaptation is designed to advance both simultaneously by managing forests to promote sustainable development and poverty reduction. Bolivia has objected strongly to linking forests to global carbon markets because this allows for the commodification of nature, which is considered sacred by Bolivian indigenous groups, and it has protected the rights of nature in its constitution.

The traditional knowledge and practices of Latin American indigenous peoples are invaluable for providing important perspectives on adapting to climate impacts. Indigenous peoples have extensive knowledge of their local environments, which they gained through thousands of years of observation, innovation and trial and error. They possess a large repository of strategies, skills, and techniques for dealing with climate variability. Following fieldwork in Peru, Emily Kirkland, a former member of the Climate and Development Lab at Brown University, discussed three cases. In the southern Andes, an archeologist named Ann Kendall is working with local communities to recover Inca-era terraces that have long been abandoned as ruins. These terraces can retain water for prolonged periods, allowing farmers to withstand droughts. In nearby Cusco, six communities have come together to conserve hundreds of native potato varieties. These native varieties are more resistant than modern varieties to heat, drought, and crop pests, making them a more resilient option during a period of climate impacts. Finally, in Peru's Piura region, the Soluciones Prácticas organization has created an innovative weather prediction system that blends modern meteorology with traditional forecasting methods. By combining

local observations of plants and animals with official predictions, Soluciones Prácticas creates seasonal forecasts that are more accurate than those
delivered by modern science alone.[86]

In each of these cases, existing efforts have to some extent been climatized (turned into a climate change issue to reflect the new emphasis on the
importance of taking climate action) with a reframing of efforts begun earlier for other reasons. The emergence of environmental issues occurred at a
time in the 1970s and 1980s that prodemocracy movements were building
in strength to oppose military dictatorships. This led many environmental
organizations in the region to implement a social justice approach, a story
that has been told most thoroughly for Brazil.[87] Some of the region's climate laws bear the marks of those movements and those times.

At the Second World Summit of Legislators in Mexico organized by the
Global Legislators Organization (GLOBE) in 2014, representatives discussed
the progress that had been made on national legislation on climate change.
According to a leading climate journalist, Lisa Friedman, climate change
legislation is "blazing a path across Latin America." Bolivia, Chile, Colombia, Costa Rica, El Salvador, Guatemala, Honduras, Paraguay, and Peru
have all either passed or announced their ambition to pass laws on climate
change to reduce emissions and adapt to climate impacts.[88] For example,
in 2012, Bolivia approved its Mother Earth Framework Law, which defines
the vision and conceptual framework for an integral development in harmony and equilibrium with Mother Earth. The law defines a high-level,
autonomous Mother Earth authority that is in the ministry of environment
and water and is in charge of the climate change agenda to promote forest
conservation, mitigation, and adaptation.[89] As is discussed in chapter 5,
Mexico was the second developing country to create a climate change law
after Brazil in 2012, and the law commits the country to reduce greenhouse
gas emissions by 30 percent by 2020 and to obtain 35 percent of its energy
from renewable energy by 2024. Mexico acted as the spark to inspire other
legislators to do the same in their countries. Andrés Avila Akerberg, who
leads the Americas chapter for GLOBE International, told Friedman, "The
initial piece of the domino was Mexico."[90]

Prior to the UN climate talks in Peru in late 2014, the former president of
Chile, Ricardo Lagos, argued that a coordinated legislative campaign should
be viewed as an essential prerequisite for sustainable development in Latin
America.[91] We agree that legislation on climate change could present a vital

means for Latin American countries to build a more democratic response to climate change while locking in actions on climate at the national level. However, this process should be not about simply creating legislation for the sake of itself but rather about creating the legal architecture within nations to facilitate improvements in policy and societal responses to climate change.

As is explained in chapter 5, Mexico's climate change law is an important step but needs to be viewed in the wider national context, given other policies and laws that may conflict or compete with it. In other countries, climate legislation has been proposed by lawmakers that has been heavily criticized by civil society groups that were insufficiently consulted or disagreed with the components of the proposed legislation. In any case, a climate law is only as good as its implementation. In some cases that we discuss later, climate change laws or policies are not implemented or are implemented partially because they clash with other legislation or policy. As the University of Brasilia's Eduardo Viola commented to us, the "decoupling between approved law and its implementation is a central feature of Latin American political culture."[92]

A Region's Emerging Clout

This brief historical tour suggests that there is a correlation between Latin American leadership on climate change and its growing presence on the global stage. Pioneering efforts that give it a lead on other regions—consolidation of democracy, relative political stability, a series of environmental and climate policy innovations, and its recent impressive economic performance—have created some of the conditions for Latin American governments and civil society to push the climate and environmental agenda. Latin American countries' voluntary emissions pledges at the UN climate negotiations are striking, as the first nonwealthy nations promising to control their emissions.[93] Their pledges came before some rich countries have acted.

Latin American countries' attempts to open up dialogue and build bridges between the global North and South have been pivotal for the advancement of the UN climate negotiations, an issue that is discussed in more detail in chapter 5. By playing a leading role in the Cartagena Dialogue, which brought together developed and developing countries at the

UN climate talks, several Latin American nations allowed new possibilities for progress, even as the North-South divide deepened and the talks threatened to stagnate entirely. We have seen from the Panama example in the Buenos Aires 2004 negotiations how Latin American countries supported the Kyoto Protocol's use of market mechanisms and then pioneered their adoption with the pricing and marketing of Clean Development Mechanism projects in the mid-2000s. Most important to us is the willingness of countries such as Costa Rica, Mexico, and Peru to put domestic emissions reduction offers on the table to pressure larger emitters that are reluctant to act, such as the US or emerging economies. These actions have developed a new discourse in the climate negotiations that all countries should do as much as possible based on their own capabilities.[94] The role of ALBA in promoting climate justice, inclusion, and respect for multilateral procedures at the climate talks has also made an important contribution, a point that becomes clearer with a fuller treatment in chapter 4.

So whither the G77 and China? The actions of the various subgroups within the G77—such as AOSIS, BASIC, AILAC, and ALBA, all of which have a strong regional presence in Latin America—may be contributing factors in deciding whether the global South's traditional negotiating bloc remains viable.[95] The G77 has been weakened considerably by splintering into subgroups, but the group continues to meet, strategize, and take joint positions throughout the negotiations.

An issue to consider after this review is the relationship between Latin America's decade of economic progress and its emerging voices on climate change. Our assessment is that economic growth and assertive foreign policies in the region have allowed countries to act more autonomously than they did previously. This stability and growth have given the region more confidence and room to maneuver and assess possible options going forward. An important new economic and political relationship with China comes up in nearly every chapter, and we believe that it supported the emergence of that newfound independence but also threatens its endurance. Several Latin American countries are becoming highly dependent on sales of their natural resources and commercial ties to that country. As is shown in later chapters, both the volume of trade and the nature of the relationship with China are important.

Finally, several Latin American countries are taking steps to confront climate change domestically, as demonstrated by Brazil, Costa Rica, Ecuador,

Mexico, and Peru. Some of their ability to do so is based on their "inadvertent pioneer" backgrounds after developing new approaches to forestry protection, ensuring the predominance of hydropower in the energy matrix, and implementing innovative urban planning—all of which can be relabeled as climate-friendly. Some of these features of their economies gave them the confidence to take action on climate change to enhance their first-mover advantage. Latin American nations face difficult challenges in balancing economic growth while tackling climate change. The positive agenda is not guaranteed and should not be overstated, given the region's growing middle class, surging energy demand, and tendency not to match ambitious climate action rhetoric with results on the ground. The values and demands of the emerging middle class will play an important role in determining the direction countries take on climate policy. It remains to be seen whether the region can support a global shift to low-carbon development outside of the UN climate negotiations, or whether given its significant natural resource endowment and the uncertain future of hydropower, it will aggressively exploit its abundant fossil fuels reserves.

We return to regionwide observations in the concluding chapter, but in the next three chapters we discuss studies of the three major negotiating groups in the region. Each includes three illuminating cases. We disaggregate the region into three groups of nations that have taken distinctive and at times competing, overlapping, and clashing positions at the UN climate talks. In chapter 3, we look at Brazil's perplexing behavior at the negotiations, its decision to join up with China, India, and South African in 2009 in the BASIC group, the ways that climate change fits into its larger foreign and national policy agenda, and its major accomplishments on reducing Amazonian deforestation. The two chapters after that look at Bolivia, Ecuador, and Venezuela as we examine the ALBA group, and Costa Rica, and Peru in an examination of AILAC and its affiliate Mexico. These cases support the core ideas of this chapter—that Latin America's diverse groups have been able to take more independent positions on climate change due to economic growth, a desire to advance a more autonomous and assertive foreign policy, and their earlier efforts on forestry protection, urban planning, and hydropower and particular interactions with civil society. Further, this independence is contributing to the fracturing of the G77, which is rarely able to speak for all the countries of the developing world. Vocal Latin American nations are beginning to fill a leadership gap in the negotiations. But the interesting cases lie ahead, so we now turn to Brazil.

3 Brazil: Climate Leader or Spoiler?

Brazil's Moment?

When Rio de Janeiro won the bid to host the 2016 Olympic Games after winning the bid to host the 2014 football World Cup for the second time, it was a crowning achievement for Brazil's former president, Luis Inácio "Lula" da Silva. "The world has recognized that the time has come for Brazil," he proclaimed.[1]

Yet the preparations for the World Cup were anything but smooth, and Brazil's defeat to Germany in the semifinal was a national football catastrophe, so the event wound up symbolizing the tensions that Brazil's political leaders and society confront in the search for fast economic growth, prosperity, and world recognition. The games went off successfully, but the World Cup was heralded as a chance to look back at the passionate football culture of Brazil, while also looking forward as the country attempts to consolidate its position as one of the new economic heavyweights of the twenty-first century.[2] Instead, it turned into a tortuous affair only partially relieved when Germany beat Brazil's arch rival, Argentina, in the final.

The challenges of hosting the World Cup and the Olympics reveal a complex story behind Brazil's playful exterior. Protests at the opening match in São Paulo exposed social discontent: Brazilians wanted to see tangible benefits for over US$10 billion of public money invested in the World Cup stadiums and supporting infrastructure.[3] The preparations went far over budget and resulted in revelations about gross overbillings and multibillion-dollar financial scandals.[4] It was initially thought that the private sector would cover the outlays of Brazil's preparations for the tournament, but the costs have fallen squarely on public budgets. Various infrastructure projects such as airport upgrades and rapid transit systems that were meant to accompany the new stadiums and boost wider economic development in host cities were delayed or canceled.[5]

As Brazil prepared for the World Cup in June 2013, the largest protests in two decades rocked the country, expressing public disenchantment with the politics and policies of the ruling class.[6] There was frustration among the general population with the inadequate provision of social services.[7] There was also a feeling of powerlessness due to widespread cases of corruption and embezzlement and the lack of transparency and financial accountability. The tensions seen in the World Cup and Olympics preparations revealed deep structural problems facing Brazil and some of the difficulties it faces in taking the next steps toward becoming a world power.[8]

Brazil considers itself a rising world power and is seeking to lead the global South. The country holds a unique position in the UN climate change negotiations. Sometimes Brazil is seen as a leader, pushing ambition and touting its own impressive emission-reduction efforts from reducing deforestation. Other times Brazil is perceived as a "saboteur" or a "spoiler," attempting to slow down and avoid any demands on the rapidly developing nations. A central goal of this chapter is to gain insights into which of these characterizations is most accurate: in what direction would Brazil like to see the climate negotiations move? To understand the country's frequently perplexing positions at the negotiations, we need to look at what drives Brazil's climate policy.

The ambivalence of Brazil's leaders on climate change cannot be overstated. On the side of ambition, President Lula presented a significant pledge in Copenhagen in 2009 and pushed for global action, acknowledging that Brazil's position was "a very bold one."[9] But after Lula was succeeded by Dilma Rousseff in the presidency, Brazilian climate ambition seems to have faded, and an old reticence seems to have set in, raising a question: were Lula's term and the Copenhagen pledge anomalies, or did they represent a longer trend toward greater commitment to action on climate change by Brazil?

We begin this chapter by reviewing some of the history of Brazil's sometimes confusing positions and behavior at the UN climate negotiations over the past two decades. Is Brazil a leader of the world or of the global South or of Latin America? Or is it simply a lone ranger, isolating itself from its neighbors and other parts of the developing and developed world? We seek to understand why Lula took an ambitious position in Copenhagen: what role was played by nonstate actors in the private-sector and civil society organizations in driving Brazil's apparent changes in national environment and climate policy through Lula's administration? Because emissions from deforestation were until recently Brazil's largest source of emissions, we focus on how nonstate actors influenced Brazilian national policy on climate change, especially its policy toward slowing the destruction in the Amazon region.

What foreign policy goals are driving Brazil's behaviors in global climate politics? As a rising power, Brazil's foreign policy and broader diplomatic goals are an essential element to understanding its climate change policies. We explore the influence that Brazil's foreign policy has on its climate policies at the UN negotiations and the ways that this issue influences Brazilian foreign policy. We attempt to understand the emergence of a powerful new bloc of countries at the negotiations in 2009, BASIC, which is made up of Brazil, China, India, and South Africa. Why did Brazil decide to join BASIC? What is Brazil's position within the group, and how does its participation in BASIC at the negotiations relate to broader changes in Brazil's foreign policy? What is Brazil's relation to its neighbors, and how do economic and political alliances like MERCOSUR and UNASUR shape its climate change policies?

Next, we focus on the history of deforestation in the Amazon and how the Brazilian federal government gained control over its chronic international black eye—illegal logging, clearing, and burning of the world's largest remaining tropical forest. Having predictability and control in the Amazon appears to have opened a window for more flexible negotiation by Lula at Copenhagen. A final section examines whether low deforestation (and higher climate ambition) is sustainable in the long term as economic stagnation and the rising power of agribusiness interests grow stronger with soaring commodity sales.

National changes in forest policy have coincided with a hardening of some of Brazil's positions on climate change in the UN negotiations, suggesting that an underlying force is driving both—President Dilma's singular focus on national economic growth. Brazil has so far avoided much of the external pressure to do more on climate change that has faced China and India, largely because it has reduced deforestation sharply since 2004 and because it can claim one of the cleanest energy systems in the world. Keeping in mind the caveats from the last chapter's discussion on the double edge of big hydro, extensive hydropower and a vast biofuels system built after the 1970s oil crisis make Brazil a low-carbon country.

Still, Brazil is one of the world's top ten emitters of greenhouse gases. Its greenhouse gas emissions have been historically concentrated in agriculture, forestry, and other land use (AFOLU), related mostly to deforestation, agriculture, and livestock. Deforestation has recently slowed considerably, to the point where forestry has ceased to be the major source of emissions. In 2010, emissions from Brazil's energy sector surpassed those from deforestation and land-use change for the first time, and from 1990 to 2012, energy-sector emissions displayed the greatest annual increases of any sector.[10] As Brazil develops, emissions related to fossil fuels for electricity production are increasing significantly and are expected to become the dominant source of greenhouse gas emissions over the next decade. Transportation is the largest energy-related emissions source, followed by industry, electricity generation, and buildings[11] Five major factors risk undermining Brazil's clean energy infrastructure: rising energy demand tied to the growing middle class, the discovery of vast offshore oil reserves known as the "Pré-sal," resistance to new big hydropower projects, persistent droughts undermining the reliability of hydropower, and problems facing the biofuel industry. These changes have had major impacts on Brazil's internal and external climate change policy.

The process is not all negatives: while it moves ahead with oil and gas exploration, Brazil is also taking promising steps on renewable energy from wind and solar, so our effort here is to develop a balanced picture of this crucial nation's direction on climate change.[12] Brazil's contribution should not be underestimated. It is not an exaggeration to say that with the Pré-sal and the Amazon rainforests, Brazil with a handful of pivotal countries could drive or doom any global efforts to stay within 2 degrees Celsius of warming.[13] At the UN negotiations, Brazil could be the hero or torpedo progress. The topics we discuss here concerning Brazil address the book's main themes and questions: What are the roots of Brazil's sometimes contradictory and often confounding positions on climate change? What is it about Brazil that made it willing to take bold action on climate change in 2009? How did Brazil become the world champion in emissions reductions, by considerably reducing Amazonian deforestation and its total national emissions? What can we learn from Brazil about the future of global climate politics and action? Can Brazil's model of social organization and politics be applied elsewhere to encourage sustainability and create lower-carbon and higher-ambition nations? In short, is Brazil a trailblazer or spoiler? We begin with a quick review of Brazil's behavior at the UN climate negotiations over the years, which regularly confounds observers and negotiators around the world.

Brazil's Bewildering Behavior at the Negotiations

In the UN climate negotiations, Brazil at times appears to be progressive on supporting ambitious international efforts to confront global warming. At other times, it has been characterized as a spoiler, blocking progress in defense of its national sovereignty under the banner of core UNFCCC principles. So which is Brazil—climate protector or spoiler?

The history laid out in chapter 2 describes several stages in the climate negotiations—the setting out of core principles at the 1992 Earth Summit, the hammering out of the Kyoto Protocol in 1997, and the scuffling in Copenhagen in 2009 (about which we present more in this chapter and the next). Our efforts to chronicle Latin America's contributions to that history referenced several of Brazil's efforts, but there are important pieces to the puzzle still to describe.

We have mentioned that President Fernando Collor hosted the Earth Summit in 1992, where the global process of climate governance was formally launched. As Eduardo Viola and Kathy Hochstetler point out, Brazil pushed hard for negotiations to be held under the UN General Assembly rather than under a smaller group like the UN Security Council or in a more technical branch such as the UN Environment Programme. Brazil's goal was to keep economic issues at the forefront to protect the rights of developing countries to economic development. Viola and Hochstetler rightly assess the huge impact of this move: "Arguably, their success on this issue has profoundly shaped subsequent climate negotiations. If politicization and a concern with economic development were Brazilian aims for the climate regime in the early 1990s, they were decidedly achieved."[14] Brazil's success in this sense has been a key part to explaining why the international community has found itself at loggerheads on the issue. The negotiations have been tied up in a largely unproductive way for over two decades and have always been far from adequately addressing global warming as required by scientific consensus.[15]

A second effort by Brazil has been to push developed countries to do much more—to act first (as they promised to do in the UNFCCC) and according to their "historical responsibility" because carbon dioxide stays in the atmosphere for roughly a hundred years after its release. In the United States, for example, key environmental laws (like the Superfund for chemical industry contamination) are built on the principle of the polluter pays. The idea is simple kindergarten ethics: whoever makes a mess should have to clean it up. In the case of chemical contamination from past industries in the US, polluters have to pay for their cleanup whether or not they knew about the dangers of their products and behaviors. Brazil pushed this approach in the Kyoto negotiations on climate change in 1997, saying that nations should have responsibility according to total emissions since the industrial revolution. However, Brazil's demand was summarily pushed off the table by the Argentinian moderator at Kyoto, Luis Espinosa.[16] The principle of burden sharing according to a nation's historical responsibility makes sense ethically and has been proposed as part of a metric by NGOs and other developing countries (and by Roberts in several writings) on who should do how much, but Brazil's strict adherence to the idea when it was clear that it had no traction has been a recipe for gridlock. Even the somewhat more moderate Indian proposal at Kyoto for emission-reduction requirements based on per capita emissions rights was dismissed before it was seriously considered.[17]

Although Brazil backed the Durban roadmap in 2011 to reach a new global climate agreement by 2015 for all countries, the country has tenaciously held to the historical accountability position, including a new push at the UN climate talks in Warsaw, Poland, in 2013. There, Brazil's historical accountability proposal was formally supported by the G77, although insiders suggest that this public display of support was superficial.[18] The position therefore led observers to conclude that this must be a tactic by Brazil to stall progress toward a binding agreement. As we observed in the Brazilian delegation's press conferences in Durban, Doha, and Warsaw, Brazil continued to chastise developed countries, touting its own significant efforts to reduce emissions from deforestation, which it saw as far superior to anything developed countries were doing.[19]

In September 2014, President Dilma was the only leader from the BASIC group to attend the Leaders' Summit on Climate Change, convened by UN Secretary General Ban Ki-moon. This was seen as an important indication of the Brazilian government's commitment to the issue. The president's speech, however, merely reiterated Brazil's ambitious measures at Copenhagen and its past accomplishments in emission reductions from stemming deforestation, but avoided making any new commitments. Rousseff reaffirmed Brazil's commitment to a universal and binding climate agreement based on common but differentiated responsibilities (CBDR). However, the speech ignored the growing role played by the energy and transport sectors in Brazil's greenhouse gas emissions, making analysts suspicious of her lack of commitment to a clean energy future.[20]

The international climate negotiations may have not been the only reason that President Dilma attended the summit. With the first round of the Brazilian presidential elections on October 5, she was also in New York to push a domestic agenda. One of her main competitors in the first round was Marina Silva, a leader on sustainable development and fighting climate change. Not attending the summit would have given Silva's election campaign an opportunity to score important points against the incumbent. As a result, Rousseff's attendance may have been as much about political point scoring and highlighting Brazil's successes on reducing deforestation for domestic audiences as it was about advancing the UN climate change talks.

Compared to its role in Warsaw in 2013, where it resurfaced the idea of historical responsibility, at the 2014 UN climate conference in Lima, Peru, Brazil was credited with adopting a more constructive approach. Brazil proposed the "recognition of the social and economic value intrinsic to mitigation activities" to overcome the logic that preventing climate change negatively impacts the economy.[21] Brazil's proposal aimed to incentivize action by "translating the results of early and additional action into units of convertible financial value," which could be used to back further sustainable development investments. Brazil believed that the UNFCCC "should develop the ways and means to recognize and promote the social value of mitigation and adaptation actions."

During her speech in Lima, Brazil's minister for the environment, Izabella Teixeira, referred to Brazil's other proposal, called "concentric differentiation." It consists of a series of three circles. The innermost is occupied by developed countries with absolute, economywide emissions reduction targets; the middle one includes emerging economies, with intensity, per capita or relative reduction targets; and the outer circle includes other developing countries with non-economywide targets. Every country should move toward the center over time, according to its respective capabilities (generally interpreted as GDP per capita). Teixeira commented that "concentric differentiation aims to ensure universal participation and promotes a continuous and sustained global effort towards increasing ambition and holding the global average temperature bellow 2 C." She went on to say that

"Self-differentiation" is not an option: it would neither be fair nor reasonable to expect developing countries to assume further obligations, while at the same time reducing the level of ambition expected from developed countries. Brazil has been doing its fair share and is ready and willing to contribute even more to the global effort against climate change. We call upon developed countries to live up to their responsibilities before the international community and to the legitimate aspirations of global civil society.[22]

The concentric differentiation approach can be seen as a mixed bag. Carlos Rittl, executive secretary of the Brazilian Climate Observatory, suggests that "while the proposal is certainly interesting for differentiating among developing countries, it still may leave major emitters such as Brazil and China off the hook, by allowing them to set targets that are not measured in absolute reductions for the post-2020 period."[23] He continued, "That would be a tragedy for the climate and also detrimental to the Brazilian economy. Brazil is far from being an innocent bystander of climate change—even by its own metric of historical responsibility." Rittl referred to Brazil's legacy of accumulated emissions in the atmosphere, making Brazil "probably the fourth top contributor to the observed global warming, responsible for about 7% of the total temperature change." This puts the nation, in Rittl's view, in the group that needs to deliver ambitious pledges in the Paris round in 2015.

On Brazil's possible pledge, the Climate Equity Reference Calculator is an interesting tool created by the organizations EcoEquity and the Stockholm Environment Institute. It seeks to benchmark how nations are doing in adequately and fairly dividing up the remaining global carbon budget before we overspend the atmospheric amount that can still be safely emitted.[24] If expectations are based on an equitable international climate agreement based on 50 percent on capacity and 50 percent on historical responsibility since 1990, the voluntary commitments that Brazil has put forward would produce only about half of the emission reductions that make up the country's fair share.[25]

Another area of Brazil's impact has been in the creation and negotiation of the Clean Development Mechanism (CDM). Brazil's insistence that the wealthy nations should pay developing countries for damage to the earth's atmosphere is based on its support of the core UNFCCC principle of parties acting according to principles of equity and their "common but differentiated responsibilities and respective capabilities" (CBDR+RC), discussed in chapter 2. This led Brazil to suggest a fund to support sustainable development efforts in the developing world as part of the Kyoto Protocol, which after negotiations with the US evolved into the CDM. The CDM took off in the second half of the 2000s (as described in chapter 2), bringing billions of dollars in development investment to some nations and sectors. Brazil was the first country to have a project approved by the CDM executive board.[26]

Most of that funding did not reach the poorest nations, however, and did not go to tree planting, as had been widely envisioned.[27] Nearly all went to large industrial projects in China, India, and Brazil. In Brazil, substantial funds flowed for cement plants, sugar mills to create biofuels, and small hydroelectric facilities.[28] Brazil captured 45 percent of all CDM funding to Latin America through 2012.[29] Given the reduced levels of participation by the rich countries since the Kyoto Protocol was largely eviscerated at Copenhagen in 2009, flows through the CDM have slowed to a trickle, and preference for new projects has been given to the Least Developed Countries Group. Therefore, the Brazilian dream of a mechanism for compensating poorer nations only marginally and temporarily materialized in the CDM.

Then there is Brazil's often confusing position on REDD+. In 2005, Costa Rica and Papua New Guinea proposed a new mechanism to keep forests standing, which evolved into what is now called reducing emissions from deforestation and forest degradation (REDD+). This was needed because under the CDM, developing countries could be funded only for planting new forests (reforestation), not for protecting existing ones. So this new proposal represented a potentially huge flow of funding that might also support the goal of poverty alleviation and protecting biodiversity across the developing world. To many people's surprise—since the Amazon represented a potential huge source of REDD+ projects—Brazil resisted REDD+ from the beginning and never joined the Coalition for Rainforest Nations. Rather, to avoid being beholden to outside powers about how they manage their own land, Brazil put forward its own mechanism, which involved a retrospective accounting where countries would receive compensation for already accomplished reductions in deforestation rates. Brazil also resisted having the market determine the prices for tying up forests in an international mechanism. The difference with the CDM was vast. Brazil's proposal required a huge amount of funding from wealthy nations in the form of grants without any exchange of the sort that underpins the CDM.

Brazil held steadfast to this proposal for years but finally softened its position as federal agencies in the country battled over who got to control CDM projects, which were turning into more lucrative projects than was envisioned.[30] A number of potential subnational REDD+ projects, such as those pioneered in the state of Amazonas, also showed the potential viability of the proposal. Brazil has played a more active role in the REDD+ negotiations since it was established as a central tenet of a new global agreement scheduled to be finalized in 2015.

From 2006 to 2010, President Lula saw an opportunity to promote Brazil's global soft power credentials and gain credit for new flexibility in the negotiations, so in Copenhagen in 2009, he promised to reduce the country's emissions by roughly 36 percent by 2020 below where it would be if it stuck to a business-as-usual trajectory. Congress quickly scrambled to codify his promises. As Viola and Hochstetler point out, this was the result of a rare constellation of domestic factors, which created "an unusual opening for progressive climate politics in 2009–2010."[31] Brazilian industries feared "border adjustment" tariffs on their products in Europe and the US if they did not act, and Lula's effort to pick Dilma as his successor was being challenged by his renegade environment minister, Marina Silva, who was running with the Green Party against Dilma. To show that he and his Workers' Party were pro-environment, Lula promised major cuts in emissions, and he made the promise in the international venue (but did not offer for them to be legally binding under the UN).

Brazil has taken positions on climate that have befuddled many observers. In defending the rights of developing countries to sustainable development, Brazil sought to position itself between rich and poor nations. However, its ability to claim leadership in Latin America is tenuous, as is described in the next two sections. Brazil's indifference to the Coalition for Rainforests Nations, which includes various Latin American countries, also reveals its lone ranger status. First, we ask why Brazil is teaming up with three of the other largest rapidly developing countries in the BASIC group and then ask how the rest of Latin America is responding.

Joining Club BASIC

BASIC (Brazil, South Africa, India, and China) was a group formed prior to the fateful 2009 negotiations in Copenhagen, consisting of the BRICS group minus Russia (which is an Annex-1 country). BASIC is not just another G77 subgroup like the Least Developed Countries. Rather it is a more informal alliance by which countries coordinate, and overlap with other groups of emerging powers and focuses on a range of strategic purposes—most consistently on pushing for a greater role in global governance.

The group was formed due to the close fit between the social and development agendas of those four countries,[32] and the climate negotiations were an excellent opportunity for them to protect their common interests. Those interests were to continue their rapid economic growth and to protect against limits that other nations, especially those in the North, might impose through trade or environmental safeguards.[33]

Especially of concern among both low-lying small island developing states and proenvironment nations in the developed North were the emerging economies' soaring carbon emissions, which threatened to undo any progress achieved by reduction efforts in developed nations under Kyoto or any successor treaty. And most alarming to the BASIC group, some of those wealthy nations (the US and the EU) were considering border adjustment tariffs for products imported from places where carbon emission rates were higher than their own. The specter of these tariffs was a great motivator for Brazil to propose major action on climate in 2009 and 2010, bringing some key industrial groups to the side of addressing the issue.[34] Led by the mining giant Vale, one group of twenty-two large corporations released an "Open Letter to Brazil about Climate Change," which called for reductions in deforestation and emissions from energy and cattle ranching. Another group, the Brazilian Climate Alliance, also called for strong climate policies and control of deforestation, even though it consisted mainly of agribusiness industry associations. A third and arguably more progressive group, the Coalition of Corporations for the Climate, demanded mandatory climate policies that would peak fossil fuel emissions between 2015 and 2020. These strong statements from private-sector groups strengthened arguments by environmental activists and built support from the general public for Lula's pledge.

At the first BASIC ministerial meeting in Beijing in 2009, BASIC countries announced a joint strategy for the Copenhagen negotiations, and in the end the group played a key role in shaping the Copenhagen Accord.[35] The now legendary moment occurred when the negotiations were foundering late in the second week as heads of state jetted in. Brackets around phrases in the UN negotiating texts mean that key areas still have not been settled. During the first week, there were about two hundred brackets in the text, but by the middle of the second week, heads of state arrived expecting to be able to settle a few last details and have a photo op at a major signing but were instead presented with a mountain of four hundred brackets.[36]

With an international embarrassment looming, the US president, Barack Obama, gate-crashed a private meeting of the BASIC leaders. The five hammered out what was to be the core of the Copenhagen Accord, twelve paragraphs that entirely reshaped the way humanity was going to deal with climate change. Rather than the old Kyoto Protocol approach of binding limits that were consistent across a group of wealthy countries, the Copenhagen language proposed a two-step "pledge and review" system whereby all nations decided what they want to do to reduce their emissions and would be reviewed periodically on their progress. A fundamental difference and a top goal of the US in pushing the Accord was that it applied to everyone—large and small, emerging or developing, and not just developed nations.

Regardless of whether this is seen as a positive new direction or a disaster (observers remain divided on this), Copenhagen represented a significant geopolitical turning point in multilateral negotiations. BASIC countries drove the process, saying that they were defending some of the key principles enshrined in the Kyoto Protocol that wealthy nations should act first and assist developing countries in decarbonizing their economies.[37] And it marked a real power shift—with the BASIC group and the US "sidelining Europe in climate change negotiations and forcing the [US] to negotiate within a very different institutional context."[38]

In Copenhagen, there was a much greater focus on the major emitters from the developing world (especially China and India) than ever before, pressuring them to make pledges. South Africa, Brazil, and even India made pledges, but the Chinese were reluctant to endorse a deal. So why did Brazil negotiate with BASIC? What does the country gain and lose from doing so? Why does it not negotiate with some of its Latin American neighbors?

Brazil's participation within BASIC clearly fits Brazil's broader foreign policy agenda to build strong South-South cooperation—and implicitly its wish to break from historical dominance of the US and Europe. For this reason, Lula regarded improving relations with China as furthering Brazil's own interests.[39] Participation in BASIC and other groups such as the BRICS supports Brazil's goal of becoming a major power. And it has put Brazil in the rooms and discussions where the pivotal moments in the last decade of climate negotiations have taken place.

Halding and his colleagues argue that Brazil's participation in BASIC is fueled by a growing acceptance that it may have to eventually negotiate concrete emission-reduction targets, and it might be better off joining forces with those in a similar situation to defer and diminish these requirements.[40] They also argue that BASIC solidarity is also helped by broader institutional inertia or so-called path dependency. The way in which the principle of common but differentiated responsibilities has been institutionalized in the Kyoto Protocol as a firewall between developing and developed countries, they argue, is an important factor. The institutionalization of this principle plays a significant role in the efforts of BASIC to resist explicit differentiation between countries on emissions-reductions and also explains the efforts of some industrialized countries to set aside the Kyoto Protocol. If the system of differentiating between countries evolves (and moves beyond a 1990 reality to one that is based on today's reality or the near future), then China, Brazil, and South Africa are likely to "graduate" into the group of nations expected to make concrete emission reductions as part of a new global agreement.[41]

BASIC has consistently articulated and supported the G77's demands for more financial and technological assistance from the North, saying that developing countries' mitigation and adaptation activities depend on it. At the climate negotiations, China has emphasized the plight of millions of its citizens who continue to endure poverty, but China has also promised assistance to developing states for their climate efforts.[42] Within BASIC, Brazil has made the most explicit statements promising climate assistance. During the Copenhagen conference, Lula spoke of a Brazilian pledge to take action to mitigate its emissions and said that Brazil would not need the world's resources to do so.[43] He also promised climate aid to some African nations developing their biofuels industries, based on the long learning from Brazil's well-established ethanol program.

If Brazil really is progressive on climate change, then it seemingly should differ from India and China, which were long considered foot-draggers in resisting emission-reduction pledges from emerging economies. After all, Brazil was the first BASIC country to offer voluntary emissions reductions. Lula pledged at Copenhagen that the nation would reduce emissions between around 36 percent below its projected emissions in 2020.[44]

Halding and colleagues argued that BASIC's cooperation is shaped by the different norms, ideas, material concerns, and relationships that affect the positions that each country brings to the negotiations.[45] At the Cancun negotiations in 2010, BASIC revealed the difficulties it was having in defining common ground and showed that it was willing to disagree publicly on particular matters, such as whether all major greenhouse gas emitters should be subject to legally binding emission reductions in a future international agreement.[46]

Brazil is different from other BASIC countries in its large proportion of emissions being due to deforestation (although this is now changing). This means that emissions-reduction obligations for its other BASIC partners might be to Brazil's comparative advantage in economic markets where they compete, particularly in energy-intensive trade-exposed sectors. Within BASIC, Brazil reportedly pushed for some kind of commitments from developing countries starting in 2020. During the Durban negotiations in 2011, Brazil attempted to build some consensus between the EU and the other BASIC countries.[47]

In Warsaw in 2013, Brazil returned to a harder line on the historical responsibility of developed countries to reduce emissions, to the dismay of the EU, which regarded the Brazilian proposal as counterproductive.[48] Viola and Hochstetler criticize Brazil as being unable to distinguish between developed nations that are taking real action on emissions reductions and finance and those that are not. "In its heavy criticism of developed countries," they argue, "Brazil has been always incapable of differentiating different performances among them. On the other side, Brazil has always done an exaggerated defense of non-Annex 1 countries' performance. This distorted and simplistic approach has undermined Brazilian credibility."[49] Our discussions with experts and negotiators and NGO representatives from across the spectrum from most to least developed countries support this observation on Brazil's positions in the negotiations.

More broadly, the question is whether BASIC as a group (or its largest countries, in particular) can become world leaders, caring for global public goods such as the global climate.[50] Andrew Hurrell and Sandeep Sengupta put the problem and the stakes this way:

If emerging powers are seen as increasingly influential and important players, their rise is also commonly viewed as having made an already difficult problem still more intractable. Their economic size and dynamism, their increasing share of greenhouse gas emissions, and their overall political salience and foreign policy activism have all become more prominent; but, on this account, they have failed to recognize or live up to the responsibilities that go with their newly acquired roles. They represent a particular class of states whose development choices are critical to the future of climate change but whose governments have all too often proved to be obstructionist and negative.[51]

So the question remains: why did Brazil join BASIC and face being labeled by other countries as obstructionist and negative in the climate negotiations, when it had a strong record of its own on emission reductions and a willingness to make its own pledge? We believe the answer lies in Brazil's broader foreign policy agenda.

The Quest for a Seat

Brazil is an emerging economy and aspires to become a major global power. Its markets have been booming, its people are diverse and cosmopolitan, and its government has the appearance of an exemplar of multilateralism, never resorting to its military to threaten its neighbors. In diplomatic circles, Brazil's presence is coveted on panels and commissions—it is perceived as an ally of the developed world and also a friend of the global South.[52] Brazilian development cooperation is small but has increased considerably in recent years, demonstrating how Brazil and other developing-country contributors are transforming the conventional aid landscape.[53]

Brazil is currently the world's seventh-largest economy. To become a major power, however, Harold Trinkunas at the Brookings Institution argues that a nation needs the ability to change the rules of the global system.[54] President Lula gave substantial attention to international affairs including climate change. He engaged closely with foreign policy matters and used the Ministry of External Relations, called Itamaraty, to build the nation's identity as a global power broker.[55] As Trinkunas puts it:

Power is relative, and shifts in the power, capabilities, and intentions of other states in the system, particularly among the existing major powers, also produce opportunities for rising powers. Opportunities may also emerge as different domains of the international order, such as climate change or finance become more or less salient in interstate relations. This provides rising powers with windows in which their capabilities might have an outsized impact relative to their historical means.[56]

Being in solidarity with other countries in the G77—and one of its largest economies, China—provides Brazil with an opportunity to exert some of this leverage.[57] G77 solidarity may explain Brazil's positions and its sometimes outsized influence in the climate talks.

The UN climate negotiations, Trinkunas argues, present an example of Brazil's transition from the target of criticism and international rules to "one of the key rule-writing states."[58] A central piece of Brazil's foreign policy has been to gain more ability to reshape the global institutions in which it feels it should have a voice. This includes in particular the UN Security Council. To gain that voice, Brazil covets a seat at the table where the big decisions are made.

Brazil has long wished to secure a permanent seat in the Security Council and thought that holding a temporary seat during a term in 2011 to 2012 gave it a good shot. As Trinkunas points out, however, rather than strengthening its case for permanent membership, Brazil's hand was weakened: "The term highlighted the tensions between Brazil's views of international politics and those of the West. Brazil's decision to caucus with BRIC countries during its term in the Security Council was not viewed positively by the [three] Western members."[59]

Lula's successor as president of Brazil, Dilma Rousseff, has shown herself to be much less interested in foreign affairs. Dilma has continued the focus on South-South cooperation by making her first official trip abroad to Argentina.[60] But she has been less concerned than Lula was with elevating Brazil's position on the global stage and has deemphasized international relations. Rousseff is making fewer visits to other countries, especially compared to Lula's extensive international travel, and is spending less money on development cooperation.[61]

To gain seats at the tables of power, Brazil should be able to show that it can lead its region. On this count, for both internal and external reasons,

Brazil has achieved little. Brazil stands apart from its region and finds itself distrusted by its neighbors, which often undermine its efforts to gain a seat. Brazil's attempts to obtain a permanent membership in the UN Security Council were thwarted by a lack of support from the US, but Mexico and Argentina also have consistently worked with other states to undermine its claim.[62] Brazil finds itself unable to wield military power, and it is "unwilling to commit its economic power to provide incentives and side payments so that other powers might follow its lead."[63] Therefore, Brazil was without either carrots or sticks to exert its leadership in Latin America. And it has been unwilling to follow other Latin American countries' lead on climate change governance.

In the economic realm, Brazil has put a lot of effort into MERCOSUR. That trade zone at first looked promising, but given the economic woes of two fellow MERCOSUR members, Argentina and Venezuela ("two of the most troubled economies in South America") and indeed Brazil's own economic underperformance, the trade bloc is not faring well.[64] Still, being the nation with the largest manufacturing and services sector in the bloc, Brazil stands to benefit from priority access to these markets. Trinkunas points out that other major trade-zone efforts like the Trans-Pacific Partnership and the Trans-Atlantic Trade and Investment Partnership, both of which include Latin American states, are proceeding without Brazil.

Politically, in breaking away from the old Washington-based Organization of American States, Lula attempted to position Brazil as "a broker of regional consensus." This started with promoting the South American Community of Nations in 2004, which became the Union of South American Nations (UNASUR) in 2008.[65] UNASUR excluded the Canada, the US, and all of Central America and Mexico, which were seen as differing profoundly in perspective by being open to global free trade and not protected, regional exchange.[66]

Still, Miriam Gomes Saraiva argues that over the long term, there is substantial continuity in Brazil's foreign policy, which is based on seeking "autonomy, universalist action, and the idea that the nation will one day become a major power on the global stage."[67] Sean Burges has argued that Brazil has outsize influence in forums like the UNFCCC because it can generate ideas that appear to draw together the interests of the developing world and in so doing either "mobilize or derail initiatives requiring a larger Southern voice."[68] Brazil, he argues, acts with "diplomatic flair," and the country positions itself "as a North-South balancer by trumpeting its 'southernness': either as representative of the global South (a position that is far from universally accepted) or by working to organize coalitions in the South around particular policy positions." He argues that by doing so, Brazil has managed to protect its sovereignty and autonomy quite cheaply, but in doing so it has ended up as a frequent "blocker" or "spoiler" of accords.[69] Brazil, he argues, has benefitted significantly from the world system the way it is currently structured, so although it complains loudly about current arrangements in a way that appears in solidarity with developing nations, Brazil has not threatened the fundamental structure of that international system.

So Brazil's larger foreign policy goals indeed appear to be driving its posture in the global climate negotiations. Its desire to be a major power and protect its sovereignty and autonomy lead it to join with some defensive countries in the BASIC coalition. This in turn leads it to resist Northern pressure to take on binding emission-reduction limits, and it often uses its southernness to defend its right to be without a binding cap, which is a only truly a right of the poorest nations in the G77. In the following chapters, we look at two groups of Brazil's neighbors that challenge different parts of this position and that have stepped away from any willingness to have Brazil speak for them in the negotiations.

Country climate negotiators are told what they can and cannot say during the UN climate talks by their head of delegation, minister, or head of state. Most of the negotiators represent those actors themselves, in their socialization and disciplinary training if not in their cabinet or ministry posts (some serve in their nations' environment ministries, and some in other agencies). In the case of Brazil, the Ministry of External Relations closely controls the tone, content, and deployment of its statements through its delegation. Brazil is no different from other nations in seeking its self-interest. However, in the case of climate change, Brazil's avoidance of commitments appears to be prolonging the global stalemate in addressing an issue that ultimately threatens the nation's economy and ecology. The fundamental questions of what Brazil is doing at home on the issue and how that drives its international posture are at the core of the next two sections.

Fewer Chainsaws, More Forest

Brazil's posture in the UN climate negotiations is influenced in part by a key issue at home—its efforts and success in reducing emissions caused by the clearing and burning of the Amazon rainforest and the drier Cerrado region. From a ten-year average of nearly 20,000 square kilometers per year being cut down through 2004, deforestation in the Amazon dropped to just below 6,000 square km in 2013, a 70 percent decrease.[70] Why did Brazil's deforestation rate drop precipitously at that time? Our understanding of the drop may help us ascertain how durable those gains will be in the future. It will also inform considerations of whether Brazil could be a model for other nations (such as Peru and Indonesia) that face daunting tasks of controlling frontier areas or highly polluting sectors. And for the central topic of this book, it is important because keeping down those rates is central to Brazil's attempts to deflect calls for it to make more difficult emissions-reductions across the economy, especially in the energy sector.

We need to examine the substantial political shift in Brazil on climate change and sustainable development. Surveys regularly point to the high level of concern that Brazilians place on environmental issues (see chapter 1). For decades, the major electronic and print media, based in Rio de Janeiro and São Paulo, have expressed great concerns about the collapse of the Amazon. Civil society and private-sector pressure led to important shifts in Brazilian policy on deforestation and climate change during the Lula government, especially before the Copenhagen negotiations in 2009.[71] After a deforestation peak in 2004, reductions have played a fundamental role in the formation of Brazil's domestic and international climate change policies. In short, the sharp drop in deforestation showed to skeptical planners in Brazil that they could control this important source of greenhouse gas emissions and that doing so could be done without subverting national development and poverty reduction goals.

Although Amazonia covers parts of nine nations, Brazil accounts for 68 percent of its land—the single most biologically diverse area in the world and the planet's largest block of remaining rainforest.[72] Brazil's biodiversity provides vital ecosystem services to the region and the world. Although the old-growth rainforests in the Amazon no longer absorb large amounts of carbon overall since it is mostly mature forest, they represent a stock of approximately 120 billion tons of CO_2 in their biomass—a huge amount that if released would spell disaster for the global climate. The region plays an integral role in Latin America's climate and beyond, creating storm systems that spread water to surrounding regions, and which produce approximately 20 percent of the world's flow of fresh water into the oceans.[73]

The Brazilian Legal Amazon region represents 53 percent of Brazil's total land area, has a population of 25 million people (up from around 11 million in 1980), and generates just under 8 percent of Brazil's total GDP.[74] So the region is vast but not the most central part of the Brazilian economy. In earlier planning efforts, the region was often seen as an untapped resource, as a mining frontier, as a vast potential breadbasket for the nation, and as a possible new economic engine.[75] The national struggle either to open up or to protect the region from the impact of world trade has teetered this way and that, between development forces and preservationist ones.[76] For decades, efforts at controlling deforestation have been fleeting in their effectiveness.

Several forces drove intense deforestation in the Amazon for years. During the military dictatorship in the 1960s and 1970s, the Brazilian government feared that the vast empty space would be coveted and potentially invaded by foreign governments, environmentalists, and commercial interests. They sought to occupy the region with economically productive Brazilians and used the region as a safety valve for landless and poor farmers from other areas of the country. Among other projects, they built the 4,000 kilometer Trans-Amazon Highway from the Northeast and the Belém-Brasília Highway to bring settlers and ranchers from the Southeast and to tie the region into the national economy. Construction contractors lobbied for and profited massively from these highway projects, huge dams, and mines, often in exchange for campaign funding or direct cash bribes to officials.[77] After attempting to settle small farmers on the Transamazon Highway and in the state of Rondônia, planners switched to large-scale ranchers in the early 1970s, some of whom cleared massive areas. Loggers and miners also needed roads to the most remote corners of the region, and the national government was largely unable or uninterested in stopping them.[78]

This was the context in which President-elect Fernando Collor de Melo was elected in early 1990. He traveled to the capitals of the wealthy nations and was asked frequently how he would stop Amazon deforestation. Foreign leaders had seen photographs of thousands of fires burning in the states of Rondônia and Pará and had heard about the struggle of the rubber tappers and their assassinated leader Chico Mendes to protect the forest against the expansion of the ranchers and road builders. Collor saw the importance of controlling deforestation for his ability to gain access to credit in international financial markets and through foreign assistance from wealthier nations. He sought to control deforestation with "command-and-control" regulations on clearing sizes and illegal land use, but some initially successful reductions in deforestation were impossible to sustain with many desperate people in a broken economy and with a growing national and global market for the products of the region, such as minerals, tropical lumber, and beef.

Deforestation rates rose again, and the Brazilian state was incapable of entirely controlling the problem. From 1994 to 2005, deforestation increased, reaching nearly record levels in 2004 (figure 3.1). The World Bank and other international funders and NGOs had been working in the region for decades and shifted to a broader, more societal approach in the attempt to create a more sustainable model of development there.[79]

In response, an interministerial committee called the Grupo Permanete de Trabalho Interministerial proposed the Action Plan for Prevention and Control of Deforestation in the Legal Amazon (Plano de Prevenção

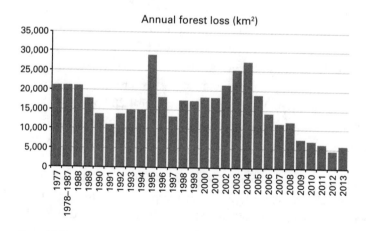

Figure 3.1
Deforestation rates in the Brazilian Amazon
Note: The second bar is the average for 1978 to 1987.
Source: Adapted from Nepstad et al. 2014; INPE 2014a, 2014b; "Calculating Deforestation Figures for the Amazon" 2014).

e Controlo Desmatamento na Amazônia Legal, PPCDAm) in 2003, and it went into effect in 2004. The Action Plan was announced by the Casa Civil (Civil House), which was one of the most powerful organs with the status of a ministry in the country and reports directly to the president.[80] The results were striking: deforestation dropped by over half in just three years. Its success was due to its inclusion of environmental agencies as well as other key parts of government, like the judiciary, development agencies, and land reform centers.[81] The PPCDAm funded positive projects through the Amazon Fund and improved and resolved land ownership issues, which were a chronic problem. It focused on environmental monitoring and control. In 2004, a remote sensing system called DETER (Real Time System for Detection of Deforestation) began providing law enforcement officials with immediate information to stop illegal clearing and burning. It also sought the promotion of productive activities that did not cause the destruction of standing forests. Having presidential support and the leadership of strong environment ministers Marina Silva and later Carlos Minc was essential to these government-led plans to reduce deforestation.[82]

Building on a large network of existing reserves, substantial new areas were set aside in protected areas of several types, many of them in active frontiers of agricultural expansion. In the next eight years, the network of reserves reached 47 percent of the Amazon, falling within different types of protected areas or indigenous lands.[83] Indigenous reserves have been recognized as a key way to protect the cultural identity of indigenous peoples and to conserve the forest; but they are often poorly patrolled by government agencies despite their status as some of the best protected areas in the Amazon.[84] A continuing problem has been that the 1,280 protected areas are often poorly managed, a reflection of extremely low public spending on the environment overall in Brazil.[85] Still, these areas of protection were a key factor in Brazil's efforts to get deforestation under control.

The story is complex, but two other sets of factors played pivotal roles in helping bring down deforestation rates sharply. Two ministers of the environment, Marina Silva and Carlos Minc (2003 to 2010), led the fight against deforestation and were open to discussion with many elements in civil society, including international and national environmental groups, rubber tappers, and local communities.[86] One highly successful campaign by Greenpeace in 2006 linked soybean producers in the Mato Grosso state to Amazon deforestation, on the one hand, and McDonald's chicken nuggets in developed countries, on the other. At the same time that they released a more detailed report, Greenpeace posted a grisly animated online video, showing a ghoulish Ronald McDonald wielding a chainsaw and being splattered with blood as trees fell and chickens were mechanically processed into McNuggets.[87] The April 2006 Greenpeace "Crime File" policy briefing called "We're Trashin' It: How McDonald's Is Eating Up the Amazon" documented how McDonald's in Europe was buying soy from Cargill's huge grain terminal in Santarém in the heart of the Amazon. It went on to describe slave labor and the invasion and pollution of indigenous lands by the farmers who provided soy to that terminal.

The Greenpeace campaign was one of several that showed the vulnerability of supply chains of huge corporations to being discredited by environmental activists. Greenpeace was also part of a larger group of civil society groups with receptive leaders inside the government. By late July, McDonald's had signed an agreement with Greenpeace to develop a "zero deforestation plan."[88] Greenpeace's "McVictory" release described how "By committing to the plan, the companies' massive buying power has created a huge demand for soy that hasn't been grown in the ashes of the rainforest. This put pressure on the 'big five' soy traders—Cargill, ADM, Bunge, Dreyfus and Amaggi to come to the negotiating table with the future of large areas of the Amazon rainforest at stake." The soy producers agreed to a moratorium on the sale of any soy produced on land deforested after the following day.[89] In 2009, another Greenpeace campaign led to a "Cattle Agreement," which similarly blocked the sale of beef produced on recently deforested land.

Soy and beef productivity and credit appear to be important factors in this story, as well. A significant change has been the intensification process by which more farmers are able to grow two or even three crops of soybeans in a single year on the same piece of land; ranchers have more than tripled the number of cows that can be reared on a unit of Amazon land.[90] This intensification appears to have lessened the pressure on forests, slowing or potentially stopping a cycle of expansionist agriculture that goes back to Brazil's colonial roots.[91] A final and critical piece of the story was that the government managed to stop the flow of agricultural credit almost completely to locations in the country where deforestation was rampant, unless they developed and enforced a tight plan to stop it.[92]

Could the government take credit for reducing deforestation, or were other events—dropping soy and beef prices, new techniques and technologies, and fears of markets being cut off by Greenpeace—transforming the economic decisions of farmers and ranchers? Clarissa Costalonga e Gandour and colleagues from the Climate Policy Initiative found that Brazil's policies explained about half the drop in deforestation but that meat and soybean prices significantly affected deforestation as well.[93] University of Brasilia professor Eduardo Viola argues that price drops may have slowed expansion of production but that deforestation continued to drop even when prices recovered.[94]

So in 2012, the Brazilian government triumphantly announced that deforestation rates had reached the lowest levels ever recorded.[95] Brazil was for years the third-largest emitter of total greenhouse gases in the world because of deforestation.[96] In 2010, Brazil announced a remarkable achievement—a 30 percent reduction in the nation's total emissions.[97] Brazil traditionally had the largest share of emissions in Latin America, with roughly half of all emissions from the region, mostly due to its emissions from land use, forestry, agriculture, and especially deforestation. However, these rankings are being reevaluated with the drop in Amazon clearing.[98] According to Brazil's first National Inventory of Greenhouse Gases released in 2004, up to 75 percent of Brazil's greenhouse gas emissions came from deforestation and land-use change.[99] With the nearly 70 percent drop in deforestation, land use dropped to only about 35 percent of the country's total emissions in 2011.[100]

Then worryingly in November 2013, the Brazilian government confirmed that deforestation in the Amazon had increased by nearly a third over the previous year.[101] The year 2014 also saw some troubling periods, but there are still debates going on about the reliability of the data. It is too early to assess whether this is merely noise around a new low level of deforestation or whether the situation threatens to deteriorate again. Daniel Nepstad's team argues that to secure its gains in the Amazon, the Brazilian government needs to develop more positive incentives for soy farmers and ranchers to continue to protect nearby forests. They argue that a mix of punitive approaches—threats of fines, jail, risk to reputations, and land-use restrictions—worked to slow the falling of trees a decade ago but that with increasing demand for these products, "we will need a new approach to keep deforestation low in the Amazon."[102]

The pro-agribusiness lobby and lawmakers in the Brazilian Congress are a powerful force and successfully pushed for a relaxing of the stiff approaches and for an expansion of the area that they are allowed to cut on each piece of property (called the Forest Code). As Denilson Cardoso and his coauthors argue, although these policies may generate collective benefits over the long-term to the benefit of society, they can impose short-term costs on specific sectors that have all the incentives to mobilize and oppose such measures.[103] So with a combination of factors driving down deforestation in the Amazon, it is unclear whether changes to any of them might cause a minor bump or a major reversion to "the bad old days" of high deforestation. In the next section, we pick up with that question in the broader context of overall greenhouse gas emissions in Brazil as the economy rises, falls, and shifts.

Do We Have Lift-off?

In 2009, the *Economist* ran a cover story with the iconic Rio de Janeiro statue of Christ the Redeemer taking off like a NASA space shuttle. Brazil, it said, was among the last to succumb to the 2008 financial crisis and the first out of the malaise, demonstrating the country's impressive economic performance, with forecasts suggesting that Brazil could overtake the United Kingdom and France to become the world's fifth-largest economy during the next decade.[104] Lula's leadership shifted the benefits of growth enough that poverty and extreme poverty in the nation fell substantially, along with the nation's infamous income inequality.

Four years later, the *Economist* ran another story, but this time with the statue of Christ the Redeemer uncontrollably plummeting back to earth.[105] Following the dizzy heights of 7.5 percent growth in 2010, Brazil's economy slowed significantly in 2011 and 2012 and made only a modest recovery in 2013 and 2014.[106] The question that the *Economist* raised was whether Brazil had blown its erstwhile progress by economic mismanagement. Our question is whether a new presidential administration and economic stagnation is driving a turn away from a proactive agenda on the environment and climate change and toward a single-minded developmentalism.

The strengths of Brazil's economy are diversity and commodities that have been strongly in demand internationally, including beef, iron ore, soybeans, orange juice and coffee. Some of Brazil's industrial strengths are in chemicals and aircraft: in some manufactures, it competes in the region, and in others it competes globally. Each of these sectors suggests issues for

Brazil's climate profile (its emissions by sector) and its policy going forward, and we briefly discuss some key ones.

Following up on the Amazon discussion, we can start with agriculture and forestry. Brazil is a global agricultural powerhouse, now ranking among the world's five largest agricultural producers and exporters.[107] However, rising emissions from agriculture threaten to undermine some of the progress made from forest protection, as is discussed in chapter 1. In 2012, attempts by the Ruralistas (pro-agribusiness caucus) in the Brazilian Congress to dilute Brazil's long-standing Forestry Code led President Dilma to veto nine articles, but the Ruralistas got most of what they wanted. Organizations in Brazil, including Greenpeace and the Amazon Environment Research Institute (IPAM), were scathing about the changes, and Marina Silva, former environment minister and presidential candidate, decried simply that "We can conclude that illegal loggers won and society lost."[108] Before Dilma vetoed some parts of the new forest code, the incident caused sufficient alarm outside the country that a presentation by the Alliance of Small Island States (AOSIS) at a UN climate change conference that year questioned whether Brazil could meet its voluntary emission-reduction and deforestation targets with the new changes to the law. AOSIS cited a study carried out in the state of Mato Grosso, which estimated an increase in deforestation up to 47 percent in 2020 if the new forestry code was put into place.[109] Silva had harsh words for her former political party, the Workers' Party: "They are hostage to the most backward elements in Congress, those who have a vision of increasing production by expanding the area of agriculture [through clearing], not through gains in productivity through technology, training, innovation."[110]

Brazil's soaring exports to China of agricultural commodities are a significant new pressure on the Amazon and thus national greenhouse gas emissions levels. China consumes more than half of the world's soybeans, and soybean prices have surged more than threefold over the past decade. China has rapidly emerged as the most important market for Brazil's soybean exports, and Brazil's soybean producers remain highly dependent on China.[111] Lacking an independent and powerful civil society, Chinese firms and government agencies are unlikely to bow to pressure the way McDonald's and Cargill did to the Greenpeace soy campaign in 2006. China's potentially large impact on deforestation in the Brazilian Amazon includes two pathways—through the direct influence of Chinese enterprises by land purchases and business startups or takeovers and through the rapid rise in exports to China of soybean and beef products by Brazilian firms on their own lands.[112] As Amazon expert Philip Fearnside and his colleagues suggest, profit earned from the soybean trade with China is strengthening Brazilian agribusiness interests, with profound effects on domestic politics.[113] These effects may include weakened environmental protection, as mining and agricultural ministries gain leverage over environmental and other social agencies.[114]

Although emissions from deforestation have recently fallen, economic growth is driving an increase in Brazil's energy emissions, particularly from power generation and transport. Economic growth has increased electricity demand, strained installed capacity, and driven demand for a greater share of fossil fuels in Brazil's power matrix. The coincidence of this growth with catastrophic droughts has created unreliability in the huge hydroelectric power facilities in the nation, creating acute shortages and a call for fossil fuel-based reliability to fill the gap during periods of high demand and low supply from renewables.

Transport was responsible for roughly 30 percent of all energy consumed and CO_2 emissions in 2007 in Brazil,[115] and things are worsening quickly: the total vehicle fleet grew by 230 percent between 1990 and 2005,[116] and sales of private cars has been up sharply since then. More recently, President Dilma has sought to boost the economy by providing tax holidays for car buyers and by keeping diesel and auto fuels cheaper.[117] The results have been predictable—a jump in auto ownership, congestion, fuel consumption, local air pollution, and greenhouse gas emissions.

In the case of electricity, after being slammed by the 1970s oil embargo because it had no native fossil fuel energy supply to turn to, Brazil developed an impressive set of renewable energy sources. First, after building a series of megadams over the last half century, hydropower accounted for 78 percent of total electricity generation in 2010 but these numbers can fluctuates substantially on an annual basis. Droughts in recent years, however, have led to wider diversification in the electricity-production mix, increasing the use of natural gas-fired power plants,[118] and the Ministry of Mines and Energy's Energy Expansion Plan for the period 2008 to 2017 calls for the expansion of fossil fuel–based thermal power stations.[119] Although hydropower accounted for 89 percent of Brazilian electricity production in the first half of 2012, this percentage fell to 74.6 by 2014, while the share of thermal power (coal, gas, biomass) in electricity generation tripled to 21.7 percent over this period.[120]

Brazil is currently planning thirty hydroelectric projects to be undertaken in the Amazon region over the next decade. Significant among them is the construction of twelve dams in the Tapajós river basin, which are projected to drive deforestation of nearly a million hectares of rainforest by 2032, increasing national deforestation rates by 8.3 percent compared to a no-dams scenario. This deforestation would cause greenhouse gas emissions to rise, attenuating the carbon savings often associated with hydropower.[121]

Second, after over thirty years of experience in producing ethanol from sugarcane, Brazil is the world leader in biodiesel exports and also has the most efficient energy production anywhere.[122] Biofuels account for 13 percent of transport fuel in Brazil, around 25.5 billion liters and one of the highest in the world.[123] There is also growing international concern that biofuels (especially those utilizing food crops like corn oil or those grown on land that was previously used for food production) were responsible for increases in global food prices. Currently, cars that can run on either 100 percent ethanol or a gasoline-ethanol blend represent 84 percent of the new cars purchased in Brazil.[124] Brazilian car owners know that because of its lower embodied energy, ethanol needs to be 30 percent cheaper than gasoline to be a good deal, so anytime it is not, "flex-fuel" car owners simply switch over to gasoline.

Brazil's low-carbon profile is being eroded, and its future is highly uncertain. A potential game changer has been the discovery of vast offshore oil reserves. Brazil's profile as an energy producer was transformed following this discovery off its coast, which now have some major fields in production and others being developed. In May 2009, the China Development Bank signed a deal with Brazilian oil company Petrobras, providing US$10 billion in loans to develop offshore fields and refineries in exchange for a guaranteed supply of oil over the next decade.[125] According to the *Oil and Gas Journal*, Brazil had 13 billion barrels of proven oil reserves as of January 2013, the second largest in South America after Venezuela. In March 2013, Brazil launched a ten-year energy plan that aims to expand oil production to over 5 million barrels a day by 2021, about 40 percent of which is to be exported,[126] but at the time of writing we expect this number to be scaled back following the ongoing Petrobras corruption scandal and low oil prices.

Mining also represents a formidable threat to Brazil's forests and its ability to keep emissions from deforestation down. As of November 2014, at least 20 percent of all strictly protected reserves and indigenous lands overlapped with areas registered as under consideration for mining.[127] In the Amazon alone, these lands of registered mining interests encompass 34,117 square km of strictly protected areas and 281,443 square km of indigenous lands.[128] Proposals currently pending in the Brazilian government include a general prohibition of new protected areas in regions of high mineral or hydropower potential. Government attempts to mitigate environmental damages caused by extractive activities within protected areas have thus far proven, as Joice Ferreira and her colleagues argue, "inadequate, poorly conceived," and failures in light of "international best-practice standards."[129] Toby Gardener, one of the paper's coauthors, commented, "The environmental damage that this proposal could generate is huge."[130]

Finally, we need to weigh the pressure that environmental groups can bring on the government to head one way or another on climate change, both domestically and at the UN climate negotiations. Brazil has a varied and sometimes influential set of environmental organizations, and at certain times in history, such as before the Earth Summit, there have been tremendous collective organizing and discussion about what the country's path should be.[131] Another important example is how civil society and the private sector have pressured the government to deal with deforestation in the Amazon that we described above. Since then, however, the movement has struggled to organize effectively around the issue of climate change: the changes to the Forest Code demonstrated the limited influence of Brazilian civil society in the face of powerful lobbying groups in congress.

The Brazilian Forum on Climate Change is a mechanism for interaction between political governance and civil society that was relatively successful in its early stages but has lost importance over time.[132] The Forum is a high-level consultative body created by decree in 2000 during the presidency of Fernando Henrique Cardoso. It is comprised of cabinet ministers, civil society representatives, academics, and businesspersons and is presided over and summoned to meet by the president, who also appoints the Forum's executive secretary. A central purpose in creating the Forum was to involve the president and his ministers directly in interactions with the main societal stakeholders in Brazil's climate agenda. However, since the government of president Lula, the Forum has gradually lost this characteristic. It still plays an important role in promoting dialogue between the state and civil society, but participation by high-level governmental officials has been restricted to formal issues and communication about the government's actions. That said, civil society and the private sector do have an influence at certain times on climate change, as was seen in the 2009 pledge by Lula and the congress's supporting legislation, when Brazil's Climate Observatory was able to have some of its ideas on the bill adopted,[133] and the business groups described by Hochstetler and Viola above had a genuine impact.

Where do these changes in various sectors of the economy leave Brazil's position on climate change in the coming years? According to Carlos Rittl of the Brazilian Climate Observatory, Brazil's greenhouse gas emissions grew 7.8 percent in 2013 in spite of low economic growth, and "70% of the planned investments on energy will go to fossil fuel in the next 10 years."[134] Tasso Azevedo, director of the Brazilian NGO Imaflora, said: "We see the tendency for emissions to rise again in 2014 even considering a stagnant economy, so if Brazil manages to resume economic growth in the future it will be hard to meet the [2020] target."[135] As we have seen, however, these anticipated reductions in land-use emissions are being replaced by increased emissions from agriculture and energy. As Eduardo Viola put it, "One thing is the plan and another is the reality." He said that we see the true face of public policies when we observe the allocation of budget resources—whether to support Petrobras for fossil fuel exploration, to strengthen the ethanol program, or to develop wind or nuclear energy.[136]

Finally, without a majority in either house after her reelection in late 2014, President Dilma sought coalitions by naming ministers from opposition parties. She "stirred up the wrath of environmentalists" by appointing agribusiness advocate Kátia Abreu—who has been nicknamed the "chainsaw queen" and "Miss Deforestation"—as her new agriculture minister.[137] Then she appointed Aldo Rebelo, a climate skeptic, as minister of science and technology.[138] We attempt to explain the Brazilian climate sphinx as we conclude the chapter.

An Uncertain Future

We have described how in the UN climate negotiations, Brazil sometimes appears to be extremely progressive on supporting ambitious international efforts on climate change. At other times, it has been called a "spoiler" when it blocks progress in defense of its national sovereignty under the banner of core UNFCCC principles. So which is Brazil—a climate leader or a spoiler?

We began with a series of questions. What are the roots of Brazil's sometimes contradictory and often perplexing positions on climate change? What about Brazil made it willing to take bold action on climate change in 2009? How did Brazil become an outlier in emission reductions, reducing deforestation in the Amazon 70 percent since 2004 and its total national emissions by a whopping 30 percent? What can we learn from Brazil about the future of global climate politics and action? Can Brazil's model of social organization and politics be applied elsewhere to encourage sustainability and create lower-carbon and higher-ambition nations? In short, is Brazil a leader (for Latin America or the world), or is it simply a Lone Ranger looking out only for itself?

Although its positions over the years at the UN climate negotiations are seemingly contradictory, Brazil's positions have been consistently organized around three bedrock issues—protecting every nation's sovereign right to national development, opposing any outside interference that might put the Amazon rainforest under international control, and stressing the historical responsibility of industrialized countries to compensate for their emissions to date.[139] We can best understand each of these positions and their various embodiments over time by understanding national politics and economics inside Brazil. These have shifted markedly from the more environmentalist and progressive years through Lula's presidency and apparently back to a more typical Brazilian nationalist and developmentalist stance since then under Dilma. As was shown at the end of the last section, the extent to which her administration is eager to secure the gains made controlling deforestation in the Amazon is questionable.

Brazil's Ministry of External Relations holds that all countries have common responsibilities in relation to climate change, that these responsibilities should reflect the amount of emissions put into the atmosphere by each nation, and that they should reflect each nation's wealth.[140] This refrain has been sung more loudly or more quietly by different Brazilian delegations over time, but there have been many years since 1992 when Brazil has used historical responsibility as a club to beat wealthy nations so they could not expect any binding limits on developing nations like Brazil itself. In this way, Brazil sought to appear a champion of the developing world.

Andrew Hurrell and Sandeep Sengupta have argued that Brazil's prioritization of renewable energy and greater ambition and cooperative stance on climate change are the result of several events—a strengthening environmental movement and public concerns about climate, the formation of "new business coalitions in favor of policy change," the important candidacy of Green parties (especially presidential candidate and former environment minister Marina Silva), and the ability of the state to control Amazonian deforestation. They argue that economic stagnation and Dilma's election and reelection have reasserted Brazil's developmentalist ideology, and they point to Brazil's efforts to build South-South solidarity as reasons that the country's delegation will return to more obstructionist approaches in the negotiations.[141]

Eduardo Viola makes similar arguments and argues that Brazil's role in the global politics of climate change has not reached its potential due to major factors, including entrenched traditional ideas and attitudes about short-term use of natural resources and a traditional conception of national sovereignty that is poorly adapted to the challenges of the global economy.[142] Viola argues that in the years around the Copenhagen meeting in 2009, Brazil transitioned from the conservative side to the moderate conservative field in global climate governance.[143] After 2004, efforts to manage deforestation declined as a result of successful policy activism by figures such as two former environment ministers, Marina Silva and Carlos Minc. David Held and his co-authors argue that as deforestation declined, a climate policy "blockage" was removed. Perceptions of the policy tradeoffs changed, and an opportunity was created for a coalition of civil society groups, businesses, and policy entrepreneurs to call for more stringent domestic climate policies.[144] The high-water mark was at Copenhagen in 2009 when President Lula announced Brazil's pledge to reduce emissions;[145] but after President Dilma took over, this momentum for climate policy appears to have halted, and the tide is flowing back out.

A quantitative look at Brazil's climate performance in comparative perspective provides an interesting angle with a similar conclusion. The Climate Change Performance Index, compiled by NGOs Germanwatch and the Climate Action Network (CAN), evaluates and compares the climate protection performance of fifty-eight countries representing the majority of global emissions. In 2006, Brazil was ranked ninth before moving up to eighth place for three consecutive years through Copenhagen. In 2010 and 2011, Brazil climbed to fourth position—and first place (three places were left blank because the authors decided that no country was worthy). So Brazil was ranked best in the world on climate change performance for two years running. In all three categories on energy and emissions levels, emissions trend, and policy ranking, Brazil was among the top fifteen countries.[146]

But then things start to shift. For the 2012 index, Brazil lost its top ranking and slipped to seventh because of increasing fossil fuel–based emissions. In the 2013 index, Brazil slipped to thirty-third place. The inclusion of data on emissions from deforestation had a significant effect on the rankings, which in part explains Brazil's downgrading. Alongside a drop in the "emissions indicator," however, Brazil scored substantially lower in the national policy evaluation. Brazil's big drop was also driven by a rise in energy-related emissions and by a much more pessimistic evaluation of national policy. Germanwatch and CAN have noted that two-thirds of all planned investments in the electricity sector between 2011 and 2020 were to fund fossil fuel or unsustainable large hydropower projects. Another important issue cited in the rankings was the discussion of revisions to Brazil's Forest Code, which threaten to undermine the progress that has been made in reducing emissions in the Amazon and the Cerrado regions. Brazil dropped further still to thirty-sixth position in 2014 and then again to forty-ninth position in 2015.[147]

In a bluntly worded 2014 article, CAN questioned Brazil's position on climate change, following its earlier impressive reductions of deforestation. It raised the point that although emissions from deforestation had dropped, Brazil should commit to emission reductions across all sectors because emissions from agriculture, energy, and transport are already higher than emissions from deforestation. Referring to emissions growth in Brazil's energy sector, which more than doubled between 1990 and 2012, CAN calls on Brazil to stop investing in fossil fuels and instead promote renewable energy.[148] Brazil has undoubtedly made much progress in reducing its emissions, but the low-hanging fruit offered by reducing deforestation is now largely harvested. Brazil could adopt a more ambitious position in relation to reducing deforestation, but this will likely harden as much tougher emissions reductions in energy and the wider economy are called for. Because there is much degraded and deforested land in Brazil, afforestation and reforestation initiatives could be pushed considerably so that by the mid-2020s, land-use change and forestry could become a substantial net carbon sink, and by 2050, it would be capable of offsetting a substantial share of the emissions from the energy sector, according to the *Pathways to Deep Decarbonization* report.[149] The administration and congress are tapping into offshore oil as a way to keep prices and inflation down and use revenues from exports for education and health, a classic trap that will drive long-term problems of many sorts.

Decisions on whether to ratify international agreements and adopt national policies to mitigate climate change are domestic political decisions. As is laid out in chapter 1, we adopt a political economy approach, which focuses on the comparative politics of climate change. This approach helps us understand complex decision-making and policy processes, differences in governance, and the power relations that mediate competing claims over resources. Grassroots activism has sometimes been critical in sharpening the focus of political actors and increasing their willingness to take proclimate stands. This was true during the Lula presidency, beginning with participatory platform building during early years for the Workers' Party and reinforced in the insurgent candidacy of Marina Silva for president in 2009. Having sympathetic leaders in ministries opened the door for climate NGOs to have an impact, as did the conjuncture around the Copenhagen negotiations.

Climate change is at once a local, national, and global phenomenon, so there are political opportunities and pressures at all levels of the political system. National governments are constrained by conflicting interests and electoral competition, such as the strong pro-agribusiness Ruralistas caucus in congress and proenvironment majorities in the country's major cities, especially in the Southeast. Subnational governments are closely tied to powerful local economic elites but also circumscribed and incentivized by what national governments will tolerate or fund. For example, by April 1, 2014, the Amazon Fund had US$380 million and had dispersed US$106 million. Much of the funding was being dispersed to state and municipal governments to strengthen their efforts to protect forest preserves and preventing forest fires.[150] Interstate coalitions at the global level (like BASIC), international institutions (like the UN and World Bank), national political processes (like urbanization or industrialization), networks, political parties, advocacy groups, and social movement organizations all play important roles.

Another bedrock of Brazil's foreign policy is a preference for multilateralism, defense of the sovereignty of states, nonintervention, and peaceful resolution of disputes in international relations. Brazil has fiercely defended its sovereignty over what lies within its borders. The rollout of the PPCDAm to stem the tide of rampant deforestation in the Amazon shows the government's attempt to control this contested space as a response to both domestic and international actors. Brazil has opposed any externally imposed targets to reduce deforestation and the emissions that accompany it—even if they bring new funds. This helps to explain the creation of Brazil's own nationally administered Amazon Fund, which allows it to reduce its reliance on multilateral agencies like the World Bank.

This perspective also helps us understand Brazil's behavior at the Rio+20 Summit in 2012, which was meant to be a major milestone in global governance of environmental issues. Despite being host, Brazil was pragmatic and did not play an active role in pushing the summit forward. It did not want to risk failure by pushing too hard on other nations, which would undermine its own foreign policy norms, and it did not want to make promises or sign up for obligations that it might regret later on.

At the UN climate talks in Doha, Qatar, in December 2012, we attended a Brazilian press conference where the former lead negotiator for Brazil, Luiz Alberto Figuereido, sat at the center of the press conference room table and challenged any other country to do what Brazil had done to reduce its emissions. The message was entirely defensive, essentially telling critics that Brazil has done its job and was beyond scrutiny. No questions were asked by the Brazilian or foreign media about how the government would exploit its new oil discoveries in relation to the UNFCCC or slow its rapidly increasing fossil energy consumption and rising emissions from agriculture. Brazil's diplomats had done their job in blocking expectations that the country and other BASIC members would take on binding commitments for future emissions reductions, and the new regime emerging around "Intended Nationally-Determined Contributions" allows this approach to continue.

Since Copenhagen, the strength and coherence of the BASIC group has become more uncertain, but its members have managed to fend off expectations of binding greenhouse gas reductions in the short term. As Brazil and China's trade and commercial ties continue to evolve, we expect that there will be a renewed need to align their positions in the UN climate change negotiations. Until recently, we would have said that this might keep Brazil in the camp of nations that resist any limits on developing nation emissions. However, China's position is shifting, as is shown by its joint announcement of pledges with the US in November 2014. For a time, South Africa was seen as more likely to take on such limits. India has resisted them strongly but might be warming to greater domestic action on climate change following a change of government in 2014.

Journalist Nicolas Kozloff argues that agribusiness and oil interests are winning out over Brazil's progressive environmental political constituencies and that this can be seen in its behaviors in Copenhagen, Cancun, and Durban in lining up with BASIC and the US in avoiding binding commitments.[151] He observes that "Brazilian cynicism has not gone unnoticed by small Pacific and Caribbean states, some of which are low-lying and vulnerable to sea level rise" and that they want binding limits on emerging economies' emissions.

Our observation since then is that Brazil does not have the support of many of the developing countries that are seeking ambition in the negotiations. This includes the small island states in AOSIS, the Least Developed Countries Group, and especially Brazil's own neighbors in the AILAC group. As is discussed in the next two chapters on the ALBA and AILAC groups, Brazil is far from being a regional leader on climate change. Brazil rarely makes statements with other countries in the region during the negotiations, so we conclude that it is a Lone Ranger and something of a climate spoiler. For at least a short time, linking up with China, India, and South Africa in BASIC has provided Brazil with a key piece of leverage to avoid having other countries tell it how to behave. This is a regrettably understandable but sad achievement.

4   "A Flea in the Ear"? The Emergence of ALBA

Standing Up for Climate Justice

On the final night of the Copenhagen negotiations in 2009, Venezuela's special presidential envoy for climate change, Claudia Salerno, banged her country's nameplate on the table repeatedly in an attempt to get the attention of the Danish chair, causing her to cut her hand. The president of the Fifteenth Conference of the Parties (COP15), Lars Løkke Rasmussen, had just gaveled the Copenhagen Accord through without full consensus and was attempting to leave the plenary hall. Raising her bloodied hand, Salerno exclaimed: "Mr. President, do you think a sovereign country should have to cut its hand and draw blood to have the right to speak? This hand that's bleeding wants to speak and has the same rights as any of those who you call a representative group of leaders!"[1]

Salerno was incensed by the emergence of the Copenhagen Accord from a small group of countries and by the rushed and nonparticipatory process that had accompanied its passage through the full plenary. As a result of the actions of Venezuela and a few other nations, the Copenhagen Accord was not adopted as a final decision of the negotiations but merely "taken note of," an obscure UN term meaning that it lacked legal power but was broadly supported. The ability of the UNFCCC to address climate change was at stake at Copenhagen. Out of fear that it would collapse without an outcome, most of the world—including a majority of Latin American countries—voted in favor of the weak Accord. Without binding limits on emissions and with the pledges that it called for expected to be starkly inadequate, the Accord was widely regarded as insufficient to avoid dangerous climate change.

The Copenhagen Accord was eventually supported by all countries except six, four of whom were from a new group at the UN climate negotiations

called the Bolivarian Alliance for the Peoples of Our America (Alianza Boliv-
iariana para los Pueblos de Nuestra América, ALBA). The group—comprised
of eleven countries, including Bolivia, Cuba, Nicaragua, and Venezuela—
blocked its official passage.[2] Ecuador stated in 2010 that it also would not
sign it.

In Copenhagen, the ALBA countries were furious at the way that the
COP15 was run and the contents of the Copenhagen Accord. At a press
conference, Ecuador's former minister of natural and cultural heritage,
María Fernanda Espinosa, stated: "We are seeing in this UN Conference
totally anti-democratic practices, which violate all the principles of the procedures of the United Nations, violate the Charter of the United Nations
and violate all the principles and norms of multilateralism."[3] Pablo Solón,
then Bolivian ambassador to the UN, criticized the Danish COP15 presidency for convening only a small group of countries for vetting the Accord,
which was developed by just five countries—BASIC and the United States
(see chapter 3). Then it went to a group of about twenty-six countries which
were selected by the chairs. "How can it be that 25 to 30 nations cook up an
agreement that excludes the majority of the 190 nations?" asked Bolivian
president Evo Morales, and he blamed the US: "The meeting has failed....
The fault is with the lack of political will by a small group of countries led
by the US."[4]

Accusations surfaced that during and after Copenhagen, several developed countries had threatened dissenting developing countries with cuts
in their foreign aid if they did not support the deal. Reports of arm twisting
were borne out by diplomatic telegrams leaked by Edward Snowden in the
WikiLeaks disclosure.[5] Venezuela's Salerno expressed to the COP15 plenary
that she had been threatened that there would be no Green Climate Fund
unless Venezuela supported the Accord.[6] The lack of ambition and political
will reflected in the Accord led the late Venezuelan president Hugo Chávez
to mock the proceedings and the US president: "Obama came, spoke and
he went out though that little door over there.... That is the emperor who
comes in the middle of the night and in the darkness, behind everyone's
back, in an anti-democratic way, cooks up a document ... that we don't
accept ... we will never accept it."[7]

And ALBA did not accept it, failing to sign the Accord and to submit pledges for mitigation actions for the period before 2020 as part of
the Accord. Following the conference, the ALBA countries said that they

"denounce ... the threat that the results of the [COP15] pose for the destiny of humanity."[8] They stated that "the process of negotiations was corrupted by the violation of the essential principles of the multilateral system ... above all those of sovereign equality between all countries."

The Copenhagen debacle reveals the strong oppositional identity of ALBA, which took a collective stand at the UN climate talks. These countries are taking various levels of domestic action on climate change, which we explore later. Here we focus on Bolivia, Ecuador, and Venezuela, which have been the most active players on the international stage. Ecuador and Bolivia have taken progressive steps to generate national policies and legislation on the environment and climate change. Both have launched pioneering initiatives with varying degrees of success and can be considered at the forefront of innovative initiatives to tackle climate change. On the contrary, Venezuela, in spite of its loud opposition to aspects of the UN and some countries, has taken limited steps at home compared to Bolivia and Ecuador.

This chapter attempts to dispel some myths about ALBA. The group should not be painted with a single brush, given the differences among its members. There are many contradictions and inconsistencies among the three leading ALBA countries—between their rhetoric and individual positions at the UN climate negotiations, on the one hand, and their actions in other policy areas on the domestic and international stages, on the other. We conclude that although ALBA is primarily an ideological grouping, pragmatism often plays an important role in its decisions. At other times, ideological considerations trump pragmatism. As a critical voice in the negotiations, ALBA speaks for issues of injustice created by unequal climate impacts, unequal responsibility, unjust decision-making processes, and inadequate assistance and support by wealthy nations. With a tendency to use fiery rhetoric, ALBA has played an important role since Copenhagen in raising these issues. Still, there is significant disagreement about whether ALBA's contributions have been positive overall during the process of reaching a new climate change agreement in Paris in 2015.

We first look at how Bolivia's climate policy and rhetoric have shifted, focusing on the World People's Conference on Climate Change and the Rights of Mother Earth that it hosted in Cochabamba in 2010. Following its rejection of the Copenhagen Accord and the Cancun Agreements the following year, Bolivia received considerable global attention, becoming the darling of many climate justice activist organizations. However, local clashes with indigenous organizations over a proposed road through their lands undercut President Morales's international profile. After Cancun, Bolivia decided it could no longer go it alone, reflecting broader foreign policy considerations and a pragmatic recalibration of the country's role at the climate negotiations and its alliances with its ALBA partners.

We then turn to Ecuador, where we discuss its radical offer to "keep the oil in the soil" in exchange for international compensation. The Yasuní-ITT Initiative's up and down history is revealing, ending with its termination and calls for a referendum on the Ecuadorian government's decision to exploit the oil reserves lying under the lands. We describe why the initiative failed and the potential fallout of its failure for Ecuador's climate policy. Finally, we analyze the complex situation in Venezuela, which is nearly completely dependent on oil. Why an oil exporter would take up a radical climate justice position requires exploration, but the policy and academic discussions are nearly silent on the issue.

We provide some background on what ALBA is and how it emerged as an important and outspoken voice at the UN climate negotiations. We conclude with a look at how ALBA joined a new bloc called the Like-Minded Developing Countries (LMDC) group with other countries including China and Saudi Arabia. We argue that climate change is only a small part of the story behind ALBA's decision to join this group. Global inequality, solidarity between G77 members and ALBA countries' national interests, Venezuelan oil diplomacy, and global aspirations all help explain the decisions.

According to a former Ecuadorian negotiator to the UNFCCC, ALBA is considered by other delegations to be "strong, potent and noisy," a "pulga en la oreja" (a flea in the ear).[9] ALBA has been effective in bringing ideas from civil society into the negotiations and occasionally blocking outcomes, but so far it has shown little ability to craft proposals that are widely adopted in final agreements. ALBA does not necessarily work as a bloc on specific issues such as REDD+ and forests, so ALBA members have adopted different positions on those, hinting at a lack of coherence but also respect for each other's specific circumstances.[10] ALBA is viewed by some as too obstructive at the climate negotiations when it uses the podium to push wider political issues, such as a rejection of US hegemony.[11] In spite of this, ALBA has played a substantive role in the talks, bringing political Left perspectives seeking to tie climate change to issues of social and economic justice and advocating for a fair and inclusive multilateral process.

What *Is* a Bolivarian Alliance?

Unlike BASIC or AILAC, the Bolivarian Alliance for the Peoples of Our America (ALBA) began as a trade group in 2004 created by Venezuela and Cuba and acts on a broad set of issues that include climate change. ALBA countries tend to negotiate as a group at the UN climate negotiations, but they also adopt individual positions on specific issues. ALBA was established to counterbalance the influence of US trade agreements and its cultural dominance and political meddling in Latin America. The name refers to the great general Simón Bolívar, who liberated much of the region from Spain in the early nineteenth century. Bolívar fought for freedom from Spanish colonial rule but also for a Pan-American union and social reforms.

ALBA would not exist without president Hugo Chávez and Venezuela's huge oil reserves. Venezuela's late president had a clear vision of a new Latin American order that can be summed up with three points. First, he held that the guiding "Washington Consensus" principle of "neoliberalism" (free trade and the slashing of government services and expenditures) was terrible for the people of Latin America.[12] Second, Latin American unity was essential to survive in a globalized world. And third, the twenty-first century must be multipolar.[13] Originally inspired by Chávez's relationship with Cuba's Fidel Castro, ALBA members also are inspired by the Bolivarian ideals of Latin American political unity, solidarity, and endogenous development. But these principles remain only loosely codified or institutionalized.[14] ALBA emphasizes respect for national sovereignty and self-determination and the creation of interstate relations based on solidarity, equality, and justice.[15] Bolivia joined in 2006 and added a new institutional agreement, the People's Trade Agreement (Tratado de Comercio de los Pueblos, TCP). Nicaragua joined in 2007, and Ecuador in 2009. Some Caribbean nations joined, as well—Dominica in 2008; Antigua and Barbuda; St. Vincent and the Grenadines in 2009; Santa Lucia in 2013;[16] and Grenada and St. Kitts and Nevis in 2014.

Like many others in the region, ALBA countries rely on their natural resources to develop. Their shared ideology is important, but ALBA functions largely due to Venezuelan oil revenues. Single members have pursued more pragmatic foreign policies, and ALBA itself can be ironically viewed as a pragmatic marriage of convenience: Venezuela uses it to advance its position in the region, while the other members use it to obtain cheap oil and financial assistance from Venezuela.[17] So although ALBA is a mechanism in which ideology and politics have a central role, it is also guided by the pragmatism of national interests of its members.[18]

Oil diplomacy is a central feature of Venezuela's foreign policy, and ALBA can be seen as (a successful) part of the effort to translate oil into influence abroad. In 2005, Venezuela created Petrocaribe, an energy agreement to provide low-interest oil sales to Caribbean and Central American countries. Petrocaribe allows countries up to twenty-five years to pay off oil bills and also can provide goods and services in exchange for oil. It has eighteen members, including Cuba, Dominica, El Salvador, Guyana, Haiti, Jamaica, and Nicaragua.[19] We discuss some of the implications of placing a climate justice ideology atop petrodiplomacy later in the chapter.

ALBA's Role at the Negotiations

In 2009, ALBA entered the Copenhagen negotiations for the first time as a bloc with a flourish. Previously, its members generally had negotiated individually or adopted joint positions as part of the G77 and China group.

ALBA was meeting regularly as a trade group in 2009, but in October at its seventh summit in Cochabamba ahead of COP15, climate change featured prominently on the agenda. Foreshadowing later positions, it stated that "in order to guarantee the full implementation of human rights, it is necessary to recognize ... the rights of Mother Earth." According to the declaration, "Developed countries have a climate debt ... with developing countries because of their historical responsibility of emissions and adaptation actions we are doomed to perform because of the global warming that they have caused."[20] To begin to pay that debt, the group declared that "developed countries ... must adopt meaningful commitments to reduce greenhouse gas emissions."[21] A special declaration on climate change defends their right to development and rejects the attempts of developed countries to transfer responsibilities for emission reductions to developing countries.[22] These points form the core of ALBA's negotiating positions and overlap significantly with global climate justice arguments taken up by a number of civil society organizations.

A cable exposed later by WikiLeaks suggests that Bolivia refused to adopt Brazil's position on the Copenhagen negotiations at a preparatory meeting before COP15. This position included BASIC's preference for voluntary pledges from countries, not a Kyoto-style set of binding emissions limits.[23] Brazil was unable to persuade Bolivia to adopt its positions, demonstrating its inability to lead in the region on climate, as was discussed in chapter 3. ALBA's radical declarations prior to Copenhagen on climate debt, its position on the exclusive responsibility of developed countries, and its adherence to the view of the rights of Mother Earth put it on a collision course with the US and the BASIC members.

ALBA (particularly Bolivia and Venezuela) has consistently portrayed itself as promoting the voice of civil society at the climate negotiations, and at key points NGOs pushing for climate justice have supported ALBA. More justice-oriented NGOs have supported ALBA's position against the Copenhagen Accord and its efforts to hold developed countries accountable for the lack of action at the UN.[24] At various UNFCCC meetings, ALBA arranged meetings with civil society, and these organizations invited ALBA delegates and other country delegations to their own events.[25] This allowed ALBA to take advantage of civil society's ability to communicate rapidly and effectively with diverse audiences and constituencies.[26] This also fits with ALBA's efforts to bring civil society voices into the UNFCCC process and at least rhetorical commitment to include civil society as part of their political project. When Claudia Salerno slammed her name plate on the table in Copenhagen or when Pablo Solón of Bolivia stood alone in opposing the Cancun Agreements, they did so with strong NGO support, which gave their positions a boost in the face of stiff opposition from other countries.

Looking back, it seems that the Danish president of COP15 and others underestimated the role that ALBA would play. As host, Denmark's job was to find a compromise approach, and this may have led it to downplay the mounting frustrations of several groups. ALBA's hard line on opposing the Copenhagen Accord forced the UN system to take another year to bring the agreements into formal adoption. The Cancun process is described in the next chapter, but ALBA countries were seen by many as troublemakers that needed to be brought back into the fold.[27]

Since Copenhagen, ALBA's principal positions have been to push for greater transparency, inclusion, and respect for the UNFCCC procedures and principals of consensus. It has common positions on the need to limit global average temperature increases to 1.5 degrees Celsius (a harder line than most), on respecting UNFCCC principles of equity and countries acting according to their common but differentiated responsibilities and respective capabilities (CBDR+RC), on maintaining the unity of the G77 and China group, on continuing the Kyoto Protocol, and on acknowledging the need for developed countries to provide significant levels of climate finance for developing countries. While the ALBA countries have some significant differences in their individual positions on the use of markets and the Clean Development Mechanism (CDM), the group continues to negotiate together on other issues. Ecuador has various CDM projects, whereas Bolivia and Venezuela strongly reject them. ALBA can be seen an important expression of political exclusion of countries from the UNFCCC negotiation process and of economic exclusion from the global economy.[28]

In the aftermath of ALBA's resistance in Copenhagen, attempts were made to reconcile with its members. Mexican ambassador Luis Alfonso de Alba visited Bolivia in 2010 as part of the extensive climate diplomacy efforts by Mexico as the incoming president of COP16 (see chapter 5).[29] John Ashton, then the UK foreign secretary's special representative for climate change, also visited Bolivia in October 2010.[30] These visits were important efforts by nations that were attempting to understand the climate politics and broader political agendas of individual ALBA countries and to let them know that they were being listened to.

Efforts by the US were less productive. In July 2010, the US special envoy for climate change, Todd Stern, spoke at the Universidad Andina Simón Bolívar in Quito, Ecuador.[31] Three months earlier, in April, it had emerged that the US State Department denied climate change assistance to Bolivia and Ecuador for opposing the Copenhagen Accord. Bolivia originally had been in line for US$3 million in climate assistance and Ecuador for $2.5 million.[32] Stern said that "the US is going to use its funds to go to countries that have indicated an interest to be part of the Accord." In response, the former Ecuadorean foreign minister, Fander Falconí, said, "We cannot allow blackmail to affect our dignity." Ecuador went on to offer $2.5 million to the US if it would ratify the Kyoto Protocol.[33] One cable from the US embassy in Belgium released by WikiLeaks stated that US official Michael Froman and former EU climate action commissioner Connie Hedegaard "agreed that we will need to neutralize, co-opt or marginalize" countries such as Bolivia, Ecuador, and Venezuela.[34] The WikiLeaks cables reveal how ALBA's leaders were perceived by the North. These visits attempted to restore good will following the US slashing of climate aid to Bolivia and Ecuador in the wake of their rejection of the Copenhagen Accord, but things have not gone well.

Bolivia has since expelled all US Agency for International Development (USAID) personnel from the country.[35]

After Cancun and before COP17 in Durban, South Africa, Panama hosted a meeting where ALBA, the African Union, and the Least Developed Countries Group announced that they would work together to ensure that COP17 strengthened the climate regime, cut emissions, and delivered on climate finance.[36] Their statement of common positions outlined that they were committed to "achieving a global goal of limiting temperature increase to well below 1.5°C above pre-industrial levels" and that "developed country Parties are to provide scaled up, adequate and predictable finance that is new and additional to existing ODA targets based on an assessed scale of contributions by 2020 that constitutes at least 1.5% of the gross domestic product of [developed countries]."[37] The next month, representatives from ALBA met in Santa Cruz, Bolivia, to coordinate their principal negotiating positions, which mainly followed these lines.[38] But the statement of common position agreed to in Panama by the African Group, Least Developed Countries Group, and ALBA unraveled in Durban. The meeting saw the Least Developed Countries join a temporary alliance with the European Union, the island states (AOSIS), and other Latin American countries such as Colombia, Chile, and Peru.

ALBA instead joined the Like-Minded Developing Countries (LMDC) group in Doha, along with China, India, and Saudi Arabia. The Like-Minded group seeks to uphold the UNFCCC's principles of national obligations according to nations' common but differentiated responsibility and equity and to push developed countries to act first on emission reductions according to their historical responsibility for climate change. ALBA's insistence on developing countries' rights to develop—given their ongoing efforts to eliminate poverty—is similar to that of China and India. Second, they claim the historical responsibility of developed countries to act first, a core "climate justice" discourse championed by ALBA. Finally, these positions allow them to challenge US and EU hegemony and frame their struggle as a fight for climate justice.[39]

Researchers suggest that the common identity within the G77 originated from a sense of inequality and of being shut out of the world's political and economic systems.[40] The G77 may be fragmenting as a bloc at the UNFCCC negotiations (as is described in chapter 2),[41] and there are many possible reasons that the smaller, poorer, and more vulnerable countries might wish to separate. However, centripetal forces often outweigh centrifugal ones: G77 members have a much larger negotiating power with the BASIC countries among them than they would without them. Venezuela for instance therefore can play a more assured role as part of the G77 and in the Like-Minded group alongside its ALBA partners and China. The next three sections look at the main ALBA countries—exploring their international postures and the national roots and contradictions that underlie them in Bolivia, Ecuador, and Venezuela.

Cochabamba and Bolivia's Shifting Climate Policy

On a global scale, Bolivia has been an important link between climate change and indigenous people's activist networks and the negotiations.[42] In Copenhagen, protestors favored President Evo Morales as the "first indigenous president in Latin America" and as the face of opposition to the weakening of the UNFCCC.[43] The Democracy Center in Bolivia suggested that Morales felt a stronger identification with social movements than with his fellow leaders in Copenhagen. Before a group of indigenous peoples, he said, "Before I was a leader, I was together with you in the alternative summits." Morales sought to use his position as president to become an advocate for the disenfranchised, saying that "if the leaders of the countries cannot arrive at an agreement, why don't the peoples then decide together?" In that moment, Jessica Aguirre and Elizabeth Cooper argue that the idea for a radically different kind of meeting was born.[44]

Immediately after leading the resistance in Copenhagen, Bolivia put in place plans to host the World People's Conference on Climate Change and the Rights of Mother Earth in Cochabamba in April 2010.[45] The location itself was symbolic: the city had gained global recognition as the place where communities had rejected privatization of water and its provision by the huge US contracting firm Bechtel. In January 2010, Morales invited governments and global civil society to attend the People's Conference.[46] The conference's objectives were to analyze the structural and systemic causes that drive climate change, agree on the project of a Universal Declaration of Mother Earth Rights, agree on proposals for new commitments under the Kyoto Protocol, and develop an action plan to advance the establishment of a Climate Justice Tribunal.[47]

In response, around 35,000 activists attended the meeting, including some from international NGOs such as Friends of the Earth and La Via Campesina International and scores of Latin American regional, national, and local organizations such as Brazil's Landless Workers Movement.[48] Heads of state showed up, including the ALBA presidents of Ecuador, Nicaragua, and Venezuela and the vice president of Cuba. There were official delegations from forty-seven countries, including Brazil, Ethiopia, India, Mexico, South Korea, and Spain.

As the event began, Pablo Solón, then Bolivia's ambassador to the UN said that the conference aimed to create a "big world alliance of social and people's movements to push the governments of the developed countries to effectively reduce greenhouse gases."[49] UN Secretary-General Ban Ki-moon (who did not attend) sent a message emphasizing how the UN seeks "dialogue, inclusiveness and transparency in the global climate discourse" and that "climate change is an ethical issue, with serious implications for the well-being of our generation and those that will follow."[50] The statement represents an uncomfortable acknowledgment of the importance of the conference and inclusion and yet also maintains some distance from the radical set of statements and images that would likely emerge.

Activists got down to business quickly, fueled by a sense of urgency expressed by Solón and Morales about the vulnerability of the nation to climate impacts. The conference was organized into seventeen official working groups, fourteen plenaries, and over 160 panels and workshops to debate proposals on climate change.[51] The People's Agreement that emerged set out a vision and a series of demands.[52] It advocated for a radical economic and political restructuring based on "indigenous" ideals of harmony with nature and neo-Marxist principles of political equality and individual rights.[53] Capitalism was denounced as the prime driver of climate change. On April 26, 2010, Bolivia submitted the main content of the People's Agreement to the UNFCCC,[54] and Morales and representatives from civil society met with Ban Ki-moon soon thereafter to promote the People's Agreement.[55]

The People's Agreement included an extremely ambitious target to reduce greenhouse gas concentrations in the atmosphere to well below 300 parts per million (ppm) CO_2 equivalent. Preindustrial levels were about 280 ppm, but current levels are just over 400 ppm. It also emphasized that in all climate change–related actions, nations should ensure the full respect of human rights (including the inherent rights of indigenous peoples, women, children, migrants, and all vulnerable sectors) and also recognize and defend the rights of Mother Earth to ensure harmony between humanity and nature. Lastly, it called on developed countries to commit to provide assessed annual contributions of 6 percent of their GDP by 2020 to address the needs of developing countries.[56]

The final statement of the conference had objectives that were nearly identical to the original announcement of the meeting and raised questions about how much of the People's Agreement was already "precooked" by the Bolivian government. Brown University's Arielle Balbus conducted a number of interviews with participants to assess this question.[57] She reports that some civil society activists, such as Christian Guerrera of Rising Tide, called the conference "prefabricated theater." Sara Mersha, a North American climate justice activist who attended Cochabamba, argued that the outcome of the conference was democratic and reflected the views of the participants.

However, the emergence of a renegade working group, Mesa 18, challenges the view that the People's Conference was a fully inclusive and democratic event. Mesa 18 emerged to discuss local issues that were not being addressed by the summit's seventeen formal working groups.[58] Following a failed bid to be included in the main conference, the National Council of Ayllus and Markas of Qullasuyu (Consejo Nacional de Ayllus y Markas del Qullasuyu, CONMAQ) and the Confederation of Indigenous People of Bolivia (Confederación de Pueblos Indígenas del Oriente Boliviana, CIDOB), launched their own discussions focusing on the environmental damage perpetrated by extractive industries in Bolivia. Mesa 18's criticisms focused on the contradictions between the Morales administration's development plans and its vision of environmental sustainability.[59] The final Declaration of Mesa 18 lambasted "the so-called progressive Latin American governments that implement mega energy and infrastructure projects." Yet the government's unwillingness to support Mesa 18 testifies to the risks of being critical toward governmental policy in Bolivia.[60] Its declarations were absent from any official communications from the Cochabamba event.

There are many ways to interpret the Cochabamba process. A cable published by WikiLeaks, attributed to John S. Creamer, the US charge d'affaires in La Paz, Bolivia, quotes a former member of Bolivia's delegation as saying that Bolivia's government position is aimed at creating an alternative development model that is consistent with Morales's anticapitalist philosophy. A Bolivian senator suggested that Morales sees environmental issues as one area where he can carve out an international identity independent from that of Venezuela's Chávez.[61] Bolivia was able to submit large parts of the People's Agreement to the UNFCCC, which strengthened its own position and portrayed itself as a champion of the people. Bolivia did make some progress in attempting to break open the elitist and closed-off negotiating process by attempting to integrate the People's Agreement into the UN process.

The act of submitting the climate justice language from the People's Agreement to UN climate negotiations in 2010 was fraught with difficulties. At a press conference in June 2010, Pablo Solón strongly objected to a negotiating text during the recent UNFCCC negotiations in Bonn, Germany. Solón noted that the draft negotiating texts produced by the chair of the Ad-Hoc Working Group on Long-Term Cooperative Action (AWG-LCA) did not reflect Bolivia's submissions, a number of which came from the People's Agreement. He said that thousands of people had created the People's Agreement, which was a landmark, consensus-based document with substantive proposals.[62] But at a press briefing on August 6, 2010, in Bonn, Solón was more upbeat, reporting that Bolivia's submissions from the People's Conference were included as options in bracketed text.[63] The text finally adopted that year in Cancun was exceedingly weak and aligned almost identically with the Copenhagen Accord, suggesting that the Cochabamba effort may have come to naught in terms of enduringly influencing the negotiating texts, at least in that round.

Although a number of the proposals in the People's Agreement were present in the new negotiating text in the Chinese city of Tianjin in the fall,[64] the proposals were barely discussed, and all were eventually wiped from the text during the Cancun negotiations.[65] In Cancun, Morales made an impassioned call for world leaders to listen to the people, citing some of the key demands of the of the People's Agreement.[66] Prior to the conference, some civil society groups commented that although submitting the contents of the People's Agreement to the official talks was beneficial, they did not see a possibility for including them in the Cancun texts.[67]

In August 2010, a journalist asked Pablo Solón whether the negotiating text was too unwieldy and included unrealistic aspects that he suggested were probably some of the proposals from the People's Agreement. Solón responded that from the Bolivian point of view, the proposals were meant to save the planet and humanity. In regards to the 6 percent of the global GDP for climate change finance, Solón said they were not unreasonable demands. Former IPCC president Rajendra Pachauri said that if the world does not spend 3 percent of the worldwide domestic product, there will be severe consequences in the near future.[68]

In the buildup to Cancun, ministers from Bolivia, Cuba, Ecuador, Nicaragua, and Venezuela issued a joint declaration. The ministers emphasized that the world could not afford a repeat of Copenhagen: "We hope that accords will be reached [at Cancun] in which developed countries ... effectively assume their obligation to reduce greenhouse gas emissions."[69]

Throughout the Cancun conference, Bolivia fought as the world's leading voice on climate justice. In the final hours, Pablo Solón was the only delegate of the 194 countries to reject the Cancun Agreements. His request to discuss the final text resulted in a collective groan and a few half-hearted boos from exhausted delegates and observers in the cavernous plenary hall.[70] Solón stated: "Allow me to express with total clarity that the Plurinational State of Bolivia ... does not accept and rejects this document, hence there is no consensus for its adoption."[71]

In response, Patricia Espinosa, then Mexican secretary for foreign affairs and president of COP16, declared that "consensus does not mean unanimity, much less the decision of one delegation to impose a veto over the will of those delegations that have come here through so much work and sacrifice."[72] Espinosa proceeded to gavel through the document regardless of Bolivia's objections at 3:15 a.m., amid a standing ovation and rapturous applause.[73] Norway's lead negotiator said to Espinosa: "You have got more praise tonight than most human beings will get in a lifetime."[74]

Bolivia rejected the Cancun Agreements for a number of reasons, including the absence of all of the People's Agreement proposals and the lack of time for negotiators to review the new negotiation texts. The Cancun Agreements did not resolve the main issue of achieving sufficiently ambitious mitigation commitments to assure the stabilization of the climate—far from it. They opened the door to an end of the Kyoto Protocol and its replacement with a voluntary pledging system. Lastly, Bolivia deemed the emphasis on the important role of carbon markets unacceptable.[75]

Pablo Solón, wrote in *The Guardian* how Bolivia was accused of being "obstructionist, obstinate and unrealistic." Solón responded that the Cancun Agreements were a "giant step backward" and would result in a temperature rise of 4 degrees Celsius or more. He stated that several nego-tiators privately supported Bolivia's position and that Bolivia was not iso-lated but rather was supported by "thousands of women, men, and young people of the social movements."[76]

Politically, the wisdom of Bolivia's objection may at first seem odd given the stakes. The Mexican COP16 presidency had little choice but to gavel over Bolivia's objections. Allowing Bolivia to block the agreement would have resulted in another train wreck of potentially larger proportions than in Copenhagen. But from scientific and procedural viewpoints, Bolivia's principal concerns were entirely legitimate, and most other developing countries commented that although the texts fell far short of their own expectations, they were willing to endorse the Cancun Agreements to keep the UN climate negotiations alive.[77]

To what extent Bolivia coordinated with its ALBA partners before it rejected the deal in Cancun is unknown to us. The unity that saw the ALBA countries stand shoulder to shoulder in Copenhagen was not on display in the final stages of COP16 in Cancun. Venezuela's Salerno stated, "We never imagined a scenario in which a country that we love so much would not feel good about this. We understand the reasons and we support many of them. [The final agreement] is not ambitious."[78] Due to ALBA's norms of noninterference and respect for sovereignty, the group decided to respect Bolivia's autonomy and agreed to disagree.

Others credit the Mexican diplomatic team for doing a better job at including ALBA before and during the negotiations in Cancun.[79] Secretary Espinosa said that ALBA maintained a position that was political and ideo-logical and did not strictly relate to the issues of the meeting. She com-mented that Mexico worked closely with ALBA, and insisted that ALBA and all Parties respect the positions of other countries, and that everyone tries to work on a common agenda.[80] During the negotiations, Ecuador and Venezuela were chosen by Mexico to cofacilitate discussions on different issues—a move that enhanced inclusion and increased these countries' participation.

Then in June 2011, six months after the Cancun showdown, Pablo Solón resigned as Bolivia's chief negotiator to the UNFCCC, publicly reported as due to a family illness. In September 2011, Solón began to speak out against the Morales administration's attempts to build a road through an indig-enous reserve called TIPNIS[81] and against heavy-handed government inter-vention. In an open letter, Solón wrote to President Morales, stating that "there must be coherence between what we do and what we say." In regards to TIPNIS, Solón says, "One cannot speak of defending Mother Earth and at the same time promote the construction of a road that will harm Mother Earth, doesn't respect indigenous rights and violates human rights in an 'unforgiveable' way."[82]

Morales was reportedly going to be proposed for a Nobel Prize based on his work on promoting Mother Earth rights, but that dream fizzled away, perhaps as a result of the Nobel committee hearing about TIPNIS. And at Rio+20 in 2012, Morales was purportedly not accepted to speak at a civil society movement conference. This represents a massive change from the heady days of Copenhagen, Cochabamba, and Cancun, when Morales was the leading hero for indigenous peoples, civil society, and climate justice.[83]

Following the resignation of Pablo Solón, Rene Orellana took over as the Bolivian delegation's chief negotiator to the UNFCCC. At Bolivia's Ministry of Foreign Affairs in November 2011, Orellana said to a group of civil society organizations that Bolivia would not again block and stand alone, as it had in Cancun. Because ALBA works on other issues beyond climate change such as trade and regional integration, unity could not be compromised for a singular issue.[84] In an interview at the COP18 in Doha in 2012, Orellana told us that Bolivia had changed its negotiations strategy but not its policy since Cancun. The change of strategy was a political decision, based on the aim of expanding Bolivia's alliances with groups such as AOSIS and African countries and playing a more proactive and constructive role. The risk of undermining ALBA unity was deemed too strong, given the extensive ties between its members and other states.[85] Since Cancun, Bolivia has promoted some innovative proposals and sought to incorporate them and its own vision into the process through talks in Durban, Doha, Warsaw, and Lima, but it has not blocked the negotiations again.

As the December 2014 Lima climate change conference wrapped up, the eighth summit of ALBA was also meeting in Havana. ALBA leaders endorsed a Bolivian proposal to host a conference on climate change for social movements that is scheduled to take place in the fall of 2015 and aims to set out proposals that would (again) be taken to the Paris climate conference in December 2015.[86]

At the time of writing, specific plans and objectives for the conference are unknown, but Morales's interest in hosting an event is consistent with his efforts to bring civil society voices into the UN climate process—following the experience of Cochabamba—even if these attempts have been criticized for being inconsistent or unproductive. This plan by Bolivia fittingly encapsulates the unique role played by the ALBA countries at the UN climate talks and their attempts to promote the participation of civil society, even if that is not the sole objective as described above, and carve out a unique space for their participation.

Ecuador's Proposal to "Keep the Oil in the Soil"

In September 2007, Ecuador's president, Rafael Correa, stood before the United Nations' General Assembly and proposed a revolutionary initiative:

For the first time an oil producer country, Ecuador, where a third of the resources of the State depends on the exploitation of the above mentioned resources, resigns this income for the well-being of humanity and invites the world to join efforts through a fair compensation, in order that together we lay the foundations for a more human and fair civilization.[87]

With the Yasuní-ITT Initiative, Ecuador agreed to leave 846 million barrels of oil lying under the Ishpingo-Tambococha-Tiputini oil reserves in the Yasuní National Park—the equivalent of 20 percent of the nation's reserves. The Initiative proposed to prevent the release of more than 400 million metric tons of carbon into the atmosphere. In return, Ecuador asked the international community for $3.6 billion, amounting to half of the oil's estimated worth.[88] As Ecuador's former minister for national patrimony, María Fernanda Espinosa put it: "This is Ecuador's contribution toward combating climate change."[89]

The Yasuní National Park is one of the most biodiverse reserves in the world. It is also home to the Tagaeri and Taromenane indigenous peoples, who are in voluntary isolation. Maintaining the oil in the ITT blocks underground would prioritize social and environmental goals and allow Ecuador to become the first developing country to propose an effective, quantifiable, and verifiable carbon-abatement model.[90] Over 70 percent of Ecuadorian citizens supported the Yasuní-ITT Initiative.[91] The proposal's path-breaking goals were based on the Andean vision of the good life (el buen vivir), an indigenous-origin concept that is based on living in harmony with nature and is now part of Ecuador's 2008 constitution.[92]

According to the plan, countries that contributed to a special UN-managed fund would receive Certificates of Guarantee Yasuní (CGYs) with the government's pledge that the crude will be left untouched indefinitely. This was a pledge, not a commitment, as the certificates could be bought back by Ecuador in the future if it decided to exploit the oil after all. The interest generated by the fund would be invested in protecting 4.8 million hectares of national parks and reserves, including the "untouchable zone" where the Tagaeri and Taromenane are struggling to reside in voluntary isolation. Social development projects in the Ecuadorian Amazon would focus on education, health, and jobs in ecotourism. A drive would be made to bring online Ecuador's hydroelectric, geothermal, wind, and solar resources.[93]

The Yasuní-ITT Initiative originated in civil society, not the Ecuadorian government. It was based on a long-running lawsuit against Chevron-Texaco that was brought by thirty thousand indigenous people and local communities members that claimed that the US company caused catastrophic environmental damages in the Ecuadorian Amazon and serious health problems. In response to this case and others, activists and scholars began calling for a moratorium on oil drilling in the region during the 1990s.[94]

Since the launch of the Yasuní-ITT Initiative in 2007 until its demise in 2013, the proposal went through various stages where progress seemed to be made, only to be undermined by announcements of deals to exploit the ITT oil blocks. Mixed messages about the shelf life of the Initiative were frequently sent. Although President Correa officially supported plan A (the initiative), this did not stop work on the exploitation of the ITT oil (plan B). In 2009, the former minister of mining and petroleum, Derlis Palacios, announced future bidding for the ITT block, stating that "If we find an immediate solution [for keeping oil underground], we will consider it. I think that we have already lost good time. We will make every necessary attempt to protect the environment, but the country needs money."[95] Immediately thereafter, President Correa again backed plan A through an executive decree that made the Yasuní-ITT Initiative official Ecuadorian policy.[96] The proposal was adversely affected by the frequent changes in its institutional structure, which saw five different commissions.[97]

The deadline to receive the funding was extended a number of times, despite blunt reminders sent out by the Ecuadorian government in an attempt to galvanize international support. The proposal was backed by various international dignitaries such as the UN secretary general, Ban Ki-moon. The German Parliament also gave its unanimous support from all political parties, and the Organization of Petroleum Exporting Countries even voiced its approval. Chile became the first country to contribute financially to the Initiative, followed by Spain, Italy, Colombia, Turkey, and Peru.[98] A major donation from Germany was initially promised but then rescinded.

The initiative suffered further setbacks when influential members of its commission resigned due to a lack of a clear strategy for how the proposal would be financed. Competing ideas on the selling of bonds at the price of petroleum gave way to the idea of selling Certificates of Guarantee Yasuní (CGYs) not at the price of oil but at the price of nonemitted carbon. The proposal was revised again to include CGYs as a guarantee for debt forgiveness, with less emphasis on carbon markets. In Copenhagen, the signing of the United Nations Development Program trust fund agreement was meant to occur but did not, because President Correa called that board's composition "an insult to Ecuadorian sovereignty."[99]

After six years, in August 2013, President Correa signed Decree 74, which terminated the trust fund of the Yasuní-ITT Initiative. Correa said, "With deep sadness but also taking full responsibility toward our people and history, I have had to make one of the hardest decisions of my administration." He continued with a broad indictment of the global polity: "It was not charity that we sought from the international community, but co-responsibility in the fight against climate change.... Unfortunately ... the world has failed us.... But let's not fool ourselves: the fundamental factor of the failure is that the world is extremely hypocritical, and the logic that prevails is not that of justice, but power."[100] The Yasuní trust fund had received only $13.3 million, which represented just 0.37 percent of the goal of $3.6 billion.[101]

The pioneering initiative was brought down by a global recession, stinginess, doubt about Ecuador's management of and commitment to the initiative, and the national imperatives of oil exploitation for development. Estimates now put the value of the ITT fields at $18 billion. Although Correa said that only 1 percent of the reserve will be affected by the oil exploration, Kelly Swing, the founder of the Tipitini research center in the Yasuní national park, said that twenty or thirty times more land in the reserve will be impacted.[102]

Surveys show that between 78 and 90 percent of Ecuadoreans are opposed to drilling in this sensitive region.[103] Civil society points to the restrictions on extracting nonrenewable resources within national protected areas and "prior consent" requirements under the Ecuadorian constitution, which in the opposing view are outweighed by the national interest as decided by the president.[104]

Alexandra Almeida, from the Ecuadorean NGO Acción Ecologica, says the Correa administration feared dropping the Yasuní-ITT Initiative prior to the presidential election due to its popularity. She says, "Carrying on with the negotiating team and the initiative to leave the oil under the ground was only a strategy to avoid losing popularity ahead of the February 2013 [presidential] elections."[105] Correa feared a potential backlash against the decision to end the initiative prior to the election so it was kept going to avoid any damage to his popularity. Correa was not willing to risk his citizens' revolution and economic plans for an environmental proposal.

Following the demise of the initiative, the "Yasunidos" collective—made up of social, environmental, and indigenous organizations—was established. The collective launched a campaign to gather the number of signatures required by the Ecuadorian constitution, to push for a national referendum and to let the people decide the fate of Yasuní-ITT. On April 12, 2014, Yasunidos delivered over 750,000 signatures to the National Electoral Council.[106] The National Electoral Council validated only 359,781 of the more than 750,000 collected, well under the 583,323 needed by Ecuadorian law, and said that some of the signatures were repeated up to nine times.[107] In late May 2014, Ecuador announced it had approved permits for oil drilling in Yasuní's ITT block, allowing Ecuador's Petroamazonas to drill there. With the permits now approved, oil companies are expected to move quickly into the ITT blocks, producing the first oil within less than two years.[108] In August 2014, the Rights of Nature Ethics Tribunal, composed of environmental justice experts from Canada, Colombia, Ecuador, the Philippines, and the United States, ruled that the Ecuadorian government's plans to exploit Yasuní-ITT violated several articles of its own constitution, which include the rights of nature, the rights of indigenous communities living in voluntary isolation, and the right to political participation.[109]

Ecuador's Yasuní-ITT Initiative was a bold and ambitious attempt to avoid carbon emissions, protect biodiversity, uphold the rights of nature and indigenous peoples, and encourage the transition to sustainable development. But economic necessity—the lack of global support, the problems of management, and the primacy of oil for Ecuador's development—reveals the fragility of such policies. Ecuador has been a progressive voice at the UN climate talks, and its visibility was greatly enhanced by the initiative and a related "Net Avoided Emissions" proposal.

The Guardian reported, however, that Ecuador had been negotiating secretly with China for US$1 billion to guarantee the supply of crude oil for PetroChina in the medium term and to provide Ecuador "access to a favourable line of credit to finance priority projects." The proposed deal was that the China Development Bank would lend "no less than US$1bn in the first phase" to "Ecuador's Ministry of Finance or an entity designated by Ecuador's government." Alexandra Almeida, from Acción Ecologica, said that "The document shows that in 2009 Ecuador's government negotiated with China to do all it could so Chinese oil companies can explore in ITT and Block 31, contradicting the Yasuní-ITT Initiative that was in effect at the time." Following publication of this article, Juan Falconí, the Ecuadorian ambassador to the United Kingdom, denied the allegations and said that *The Guardian's* claims are baseless, were made without any credible evidence, and were based on a fraudulent government document.[110]

Following the end of the Yasuní-ITT Initiative, claims that the uncontacted indigenous groups in the Yasuní were effectively abandoned by the Ecuadorian government posed serious questions about the rights of these indigenous groups. The 2008 constitution, which was the first in the world to include the rights of nature, also appears to be undermined with the decision to expand oil exploitation in the Yasuní National Park. The Ecuadorian government was threatened by the Yasunidos' plans to force a public vote on the future of exploitation in the Yasuní. Because oil revenue accounts for more than 50 percent of Ecuador's export earnings and about a third of all tax revenues, this resource is important for the nation's ability to maintain social spending. As Uruguayan writer Eduardo Gudynas argues, Ecuador had to continue seeking bids for oil field concessions, and oil companies demand firm investment conditions to ensure that the blocks they acquire can be effectively exploited. These assurances would be meaningless in light of the possibility of a people's referendum that could prevent oil exploration in any part of the country.[111]

The Yasuní-ITT Initiative has gone full circle. The original idea was created by civil society, taken up by the government, taken to the international community, canceled by the government, and finally reclaimed by a civil society that sought to salvage it. Tensions between the government and these civil society groups are escalating. The government has closed down the office of the Pachamama Foundation in Quito, which works closely with indigenous groups in the Amazon, on allegedly baseless and politically motivated charges.[112]

Oil and Venezuela's Mercurial Climate Posture

In front of thousands of delegates in the plenary in Copenhagen, the late Venezuelan president Hugo Chávez proclaimed, "Let's not change the climate, let's change the system! Capitalism is a destructive development model that is putting an end to life; it threatens to put a definitive end to the human species."[113]

Since Chávez's election in 1999, Venezuelan politics have followed the democratic revolutionary principles of a Bolivarian revolution that was defined by the soldier-turned-socialist "father of the people" Chávez. This Bolivarian socialist lens is the one that Venezuelan representatives adopt when speaking about climate change—that environmental protection and principles should be based on the recognition that the effects of climate change affect largely the poor and most vulnerable.[114] This core climate-justice argument states that developed countries caused the problem and so they should be the ones to stop it and provide the funding, technology, and support to help developing countries adapt to climate impacts. Venezuela rejects carbon trading and states that any future climate agreement should be based on justice, equity, and the principles of the original UNFCCC.

At the UN climate negotiations, Venezuela emphasizes its special national circumstances due to its oil, which poses significant challenges to the Venezuelan economy and puts it in a disadvantaged position for addressing climate change.[115] Venezuela is unmistakably a petrostate. Oil accounts for roughly 95 percent of Venezuela's export earnings, more than 50 percent of its federal budget revenues, and around 30 percent of the entire gross domestic product.[116] Trade partners such as China, the Petrocaribe members, and the US make oil a key bargaining chip and commercial and diplomatic tool. Venezuela's second socialist plan 2013–2019 is explicit about oil's crucial role to drive the transformation of the nation toward Bolivarian socialism and build its foreign relations with China and Petrocaribe partners.

Venezuela and China formed a strategic alliance in 2001. In 2008, Chávez said that China required considerable amounts of energy and that Venezuela was committed to providing it.[117] China has lent Venezuela approximately $46.5 billion between 2005 and 2012.[118] In 2010, the China National Petroleum Corporation signed a deal to help Venezuela develop a major Orinoco oil field with the aim of reaching 10 million barrels a day by 2030.[119] Venezuela is now the China Development Bank's (CDB) largest foreign borrower, and all of the lines of credit are secured against oil supply contracts,[120] often at prices locked in at current rates for the entire life of the loan. From just 49,000 barrels a day in 2005, oil exports to China were planned to reach 1 million barrels per day by 2015, a twentyfold increase in a decade.[121]

In 2005, Venezuela created Petrocaribe, an energy agreement to provide low-interest oil sales to Caribbean and Central American countries. The Caribbean nations have the highest electricity costs in the Western Hemisphere and are net energy importers that spend over 10 percent of their GDP on oil imports. Petrocaribe allows countries up to twenty-five years to pay off oil bills and to provide goods and services in exchange for oil. Petrocaribe plans call for building or repairing some twenty refineries in the next ten years.[122] According to the former president of the Dominican Republic, Leonel Fernández, "Venezuela is teaching an impressive lesson to the world that solidarity and generosity can prevail over speculation, greed and unquenchable thirst for wealth."

The use of oil as a central pillar of Venezuelan diplomacy and interest in the Caribbean is not new.[123] Since the 1970s, Venezuela has deemed the Caribbean to be a natural area of influence. Petrocaribe has become a cooperation instrument at the heart of ALBA by seeking to counteract bilateral trade negotiations between the US and Caribbean and Central American countries.[124] But with the exception of Cuba, Caribbean countries have not aligned themselves in an open and unified manner with the anti-imperialist or anti-US positions defended by Venezuela and ALBA.[125] Despite the official reports, it is unclear whether member countries are really receiving all the promised shipments of oil and whether proposed projects are being executed, with one source pointing out that Cuba has been reselling part of its oil.[126] Further, a number of Caribbean countries are part of the Alliance of Small Island States (AOSIS) at the UN climate negotiations and have adopted more ambitious positions than Venezuela and have been openly hostile to OPEC's stances.

Harold Trinkunas at the Brookings Institution argues that the continued dependence of Central American and Caribbean nations on Petrocaribe is risky because subsidized oil creates disincentives for adopting more advanced technologies and investment in new sources of energy and creates energy dependency on Venezuela. Subsidized financing, he argues, has led to rising levels of debt owed to Venezuela by the members.[127] Now at risk of descending into hyperinflation, Venezuela appears to be cutting back its subsidies to Central American and Caribbean countries, which Andreas Oppenheimer argues "is likely to severely curtail its regional clout."[128]

What is less clear is whether this shift will increase interest in low-carbon solutions in these partner countries. Venezuela is not likely to be in favor of a strong UN-led climate change regime that promotes a global low-carbon future that would hinder its oil sector. Speaking in an interview in Doha, Venezuela's lead negotiator, Claudia Salerno, said in reference to Venezuela's oil reserves that oil creates a "huge responsibility," that Venezuela represents only "0.48% of the total emissions" in the world, and that Venezuela is "an extremely green country."[129]

These numbers look dubious. According to the World Resource's CAIT emissions database, Venezuela in 2011 was responsible for 267 $MtCO_2e$ from fossil fuels (and 381 $MtCO_2e$ with deforestation), which is 0.62 percent of global greenhouse gas emissions (and 0.84 percent of global emissions counting deforestation). This includes only emissions from fuels burned inside Venezuela, not those delivered and burned elsewhere. According to Venezuela's First National Communication to the UNFCCC, submitted in 2005, emissions from the energy sector are responsible for around 75 percent of emissions, followed by the agricultural, waste, and industrial sectors; the 2011 figures put that at about 70 percent of emissions from fossil energy.[130]

Although the document on what Venezuela has done at home on climate change is unreliable and sketchy, our assessment is that Venezuela has made little real progress on climate change, compared to other large emitters in the region such as Brazil, Mexico, or its neighbors such as Colombia. The Venezuelan government has distributed over 70 million energy-saving lightbulbs as part of a national energy-efficiency initiative.[131] Hydropower accounts for around 70 percent of its electricity generation. A program to combat desertification called Mission Tree has reforested around 35,000 hectares with nearly 30 million trees with a goal to plant an additional 20 million trees by 2015. But Venezuela has no piece of legislation that comprehensively confronts climate change. There is no national law to mitigate energy consumption, advance renewable energy, or increase energy efficiency.[132] Venezuela does not yet have a national plan to address climate impacts, despite the vulnerability of its electricity system, based largely on hydropower, to climate impacts such as droughts. In 2012, Venezuela announced plans to limit greenhouse gas emissions across four sectors, including its petroleum industry. Some observers suggest that these plans have little chance of being implemented.[133] According to ClimateScope 2013, which assessed clean energy investments in the region, Venezuela ranked twentieth out of twenty-six countries in its ability to attract capital for low-carbon energy sources and efforts to build a green economy.[134]

According to a Venezuelan scientist who spoke to us anonymously, the government lacks any policy on climate change. Venezuela has submitted only one national communication to the UNFCCC, whereas most Latin American countries have submitted at least two and in some cases three or even five. Further, the data in the national communication are allegedly from the 1990s, so Venezuela's claim of representing only 0.48 percent of global emissions seems to be a politically motivated understatement.[135] Even using government-provided statistics, Venezuela's per capita emissions stand at approximately six tons of CO_2 emissions per person, above the world average.

Chávez's second socialist plan for 2013 to 2019 was passed into law by Venezuela's National Assembly in late 2013.[136] The plan includes some ambitious objectives—to build an "eco-socialist and productive economic model, based on a harmonious relationship between man and nature," "continue struggling for the preservation, respect for and strengthening of the climate system constituted by the UNFCCC and its Kyoto Protocol," contribute to the "creation of a big world movement to eradicate the causes and reverse the effects of climate change," "dismantle international carbon markets," and "design a national mitigation plan and national plan of adaptation."[137] These are impressive goals, but the means of implementation is unclear.

At the UN climate talks in Doha in 2012, rumors circulated that Venezuela was considering putting forward its candidacy to host the COP20 in 2014. Peru also was interested in hosting the conference (following its 2010 defeat to Mexico to host the COP16). In 2013, Peru and Venezuela promoted their candidacies. In June 2013, the United Nations' Group of Latin

American and Caribbean Countries met to determine who would host in 2014, and after a lengthy discussion, Venezuela rescinded its candidacy, following the death of President Chávez earlier in the year. Peru was confirmed COP20 president.

Earlier that month, over sixty civil society groups from Latin America signed a declaration in favor of Peru.[138] According to the declaration: "Peru has been a progressive voice … on climate change and has demonstrated a willingness to listen and offer counsel in the international negotiations … [which] places it in a solid position to host COP20."[139] Even though Venezuela has attempted to position itself as one of the principal defenders of Mother Earth and promoting civil society, the declaration and its signatories stated a preference for Peru.

So instead, Venezuela offered to host a "Social Pre-COP," consisting of two conferences that aspired to give civil society voice in the UN process, bringing together activists and ministers from around the world. Claudia Salerno explained to the US news program *Democracy Now!* that Venezuela would host "the first formal consultation of every single social movement involved in the climate change agenda," at which ministers would talk to each other and also their people about the agreement the world wants to see.[140]

But compared to other Latin American countries such as Brazil and Peru, Venezuela's civil society has little capacity on climate issues, which posed problems for a strong and credible turnout at home.[141] Further, the Venezuelan government was not willing to coordinate activities or include national groups that were not in favor of its policies in the preparations for or during the Social Pre-COP. The timing of the Social Pre-COP came at a very difficult moment. In early 2014, Venezuela was wracked with protests, and a Human Rights Watch report in May claimed that Venezuela was committing systematic human rights abuses. Wanting the opportunity to project its own vision of the climate change issue even if it could not host the full COP, the Social Pre-COP was a way for Venezuela to save face and put its mark on the process consistent with its former role. Especially in Copenhagen and Cochabamba, Venezuela's emphasis on climate justice resonated strongly with civil society. Moving the event away from Caracas to Venezuela's Margarita Island reflected concerns about safety in the capital city and possible disruptions by domestic organizations. In line with the second socialist plan, which includes an objective to contribute to the creation of a big world movement on climate change, the organization of the Social Pre-COP was consistent with national climate policy.

The Social Pre-COP preparatory meeting in July 2014 and the main Social Pre-COP in November that year were controversial events befitting of Venezuela's contentious role at the UN climate negotiations. On the one hand, they were celebrated as an unprecedented attempt to establish a dialogue between civil society with national governments prior to the UN climate conference in Lima, Peru. According to one participant, ministers and negotiators from forty countries and representatives from eighty civil society groups from around the world participated.[142]

Venezuela's Social Pre-COP had the theme "Change the System, Not the Climate" and argued that an overhaul of the global capitalist system is necessary to combat climate change effectively.[143] Civil society groups in Venezuela, however, have largely opposed the Venezuelan government's stance on climate change. For example, the Venezuelan Network of Non-Governmental Environmental Organizations (Red de Organizaciones Ambientales no Gubernamentales de Venezuela), the predominant network of Venezuelan civil society groups, rejects the ideological bias that Venezuela imposed on its pre-COP, stating that a discussion that reduces climate change to issues of socialism versus capitalism oversimplifies climate change and masks the true demands of citizens.[144] The network believes in coresponsibility and also argues that any unbridled exploitation of natural resources is unacceptable.

Although civil society groups fought hard at the pre-COP to include a statement that the international community should leave 80 percent of oil, coal, and gas reserves in the ground, the final text, revised by the Venezuelan government, left those provisions out.[145]

The main output of the November meeting was the "Key Messages for COP20 and the Ministerial Meeting of the Social PreCOP 2014." The document says nothing about the phaseout of the use of fossil fuels, which was a key theme discussed during the earlier meetings. Venezuela therefore decided to call the key message document a presidential summary rather than a consensus document between civil society and ministers in attendance.[146] Mauro Fernández, a member of Greenpeace, commented that Greenpeace was not able to support the "Key Messages" document presented by Venezuela given its omissions of certain elements (such as the reference to the gradual phasing out of fossil fuels) that were red lines for various groups. Fernández also criticized the organization of the meeting, which was led by the Venezuelan government during the initial stages, rather than by civil society, as was the case during the July preparatory meeting.[147]

The Social Pre-COP failed to create a national dialogue between the Venezuelan government and national organizations and those from around the world.[148] Some of Venezuela's leading environmental organizations were not invited to the Social Pre-COP because of their opposition to government policy. Therefore, the international NGOs that attended the Social Pre-COP missed an opportunity to work with national groups. Such connections are regarded as important outcomes of international conferences of this sort.

Venezuela seems to have organized the Social Pre-COP to do more than simply attempt to promote the role of civil society groups in the UNFCCC process and to create a new global movement to fight climate change. Venezuela also saw the Social Pre-COP as a means to gain credibility within the global climate community and perhaps to deflect attention from its lack of domestic action on climate change. However, the "Key Messages" reflect a level of pragmatism, especially given the omission of any reference to fossil fuels.

In Lima, the authors met the reportedly only member of Venezuelan civil society who attended the COP20. María Eugenia Rinaudo was working as part of the Adopt a Negotiator group, which for the first time had a Venezuelan civil society representative following the Venezuelan delegation. Her attendance at the COP was funded by the Adopt a Negotiator group, and she did not receive any government funding. It is unfortunate that despite the substantial sums that Venezuela spent on organizing and hosting a Social Pre-COP—which included funding the international travel of global NGO representatives —it could not do anything to support greater participation of national NGO representatives at the Lima climate change conference.

In the wake of what was a disappointing Social Pre-COP, Venezuela lost credibility at the UN climate negotiations because its motives were revealed to extend beyond simply attempting to support civil society. Civil society groups in attendance felt betrayed by the release of the "Key Messages" document, which did not reflect their positions. This exposes a contradiction between Venezuela's climate positions at home and its actions at the UN climate change talks.

Venezuela's interpretation of climate justice presents a paradox and challenge to global civil society. Given that Venezuela holds the world's largest oil reserves—which represent a substantial portion of the available amount of carbon that can safely be put into the atmosphere (the global carbon budget)—its role on climate change could prove decisive for global society. As 350.org leader Bill McKibben put it in an influential 2012 article, although President Chávez insisted that "climate change is undoubtedly the most devastating environmental problem of this century," he forged ahead with plans to develop the vast Orinoco tar sands as "the most significant engine for a comprehensive development of the entire territory and Venezuelan population." McKibben pointed out that the Orinoco deposits are larger than the controversial tar sands of Alberta, Canada, and that both deposits together could fill up the whole carbon budget.[149] The McGlade and Ekins study of "unburnable carbon" in *Nature* discussed earlier suggests that major proportions of Venezuela's fossil fuels reserves are "unburnable" if we are going to avoid dangerous climate change.[150]

Sitting atop the world's largest known oil reserves, Venezuela is in alignment with China and the Like-Minded Developing Countries group in resisting efforts to create obligations for developing countries. Venezuela's notions of climate justice—as revealed in its actions—appear to clash with those of vulnerable nations that face rising sea levels and other impacts of soaring atmospheric carbon levels. As the next chapter shows, some countries have raised concerns about using development as an excuse for undermining higher ambitions for emissions-reductions at the climate negotiations.[151] Venezuela's decision (with its ALBA partners) to join the Like-Minded Developing Countries group with China and others seems consistent with its goals of holding developed countries to account while stalling progress that threatens its national interests. Given Venezuela's current ideological preference for exporting oil to China, the country's partnership with China serves its own interests in two ways: Venezuela can export oil to a preferred ally and thus secure much-needed loans, and it can position itself alongside China at the UN negotiations to avoid an aggressive climate treaty that might be seen as undermining its own economy and arguably China's as well. Chinese trade and commercial ties with Venezuela may be strengthening the relative power of political and commercial domestic constituencies and of "dirty" ministries (for example, ministries of mining and energy) compared with environmental and climate change ministries and departments. It appears that these dirty ministries have nearly complete influence over Venezuela's domestic and foreign policies on climate change.

Venezuela's actions have often polarized global opinion. To Venezuela's supporters, its positions and discourse on climate justice express exactly what is wrong with the world and how the end of capitalism and US neoliberal influence is the only possible way to save the planet. To its detractors, Venezuela's ideology and calls for the complete dismantling of the dominant economic system is out of sync with how the UNFCCC works and what it can realistically achieve. Venezuela's weak domestic climate change policies and radical demands at the UN talks raise claims of hypocrisy.

Looking ahead, Venezuela's tenuous position of blending an ideological perspective with pragmatic choices to protect its national interests will come under greater scrutiny as the world struggles to tackle global warming. Venezuela's oil reserves and what it does with them (and those of other major oil producers) may become a modern day equivalent of the criticism that Brazil faced in the 1980s when the world watched the Amazon burn from space—a matter of collective human survival that fundamentally challenges national sovereignty. By not developing low-carbon policies now such as promoting renewable energy including wind and solar, Venezuela is putting itself in an ever more vulnerable position.

Assessing ALBA's Impact and Future

ALBA began as a trade and solidarity pact of left-leaning nations in Latin America led by Venezuela and its oil wealth to provide a counterweight to the free-trade agreements promoted by the US. ALBA burst onto the global climate negotiations scene in Copenhagen in 2009, most visibly as a blocker of the majority's desire to settle a deal—any deal. Working with NGOs from around the world, ALBA raised important issues of climate justice and brought them into the formal negotiations after the People's Conference in Cochabamba. The central climate justice message was that the Northern countries caused climate change, nations in the South did not, and the poor nations are suffering worst and first from the impacts. A core climate justice idea is that the North owes the South a huge "climate debt" that should be paid with massive support for developing nations to deal with the impacts and to green their development infrastructure. One of the more contentious positions of ALBA has been its emphasis on lambasting the global North for creating climate change and for failing to take action as it agreed to do in the UNFCCC. Some of ALBA's arguments, both from science and climate justice perspectives, are legitimate. They also fit with the projects of these nation's governments, placing themselves in opposition to US-led imperialism, whether mercantilist, capitalist, or environmentalist. Given the polarized nature of the climate negotiations, this North versus South approach has become increasingly unconstructive, as is discussed in the following chapter.

For its relatively small size, ALBA has had a large impact by bringing important issues before the world by attempting to block an unjust and inadequate pact at Copenhagen and through Bolivia's continuing resistance at Cancun. ALBA has brought significant issues to the UNFCCC draft texts, but the group has had less success in securing passage of such issues in final agreements. Since its rapid crescendo in 2009, ALBA's voice has lost much of its potency, in part because of mounting political, economic, and social problems in Venezuela. After over a decade in office, President Chávez began to confront more serious challenges, including a worsening economy, a sharply deteriorating security situation, and a cancer diagnosis that led to his death in March 2013.[152] Along with other ALBA countries (Ecuador and Bolivia), Venezuela's civil society organizations have grown increasingly critical of what they see as their governments' curtailing of civil liberties, such as the right to protest and freedom of the press. These violations challenge the relationship between ALBA countries and global civil society organizations, which for years strongly supported their climate justice focus.[153]

Still, the 2010 Cochabamba People's Summit was largely a success for Bolivia. The presence of around 35,000 activists was a significant achievement and demonstrated a high level of frustration with Copenhagen and the UNFCCC process and strong global commitment to this issue. It allowed Bolivia's Pablo Solón to fight for the inclusion of many of the demands from ALBA and civil society into the negotiating texts in Tianjin in early fall of 2010. However, they were all removed from the table in December. The Democracy Center's Jim Shultz, has questioned whether the People's

Conference went far enough in challenging "the complicated political calculus within those key countries," noting that coming up with declarations and demands is straightforward but that the climate justice movement's approach to going beyond declarations to amass real power remains the principal challenge.[154] By standing alone in the world by rejecting the Cancun Agreements, Bolivia could argue that it did not turn its back on its positions from Copenhagen and Cochabamba and was following the will of the thousands of people that had gathered there and the millions more that their groups represented.

In Ecuador, a brave experiment in attempting to gain the world's support for the Yasuní-ITT Initiative to "keep the oil in the soil" was proposed with much fanfare in 2007 but eventually had to be abandoned. Alberto Acosta, Ecuador's former minister of energy and mines and one of the main architects of the initiative, said that "Ecuador and the world have lost an opportunity to shape a revolutionary initiative.... It was a giant step on the road toward post-extractivism."[155]

Venezuela's oil supplies—traditionally among the cheapest to extract in the world—gave President Chávez tremendous latitude to expand his global influence while prices were high. Counterbalancing the US's influence in the region was a top priority, and the arrival of ALBA at the UNFCCC negotiations afforded charismatic negotiators Claudia Salerno and Pablo Solón a platform for taking strong positions in favor of participatory decision making and for placing full responsibility for climate change on the developed countries. Venezuela's second socialist plan for 2013 to 2019 states that oil is the engine for powering Venezuela's path toward Bolivarian socialism. There are major objectives for fighting climate change and reshaping global capitalism outlined, but few concrete steps are being taken toward realistic action. Venezuela's weak domestic policies on climate seem inconsistent with its demands at the negotiations. Allegations have been leveled at Venezuela that the country is attempting to hold up the negotiations or block outcomes. Some of these claims are similar to accusations made for years against Saudi Arabia—that oil vendors do not want any controls on the sale of their main product. Civil society groups backed Peru over Venezuela for hosting COP20, even though Venezuela took a more populist climate justice position than Peru.

In the end, ALBA countries are primarily extractivist economies with major fossil fuel sectors in their economies, and for some observers, this calls much of what ALBA does into question. Eduardo Gudynas has commented at length about the fate of the Yasuní project, tying its problems to the bigger issue of the region's dependence on natural resources extraction. His observations could as easily be about Bolivia, Ecuador, or Venezuela:

Present day extractivism is only possible by reigning in democratic plurality. Few projects would surpass rigorous environmental and social regulation, as they always have great environmental impacts and few people in local communities would agree to sacrifice their lands. This issue is more serious for progressive governments, since the vast majority of extractivist rationale is based on conservative arguments tied to the market and reinforcing global commercial subordination. These arguments are therefore contrary to the very essence of the left. All this means that a progressive government, when forced to seriously discuss its appetite for petroleum or mining, must shed its clothes and reveal its most intimate mercantile thoughts.[156]

Gudynas makes the major point that "for the progressive Governments or for the new left governments, environmental issues have become a flank of serious contradictions. Their strong support to extractive activities to fuel economic growth is aggravating environmental impacts, triggers serious social protests, and perpetuates the subordination to be suppliers of raw materials for globalization."[157] Environmental issues represent a similar contradiction for neoliberal capitalism, and industrialization as the goal of development raises similar issues on the left and the right. Gudynas argues that resource dependency creates more difficult cognitive dissonance for left-leaning governments, which claim to support social movements. For Bolivia and Ecuador, the irony is even greater because they have constitutional protections for the rights of Mother Earth.

A leading Venezuelan leftist thinker finds it problematic that ALBA tends to hold capitalism responsible for climate change. Edgardo Lander argues that this framing can be used to make the case so that "so-called socialist governments [can] wash their hands in relation to their own responsibility." He suggests that this is case for Venezuela, where the responsibilities of the global North are emphasized, which tends to obscure the consequences of an oil-based model of state socialist extractive development.[158]

We are witnessing an increasing alignment of interests between ALBA countries and China, and we believe that China is an important part of this story. There is strong interest in Chinese investments in extractive industries in Latin America that fuel China's development at home. And in the climate negotiations, there is an alignment between ALBA's and the

Like-Minded Developing Countries group's opposition to any binding limits on any of the 134 members of the G77.[159] This position is at odds with the long-term interests of the vulnerable countries of the earth, which may gain grants or loans from China or highly subsidized oil from Venezuela at the price of their long-term future.

So ALBA countries' political projects in building twenty-first-century socialism has sometimes crashed up against economic and political realities and resulted in pragmatic decision making. At a more fundamental level, having postcolonial economies based on substantial natural resources presents both an opportunity and a great danger. Latin America is sometimes an important player in the UN climate negotiations, but the region's extractive economy creates contradictions and inconsistencies at home that drive what may seem like inconsistent positions. The next chapter looks at a different set of Latin American countries that have decided that resisting binding action for developing countries would damage the global climate and also their own economies. Their divergence from ALBA and Brazil is clear and sometimes uncomfortable.

5 The Revolt of the Middle: Mexico and AILAC

Latin America's Other Path?

Prior to the 2013 UN climate change negotiations in Warsaw, Poland, members of the Independent Association of Latin America and the Caribbean States (Asociación Independiente de América Latina y el Caribe, AILAC) met in Lima, Peru. Manuel Pulgar-Vidal, Peru's minister for the environment and president of the COP20 described AILAC's aspirations to grow their economies, tackle poverty, and be inclusive. He said, "We want to represent a model for the region ... to play in the big leagues. We are a team that looks to be proactive and influence the [climate] negotiations."[1]

In the last two chapters we looked at Latin America's two other main negotiating blocs—Brazil and its participation in the BASIC group of large emerging economies and the left-leaning Bolivarian Alliance for the Peoples of Our America (ALBA). We now turn to Mexico and AILAC. AILAC was launched in 2012 and includes Chile, Colombia, Costa Rica, Guatemala, Panama, Paraguay, and Peru. The bloc is part of the G77 and China group but often diverges from its negotiating positions, reflecting the fragmentation of the larger bloc.[2] This chapter aims to explain Mexico's and AILAC's positions and the roles that they have played in the talks. Mexico and AILAC have participated together in the informal group called the Cartagena Dialogue for Progressive Action, which is discussed below. At times, Mexico and AILAC negotiate separately at the talks but share a number of common positions.

AILAC has been dubbed the third way at the UN climate negotiations, given its role in seeking to build bridges between developed and developing countries. As G77 members, AILAC's statements emphasize that developed countries need to increase their level of ambition on emissions-reduction targets and provide climate finance and technology transfer to developing countries. At the same time, AILAC has a more flexible and dynamic interpretation of the thorny concept of common but differentiated responsibilities and respective capabilities (CBDR+RC), a phrase that has tied up the UN climate negotiations for decades. AILAC promotes the idea that emissions-reductions need to be adopted by all countries based on historic, present, and future responsibilities and capabilities. Its interpretation of CBDR+RC favors doing away with the firewall between North and South, which ALBA and Brazil have previously fought to maintain. Rather, AILAC countries have put forward 2020 emissions-reductions pledges backed up by some bold domestic action plans on climate change. They maintain that the principle of CBDR+RC should be respected, responsibility should be differentiated, but it should not be a brake on action by developing countries. In 2008, some AILAC countries (with Brazil and Mexico) were among the first developing countries to put forward domestic voluntary emission-reduction pledges, as is discussed in chapter 2.

Our goal throughout this book is to understand the roots of different countries' and blocs' positions. Mexico and AILAC countries are market-oriented, with economies relatively open to free trade and lighter compared to Brazil and ALBA countries on regulation and state intervention in the economy. Politically, these governments are largely centrist—either center left or center right—and therefore differ considerably from the political projects of their ALBA neighbor countries such as Bolivia and Ecuador.

Like Brazil and ALBA, AILAC countries' foreign policy is increasingly independent of the US, which is reflected in the growing presence of new trade and diplomatic partners such as China.[3] Chile, Colombia, Mexico, and Peru created the Pacific Alliance in June 2012 (with Costa Rica and Guatemala both considering joining), largely to increase trade and commerce within the region and with Asian markets.[4] There is considerable overlap between those members of AILAC and the Pacific Alliance, and they share some common positions on climate change and trade.[5] These Latin American countries and Brazil also were early proponents of the Clean Development Mechanism, which operated as an important incentive for domestic climate change policy in the early 2000s. Based on that experience, most of these countries have pressed for the development of market mechanisms that allow them to combine buying and selling carbon offsets with domestic emission reductions.[6] AILAC countries have promoted their domestic efforts on climate change through the international climate regime in a way that supports an ambitious multilateral treaty: they hope that their bold actions will inspire the same in other, larger players. As middle-income countries unable to throw their military or economic weight around, they see respect for a rules-based international system based on multilateralism and cooperation as vital.[7] Trade integration and multilateralism are two ways they see to strengthen those rules.

The following section looks at the Cartagena Dialogue for Progressive Action. This innovative North-South group is led by some Latin American countries, which played an instrumental role in its creation. We then turn to Mexico's presidency of the COP16 in 2010, where the country secured a diplomatic triumph that was widely credited with salvaging the multilateral process on climate change. We examine the roots of Mexico's support for its UNFCCC positions and its path-breaking domestic climate policy. We then look at the emergence of AILAC in 2012 and its role, positions, and impact at the UN climate change negotiations.

The sections on Costa Rica and Peru reveal AILAC's unique efforts and difficulties. Costa Rica, which is said to be one of the greenest countries on the planet, put forward an ambitious bid to be the first developing country to become carbon neutral by 2021. However, its quest for economic growth and new commercial ties with China has threatened Costa Rica's climate leadership and environmental image. Finally, we look at Peru's preparations to host the UN negotiations in Lima in December 2014, focusing on the apparent disconnect between the Peruvian ministry for the environment charged with organizing the COP20 and the domestic policy situation in Peru.

By examining Mexico's and AILAC's path-breaking roles and some of the contradictions and tensions inherent in climate leadership, we attempt to understand the durability of that leadership. This examination gets to the book's core questions on what it is about Latin America that makes some of its nations willing to take bold action and whether those actions will be politically sustainable. We begin with the Cartagena Dialogue's pioneering effort to build consensus between developed and developing countries.

Bridging the North-South Divide

The Copenhagen climate conference in 2009 was a harrowing example of how a UN climate negotiation can stumble toward the abyss of disunity, only to salvage just enough momentum to keep a "zombie" process alive for another year. Frustrated with the direction that the talks were taking, an informal group met in the final days of Copenhagen.[8] Then in March 2010, it held its first official meeting in Cartagena, Colombia. The Cartagena Dialogue for Progressive Action is an informal space rather than an official UNFCCC group and welcomes any country that is willing to work toward an ambitious and legally binding regime; it is committed domestically to becoming or remaining a low-carbon economy. Participants work together within and across formal UNFCCC negotiating blocs to discuss openly and constructively the rationale behind each other's positions, exploring areas of convergence and potential areas of joint action.[9]

The Cartagena Dialogue includes participants from Africa, Asia, Australasia, the Caribbean, Europe, Latin America, and the Small Island States. Chile, Colombia, Costa Rica, the Dominican Republic, Mexico, and Peru have participated actively from the outset.[10] The meetings of the Cartagena Dialogue allow countries who seldom come into contact with each other additional opportunities to interact, opening lines of communication that did not previously exist. The Cartagena Dialogue has successfully forged a middle ground for debate because it is inclusive, small, informal, flexible, and closed to the media and observers.[11]

The Cartagena Dialogue had a significant impact at both the COP16 and COP17. In Cancun, countries in the Cartagena Dialogue met frequently in subgroups to search for consensus and explore strategies for working with inflexible countries.[12] As the COP16 entered its final stages, countries from Australia, the Caribbean, the EU, and Latin America jointly reviewed the draft texts before the closing plenary and decided they would accept the Cancun Agreements. This had never been done before, and it would have been considered heresy given the fraught North-South divide between countries to suggest that such a thing even be attempted.

Consequently, Latin American countries participating in the Cartagena Dialogue have been labeled by some other developing countries as sellouts that are in cahoots with the opposition.[13] However, Cartagena members from developing countries do not feel that they are betraying their fellow countries in the South, and suggest that their critics may have missed the point about the Dialogue's aim. Bangladesh, speaking on behalf of the Dialogue in Bonn, Germany in June 2013 spoke about the importance of Dialogue meetings for understanding other parties' positions and allowing countries to work in "the best spirit of cooperation to find common ground for action by all," consistent with the core principles of the UNFCCC.[14]

Although the Cartagena Dialogue has had some successes, particularly in Cancun and Durban, participating countries inevitably have distinct agendas and priorities. Latin American countries have pushed for greater emphasis on adaptation and climate finance to balance the emphasis placed on mitigation by European countries. As is shown in the next section, the Cartagena Dialogue played a crucial but understated role in the Mexican presidency of the 2010 negotiations in efforts to rebuild trust after the mess at Copenhagen.

Mexico "Saves Climate Multilateralism"

The scene in Cancun for the 2010 UN negotiations was vastly different from that of Copenhagen the year before. In Copenhagen's Bella Centre, civil society booths and events were all inside the same halls as the official negotiations. As the tone grew more desperate during the two-week marathon, campaigners grew bolder in the actions they were willing to take to try to push for an ambitious agreement. The international group Avaaz and others staged near daily protests inside the hall. They and other civil society protestors became increasingly disruptive until all observer organization representatives were removed from the venue for the final three days of the talks when heads of state arrived.

By contrast, the Cancun climate negotiations were held in the extravagant and fortified Moon Palace hotel, which was a twenty-minute bus ride from the Cancunmesse convention hall where thousands of UN accredited civil society participants were set up. Parallel events organized by nonaccredited civil society groups were restricted to venues even farther away, which presented a logistical challenge for those trying to access them. Although many wealthy nation delegates stayed at the Moon Palace, other delegations and observers stayed in hotels along the sprawling beach complex. For participants who were staying at the far end of the beach, getting to the Cancunmesse and especially the Moon Palace required taking a one-hour journey in UN-charted buses on roads lined with Mexican security forces heavily armed with machine guns mounted on Humvees.

The Cancunmesse convention center included several lavish and exotic displays organized by governments. Mexico showcased its national policies on climate change and its credentials on green growth at events with a packed crowd of local press and distinguished foreign dignitaries. Ecuador attempted to attract interest in its pioneering Yasuní-ITT Initiative at a dedicated display (see chapter 4), and the Brazilians competed with the Mexicans for the limelight with an exuberant Amazonian-styled pavilion complete with a mock rainforest, live bands, and cocktail parties.

Regrettably, even farther away were other civil society venues. The Mexican government organized an official event at a stadium, and the climate justice movement (led by the international land rights group La Via Campesina and a coalition called Klimaforum) sponsored two separate events at an even greater distance. Although the Mexican government consulted with some civil society groups prior to the conference, it feared that civil society groups at the Moon Palace could result in confrontations, which had led to the eviction of civil society representatives in Copenhagen. Around three thousand protestors from thirty-six countries converged on Cancun in caravans to participate in the Alternative Forum for Life, Social, and Environmental Justice led by La Via Campesina, a network of organizations that focused on small farmers and rural workers. Diálogo Climático-Espacio Mexicano convened a march in downtown Cancun on the Global Day of Action, and Klimaforum held various sessions over many days at its Global Ecovillage, where one hundred to three hundred people from forty countries participated daily.[15]

All three groups were critical of what they saw as the "false solutions" (such as carbon trading) that were being proposed at the talks, critiquing corporations and neoliberalism and seeking solutions from "traditional" knowledge.[16] Arielle Balbus from our lab group attended these events and reported that the discourse at La Via Campesina, which included the Mexican revolutionary group Zapatista Army of National Liberation (Ejército Zapatista de Liberación Nacional, EZLN), was more radical and that both events produced declarations denouncing the Cancun Agreements and proposed their own solutions.[17] These declarations and protests were never seen by those inside the Moon Palace. In short, the physical plan for the events of 2010 was fragmenting, marginalizing, and disempowering to civil society, which had for two decades been seen as an important impetus to action at the talks. The Mexican government's management of the conference was critiqued daily by participants as exclusionary in a new and worrisome way for the UNFCCC.

As incoming president of the COP16, Mexico would normally take over leadership only at the next session, in Cancun in December 2010. However, following the fiasco in Copenhagen, Mexico began its work in earnest immediately after the COP15. President Felipe Calderón decided that Mexico's secretary of foreign affairs, Patricia Espinosa, would host the COP, breaking with the tradition that the incumbent minister of the environment usually hosts the proceedings. Because Calderón appreciated that the process required extensive diplomatic expertise, he appointed one of the country's most experienced diplomats, Luis Alfonso de Alba, as its special representative for climate change. De Alba, a career diplomat, had been unanimously elected first president of the UN Human Rights Council in 2006, in which position he developed close relationships with various countries on the issue including Ecuador and Nicaragua, allowing him to reach across many balkanized groups in the UNFCCC.[18]

De Alba began to hold formal and informal meetings in Mexico and around the world. In addition to meetings in Mexico City, he also traveled to Bolivia, Germany, India, and the US and held meetings with groups such as the African Group and AOSIS. Backed up by a team of twenty, de Alba and the Mexican delegation were on the road for more than 250 days in 2010. They focused on a two specific elements. First, they met with countries that disapproved of the handling and results in Copenhagen and that needed assurance that the COP16 would be inclusive to all. They met with the power brokers about the key elements of negotiations. A former adviser to the delegation of the Marshall Islands in Cancun said following the COP16 that "looking back, the reasons for this comparative success are very clear.... Patricia Espinosa, and her impressive team of diplomats listened and listened and listened. And by this simple act, they helped rebuild the trust and spirit of compromise that had been shattered in Copenhagen."[19]

Second, they brought down the excessively high expectations that had doomed Copenhagen and refocused on a pragmatic approach. De Alba described the strategy this way: "I certainly lowered the expectations. But in the sense of having a very pragmatic approach.... We need to be realistic, no good to raise expectations that cannot be met." Also, instead of simply hosting the negotiations and letting countries negotiate between themselves with little involvement from the presidency, Mexico decided to facilitate the negotiation process with its own proposals.[20]

The leadership of the Mexican president, Felipe Calderón, was also crucial. Calderón described climate change as an issue of significant personal interest, often recounting that his interest in the environment from an early age had been boosted by his father's concerns about changing weather patterns. Climate change also provided Calderón with a Mexican global policy issue that created a distraction from the escalating violence of its drug cartels.[21] He considered climate to be not only an environmental issue but also something that cuts across multiple ministries and sectors. He saw hosting the COP16 as an opportunity to boost his efforts to push domestic climate legislation in Mexico because he was without a majority in Congress and could not drive through a bill on his own.[22]

In contrast to the COP15, countries described the process run by the Mexicans as transparent, which bolstered trust. Countries felt that they were consulted in an inclusive manner during the proceedings and were not worried that a "secret text" would emerge and undermine the work they had done collectively (as occurred in Copenhagen).[23] As *ClimateWire's* Lisa Friedman reported, "Negotiators said there wasn't a single moment when the talks seemed to turn. Rather, they said, it was the Mexican host government's insistence on cloistering diplomats for long stretches of time and deftly creating small working groups, while throwing open the door to any country that wanted to step in and be heard."[24]

In 2010, Mexico also began to participate in the Cartagena Dialogue. Mexico's involvement with the Dialogue prior to and during the COP16 appears to have been an important reason behind the successful outcome in Cancun, given the group's emphasis on compromise and bridging differences between North and South. Involvement in the Cartagena Dialogue also helped Mexico to secure regional leadership in Latin America, which allowed it to work closely with those countries that eventually came together to form AILAC. Siwon Park of the Korean Environment Institute put it this way:

Working with groups including the Cartagena Dialogue, Mexico learned the reasoning behind each country's position and explored areas of convergence where joint action could emerge. Mexico's regional leadership was particularly important for the success of the Cancun meeting. It sought after close communication and cooperation with countries in Latin America, with which Mexico exercised an effective leadership throughout the COP meeting.[25]

Secretary Espinosa was a crucial influence in publicly leading the proceedings and setting the tone of cooperation. Her words revealed the level of distrust her team faced: "There will be no separate or parallel Ministerial process ... and no duplication of negotiations," she promised. "The

Mexican Presidency will help facilitate communication among ministers, through constant dialogue with all.... There is no hidden text and no secret negotiations. The Mexican Presidency will continue to work with full transparency and according to UN procedures."[26] Late in the meetings, when inclusive process often breaks down, Espinosa restated her pledge: "There will be no parallel or overlapping discussions and I will continue ensuring that all positions are taken into account. The Mexican delegation ... will remain accessible to every delegation."[27]

The proceedings also benefited from the good working relationship between Mexico's Espinosa and the UNFCCC executive secretary, Costa Rican national Christiana Figueres. With only two years separating them in age and the convergence of language and cultural values, Espinosa and Figueres worked positively together and used many methods to achieve consensus, including plenary meetings, ministerial consultations, and bilateral agreements.[28] The Mexican presidency identified key countries to assist in generating advances in Cancun. In large meetings, negotiators use written statements, which can limit interaction and discussion, so large meetings with more than twenty-five people were at times avoided in favor of smaller meetings. As Park notes, parties appreciated the inclusive and participatory process. Mexico organized meetings in small groups led by the president and a few ministers whom it selected. Small informal consultations and "confessionals" (in which individual delegations were asked their positions) were conducted by pairs of ministers and by the COP president, informal plenaries kept all participants informed, and a text was written or issued by facilitators and eventually put together by Mexico and the UNFCCC secretariat. The Mexican team played an unprecedentedly strong leadership role at the COP16, which was designed to rebuild trust. A balance was kept between the negotiation groups, and in the end, de Alba reported to us that BASIC and the G77 and China were satisfied with how Mexico conducted the proceedings.

As opposed to what happened in Copenhagen, only Bolivia rejected the Cancun Agreements, as is described in chapter 4. Why did the other ALBA countries side with Mexico and not Bolivia? ALBA countries feared a repeat of COP15, where a small group of countries reached a deal behind closed doors. Mexico presented a draft text with six hours to go before the final plenary, which gave countries more time to express their doubts and concerns. There was also a sense that the COP16 was being held on Latin

American soil, which generated regional interest in seeing a positive result from the process and led particular countries to feel that they owed Mexico the respect with which they themselves were treated by their hosts. These countries knew they would be working with Mexico on a long series of issues in the future and therefore did not want to sabotage the Cancun conference. Away from the climate talks, Espinosa's leadership on foreign policy also focused on rebuilding diplomatic relations with Cuba and Venezuela, relationships which had become strained in the previous administration.[29]

One of the most controversial issues to arise in Cancun was Espinosa's decision to gavel through the Cancun Agreements, despite the objection of Bolivia's chief negotiator, Pablo Solón (see chapter 4). Solón did not express concerns with the proposed package of elements in the Cancun Agreement until the final plenary.[30] In response, Espinosa said: "Consensus requires that everyone is given the right to be heard and have their views given due consideration, and Bolivia has been given this opportunity." She went on to state that "Consensus does not mean that one country has the right of veto, and can prevent 193 others from moving forward after years of negotiations on something that our societies and future generations expect."[31]

Although Mexico's approach was controversial, it was a creative interpretation of the decision-making rules of the institution and received general acceptance by other parties.[32] Nele Marien, a former member of Bolivia's delegation, argued to us that countries in Cancun agreed to be less democratic to ensure that progress was made.[33] Speaking in London six months later, secretary Espinosa stated: "in a world that shares democratic values, where all countries have an equal status, the veto is the least democratic way to face common challenges, particularly when all efforts were made in good faith to accommodate the positions of all parties."[34]

So was Cancun a victory or a disaster? We suggest using four main elements to address this question. First, as de Alba noted about the substance of the Cancun Agreements, he would side with Bolivia that the agreements lacked adequate ambition and were flawed on a scientific basis in terms of achieving deep decarbonization to ensure a safe climate.[35] As is discussed in chapter 4, the Cancun Agreements in terms of ambition can be considered a "giant step backward." But pragmatism was essential, given the challenging political conditions (including those in the perennially difficult US, where the US Senate was seen as unwilling to ratify a binding treaty) for passing a climate change accord. Mexico was candid about this as part of its discourse of lowering expectations. Having countries pledge reductions voluntarily by the Cancun Agreements was seen as a way to leave the door open for greater ambition in the future, instead of pushing for something unobtainable, which would have caused the process to unravel.[36]

Second, Cancun was perhaps not about reaching an agreement that would save the planet but was primarily about rescuing the discredited UN climate negotiations to fight another day, following the debacle in Copenhagen. That can be seen as a positive, and we agree that the "perfect is often the enemy of the good." In the case of the Cancun Agreements, however, the good was barely above terrible from the point of view of the scientific adequacy of the climate action that it codified. With the benefit of hindsight, we can say that getting the UN negotiations back on track was essential for building trust for the Durban climate conference in 2011, which created a timetable to reach a new agreement in 2015. The value of that process will be known in the future based on its ambition, buy-in, workability, and follow-through.

Third, civil society groups were unfortunately kept largely on the periphery in Cancun. This can be considered a main failing of the COP16. Although there were probably legitimate security concerns given the appalling drug-related violence in Mexico and concerns that demonstrations might derail the process, the deliberate exclusionary strategy that geographically isolated even UN-recognized civil society observer groups and restricted their voices in the process was very regrettable. The UNFCCC process needs to be more inclusionary and democratic and incorporate more participatory processes for civil society groups. On that score, the COP16 made little headway and can be considered a serious setback for engaging civil society with what often is an exclusionary process. The demands of the People's Agreement produced in Cochabamba (see chapter 4) were entered into the process by the chairs of the working groups building the texts but later were struck from them in Cancun as the negotiations advanced. Civil society demonstrations in Cancun were largely ignored by those inside the Moon Palace, whose focus was exclusively on diplomatic maneuverings and consensus building among governments.

Fourth are the national impacts of success in Cancun. For Mexico's domestic climate change legislation, the COP16 provided a transformative lift.[37] Following on the COP16's success, four draft laws were put forward to Mexico's congress by its major political parties, and they eventually led to the approval of the General Law on Climate Change in April 2012.[38] Mexico's climate change law includes targets to reduce greenhouse gas emissions by 30 percent below a business as usual scenario by 2020 and 50 percent by 2050 (conditional on international support), and it states that 35 percent of electricity should come from renewable sources by 2024.[39] Remarkably, support for the package was nearly universal: the bill passed in Mexico's lower house with a vote of 128 for and ten against and was later passed unanimously by the senate by seventy-eight votes to zero. President Calderón signed it shortly afterward. Porfirio Muñoz Ledo, a founding member of the Democratic Revolution Party (Partido Revolucionario Democrático, PRD) told the BBC, "Mexico has a long tradition in multilateral politics.... this legislation is a strong commitment coming out of Cancun."[40]

In August 2014, however, Mexico's president, Enrique Peña Nieto, signed into law historic energy reform legislation that opens up the country's oil and gas industries to private investment to boost economic growth and production. The reforms also include plans to reduce fossil fuel subsidies, which could provide a more level playing field for renewable energy. They also end the state's seventy-six-year-old monopoly on the energy sector and attempt to boost oil production by 45 percent by 2025.[41] The energy reforms could increase Mexico's long-term oil production by 75 percent.[42]

Greenhouse gas emissions in Mexico are rising due to an increasing use of fossil fuels. The largest source of emissions is the combustion of fossil fuels, and the greatest contributors to this category are the transport sector and electricity generation. Approximately 30 percent of all energy use is dedicated to transportation, and close to 70 percent of that energy is consumed by passenger transport. This trend reflects the increase in vehicle ownership, which doubled from 2000 to 2010 to approximately 207 vehicles per thousand people. This increased ownership has caused greenhouse gas emissions from the transport sector to increase at an annual rate of 3.2 percent between 1990 and 2010.[43]

At the Lima climate conference in December 2014, the Mexican delegation informed civil society representatives that there is a potential conflict between the climate law and energy reforms and that an investigation into how the two might interact was pending. One of Mexico's top environmental organizations, the Mexican Center for Environmental Law (Centro Mexicano de Derecho Ambiental, CEMDA) has voiced concerns that the energy-reform legislation could undermine progress toward achieving progress on the climate law by backing the expansion of fossil fuels.[44] CEMDA's Gabriela Niño commented that the energy and climate agendas in Mexico seem to be going in different directions.[45] Analysts have questioned the likelihood that President Peña Nieto will implement the climate change law amid resistance from industry, and have highlighted his focus on accelerating economic growth and increasing oil and gas production. Carlos Ramírez, from the Eurasia Group, commented on the climate law's ambitious targets: "The goals are certainly very aggressive ... [and] it will not be the first time ... that a law approved by the Congress has goals that are out of reach for the country."[46]

Nevertheless, the climate agenda appears to be advancing under the new president. In June 2013, President Peña Nieto presented a National Climate Change Strategy which aims at developing "green growth" in Mexico. The plan focuses on eight axes of action, including reducing vulnerability to climate change, increasing the capacity of ecosystems to adapt to climate impacts, accelerating clean energy, reducing energy consumption, and transitioning toward models of sustainable cities.[47] Recently, Mexico unveiled plans to provide 33 percent of its energy from renewable sources by 2018. Preliminary estimates from the World Wide Fund for Nature (WWF) show that the target could reduce emissions from the power sector by 15 percent. Vanessa Pérez-Cirera, WWF-Mexico's climate and energy program director, says that "doubling the country's renewable electricity output over 6 years will be an achievement with its ever increasing energy demands."[48]

Despite Mexico's impressive advances on climate and clean energy policies and the introduction of a carbon tax in January 2014, analysts suggest that Mexico's efforts are not yet sufficient to meet its conditional pledge, which consist of 30 percent emission reductions relative to business as usual in 2020. Research suggests that Mexico will achieve roughly half of the conditional pledge with currently implemented policies.[49]

At the Cancun climate negotiations, a recovering multilateral process hit rock bottom and began a recovery with small steps—weak efforts at reducing carbon pollution, greater exclusion of civil society in the talks, positive outcomes inside Mexico in the years that followed COP16, and stronger trust in the UN process for future negotiations. The legacy of Cancun is not yet decided, but the trajectory of the negotiations in the future may turn partly as the result of Mexico's leadership style and a small yet assertive negotiating group, many of them members of the Cartagena Dialogue, that are taking a line similar to Mexico—AILAC.

AILAC's Green Shoots in Doha

The emergence of the Independent Association of Latin America and the Caribbean (Asociación Independiente de América Latina y el Carbibe, AILAC) in Doha in 2012 was a significant development in the UNFCCC negotiations, belying the relatively small size of AILAC's member countries. AILAC promotes a flexible and ambitious approach to advancing the UN climate negotiations and is willing to move beyond the hard line taken by Brazil, ALBA, and others that rich nations must act first before developing countries also take action. Our observation is that this surprising approach could be a key to unlocking the negotiations.

But where did the group come from? A number of middle-income Latin American countries had been making ad hoc joint statements since about 2005, and several joined the Cartagena Dialogue process. Sometimes Mexico, the Dominican Republic, and some other Latin American countries joined. The region was not yet balkanized into fixed negotiating groups. These Latin American countries—which were to become AILAC—initially sought to distinguish themselves from Brazil, which they felt often did not reflect their positions or interests.

In 2006, Jose Alberto Garibaldi, a climate adviser to a few Latin American governments, set up the Latin American and the Caribbean Workshops to Increase the Scale of Responses (LAC-WISR) to provide a space for informal discussions between negotiators and researchers from multilateral organizations and Latin America countries. Chile, Colombia, Costa Rica, Mexico, Panama, and Peru attended, and other regular participants included Argentina, the Dominican Republic, Guatemala, Paraguay, and Uruguay. The meetings built capacity, and participants wrote joint position papers, which countries decided whether to support later on. This approach, which later was adopted in the Cartagena Dialogue group, propelled several of the participants of LCA-WISR into key positions within the negotiations process, such as the election of Christiana Figueres as executive secretary of the UNFCCC.[50] The workshops contributed to the formation of AILAC.

Some of these countries took on mitigation pledges, a significant development because they were not obliged to do so under the Kyoto Protocol. This implied breaking ranks with the G77 and China group, which called on developed countries to act first before they would accept binding limits on their emissions.[51] Costa Rica, Mexico, and Peru put forward planned mitigation actions in 2008, which were made as part of country pledges in connection with the deal expected to come from Copenhagen in 2009. This developed a new narrative based on the idea that all countries had to do as much as possible based on their own capabilities.[52]

Peru was the first developing country to announce a voluntary emissions-reduction pledge in 2008, offering to reduce to zero its net deforestation of primary forests by 2021.[53] At the COP14 in Poznan, Poland, Peru's then minister of environment, the late Antonio Brack, expressed his country's willingness to achieve a zero net deforestation rate within ten years.[54] Brack told the BBC: "We are an important country with a large area of forest that has a value…. This is Peru's contribution to mitigating climate change."[55] Then Costa Rica put forward a pledge to become carbon neutral by 2021 by offsetting emissions through reforestation and by reducing emissions in the waste, transport, and agricultural sectors.[56] In 2009, other Latin American countries stated that they would make additional commitments in exchange for further commitments by developed countries. This was done with the view that such a course of action would increase the demand and viability of carbon markets (from which they might gain investment), while at the same time reducing climate impacts.[57]

At Copenhagen, a landmark side event took place promoting this new discourse, with a heavy Latin American presence. The meeting called for a global climate regime that would allow middle-income countries to do more on mitigation. The case argued that these countries have more to gain in an ambitious but differentiated regime to which they contribute substantially rather than in a weaker and less ambitious one to which they contributed little and are rendered more vulnerable to climate impacts. Garibaldi, who played a seminal role in creating AILAC, presented a report called "The Economics of Boldness" that focused on mitigation in middle-income countries, arguing that these countries are best placed if they engage in mitigation activities. Garibaldi illustrated that engaging in "bold and early" activities can reduce the costs of mitigation and, in some instances, can result in a net gain. Eduardo Durand, from Peru's ministry of the environment, explained his country's vulnerability to the effects of climate change and argued that more engagement with mitigation will lead to less need for future adaptation. Colombia's Andrea García stated that the "middle can be beautiful" and urged that the COP provide a means for middle-income countries to engage in mitigation.[58] They hoped their own actions and pledges might persuade larger emitters to do more.[59]

At the Durban climate conference in 2011, the negotiations went into extra time as delegates scrambled to secure an outcome. Colombia considered the deal too weak and nearly rejected the agreement.[60] Other Latin American countries that later became AILAC followed Colombia. This led to the final huddle centered on India's environment minister, Jayanthi Natarajan, surrounded by delegates. The Alliance of Small Island States (AOSIS), Colombia, the EU, and the Least Developed Countries Group favored a text that emphasized a legally binding agreement. India pushed for less robust language on the legal nature of the deal. Colombia, the EU, and other Latin American countries were able to work together at this crucial moment and coordinate their intervention due to their shared position and also due to their participation in the Cartagena Dialogue, which made these coordinated interventions more likely due to the increased trust and communication between delegates.[61] In the aftermath of Durban, leading think tank E3G heralded the EU's diplomacy in pushing the negotiations toward a successful outcome.[62] In other reporting from Durban, a temporary alliance that was referred to as the "axis of ambition" was made up of AOSIS, the EU, some Latin American countries, and the Least Developed Countries Group. The lack of precision in naming those Latin American countries, which played an important role in Durban, provides a good example of why these Latin American countries took steps to create AILAC—to enhance their visibility, identity, and influence.

Finally, at the Doha negotiations in 2012, AILAC was officially launched as a self-described "revolt of the middle." Emboldened by their collective experiences and their willingness to take on domestic climate actions, these countries decided to stop waiting for emissions reductions or financial support from the rich nations and launched an ambitious case for low-carbon development of their own. As Monica Araya, a former adviser to the Costa Rican delegation told El País, "[The negotiations are] always told as a battle of North versus South ... but each time this explains less and less of what's happening."[63] She continued, "There is an alliance of countries that want all nations to take on binding obligations, and that the negotiations process is adapting to a changing world."[64] Isabel Cavelier, from Colombia's Ministry of Foreign Affairs and former head of AILAC's support unit, said in 2012, "We think we can show the world that we are developing countries, we have a lot of problems at home, but we are ready to act. If we can show that we can take the lead, and we're not waiting for the rest of the world, then we can [set] an example."[65]

A crucial aspect to AILAC's perspective is that domestic action boosts ambition at the multilateral level, where action contributes to the political space back home to build a low-carbon economy. Ned Helme, president of the Washington, DC–based Center for Clean Air Policy, said, "When you do this work on the ground, you begin to see the benefits and I think that's what's happening." He said, "It means you can feel safer stepping up on climate when you know the kinds of things you'll need to do mean not just more costs. They'll bring benefits, economic benefits to your country." Or as Monica Araya put it even more bluntly: "It's almost as if, in the [UNFCCC], ambition is a concession. We need to reverse that idea. We want ambition to be framed in terms of self-interest."[66]

Costa Rica's former minister of the environment, René Castro, made clear in his intervention at the Doha conference that funding from the developed countries could catalyze the transition to a greener path: "We need to find a solution to the current silence on climate finance. Many developing countries are engaging in NAMAs [nationally appropriate mitigation actions] and adaptation projects, and are deeply worried about the lack of fund-predictability post-2012 when the fast start finance period ends.... [We need] clarity on how the commitment will be translated into a clear, credible trajectory that will build trust in the developing world."[67] The willingness of AILAC countries to go out on a limb, in other words, requires credible promises of support for their actions.

AILAC considers that all countries should contribute to emission reductions but that each country's capacities and responsibilities are differentiated, which needs to be reflected in the negotiations. Garibaldi notes that "The group allows [them] to give a fresh view of the fundamental challenges the Convention sought to address, and the need to face them through increased collective action by all."[68]

AILAC has generally positive relations with countries in the EU, particularly the United Kingdom (UK), given their mutual participation in the Cartagena Dialogue. The UK has sought increased engagement with AILAC, particularly on increasing the ambition of emission-reduction targets and the use of markets. And according to one official, the UK regards AILAC as a "vital linchpin between progressive developing and developed countries."[69]

AILAC's development has not been straightforward. In 2014, it was finally able to form a technical support unit to advance its work following delays of over a year. There are also asymmetries between AILAC members: Chile and Colombia have been the clear leaders of the group, Costa Rica and Peru have their smaller delegations and therefore have been less involved,[70] and Guatemala and Panama have been largely followers. There are important uncertainties. For example, the inauguration of a new president in Costa Rica in May 2014 raised doubts about whether its carbon-neutral target for 2021 remained feasible and has opened some ambiguities about that country's level of involvement in AILAC (see the next section). Although most AILAC countries have put forward voluntary emission-reduction pledges that have been accompanied by domestic policies on climate change, the level of implementation remains a challenge.[71] Colombia's first minister of the environment, Manuel Rodríguez Becerra, argues that a number of climate policies in the region are more symbolic than real. He agrees that Colombia is highly vulnerable to climate change but says the government's mining and economic policies are pulling Colombia toward greater vulnerability, not less.[72]

Given the tense, drawn out, and difficult UN climate negotiations, the emergence of AILAC—committed to a legally binding agreement in 2015, touting their domestic actions, and reaching across the North-South divide—has been celebrated by some negotiators and analysts, including ourselves.[73] Paraguay joined AILAC in June 2015, and other countries are considering doing so; this is a positive indication of AILAC's growing presence. At the COP20 in Peru, some of AILAC's main positions were advanced, as is discussed further in the section on Peru. However, there are questions about whether AILAC's proambition rhetoric can stand up to the realities of national and international politics.

Costa Rica's Oil Refinery and Carbon Neutrality Goal

Costa Rica has been heralded as a pioneer on green issues and a leader on climate change. Known as a Mecca for ecotourism enthusiasts due to its biodiversity and abundant nature reserves, Costa Rica has achieved impressive reforestation results and obtains over 90 percent of its electricity from renewable energy.[74] The nation has achieved high levels of human development in the form of literacy, life expectancy, and gross domestic product per capita per unit of greenhouse gases emitted.

During the 1980s and 1990s, Costa Rica had one of the highest rates of deforestation in Latin America. By 1980, Costa Rica had lost nearly three quarters of its forest to the spread of logging, peasant farming, and ranching. But the combination of various factors, such as the collapse of export markets for meat and the end of the conflict in Central America, led to opportunities for emerging social and environmental movements. The government created the first national-level program for payments for environmental services in a developing country,[75] aiming to reverse the incentives that were driving the destruction of forests. The program pays owners of forests for some of the value of keeping them intact, such as flood control, water supply for cities, and reduction of the release of carbon emissions. Costa Rica is now considered a global leader on lands receiving payments for environmental services. Protected lands cover over 600,000 hectares, and according to Costa Rica's Second National Communication to the UNFCCC, the country has 166 protected areas, which cover 26 percent of its land area.[76] Forest cover sprang back from only 21 percent of its national territory in 1986 to 51 percent by the late 2000s.[77]

In 2007, Costa Rica sought to distinguish itself on the world stage with its position and action on climate change. To coincide with the year of its two hundredth anniversary of independence from Spain, it made a pioneering pledge to become carbon neutral by 2021 by sharply reducing emissions in the waste, transport, and agricultural sectors and by offsetting remaining emissions through reforestation. The former Costa Rican President Oscar Arias, codified the Carbon Neutrality Initiative in Decree No. 33487-MP as part of his Peace with Nature policy. The initiative was a skillful effort to capitalize on the two attributes for which Costa Rica is famous—peacefulness and environmental protection.[78] Costa Rica's Second National Communication states,

The National Carbon Neutral Policy is a defiant challenge. Delay actions will impose higher costs in the future....Taking actions now will facilitate a head start and build national capacities to become a low and neutral carbon emission economy.[79]

The pledge far exceeded those made by what had always been the most progressive group, the EU, which promised to reduce its emissions by 20 percent by 2020.[80] José Vásquez from the World Wildlife Fund told the BBC, "Costa Rica has been the only country in Central America ahead of everyone else, in terms of protecting the environment.... The only thing I see is a little bit problematic is [going carbon neutral] by 2021. It's a huge target."[81]

Due to Costa Rica's large hydroelectric capacity, it has one of the cleanest energy matrices in the world, but greenhouse gas emissions from energy are increasing as a result of the growing consumption of fossil fuels for transportation. The country is struggling to decouple its economic growth from emissions. The 2008 to 2021 National Energy Plan aims to diversify the energy matrix by promoting sustainable transportation, the development of renewable energy (including solar), energy efficiency, and the reduction of fossil fuel consumption.[82]

Despite his apparent enthusiasm for the carbon-neutral pledge, President Arias's commitment to the environment was questioned by environmental organizations.[83] Arias's successor, Laura Chinchilla, cut off funding for the initiative after her 2010 inauguration.[84] The costs of the carbon-neutral pledge potentially would run into the billions of dollars, and the government has said that it cannot deliver success by 2021 without substantial financial assistance from international donors (as was also noted by former environment minister René Castro's statement in the previous section).[85] The manner by which Costa Rica calculates its emissions for its carbon-neutral target has also drawn difficult questions, particularly on its energy generation.[86] The transport sector, which generates nearly 70 percent of Costa Rica's carbon emissions, presents a major obstacle. To offset these emissions, the carbon neutral plan stipulated that 20 to 25 percent of the country's transport would need to switch to carbon-neutral alternatives by 2014.[87]

At the UN Leaders' Summit on Climate Change in September 2014, President Luis Guillermo Solís reaffirmed Costa Rica's commitment to become carbon neutral by 2021. Solís said that his administration would push for a new bus system that runs on biofuels and an electric railway. Solís stated that after the Reventazón Hydroelectric Project is operational in 2016, Costa Rica's electrical matrix will be 100 percent renewable.[88] Despite this goal, Mariana Porras from the Ceiba Association of Ecological Communities and Friends of the Earth Costa Rica said, "Right now carbon neutrality is more of a political goal than an environmental one.... It is letting the country appear green without actually addressing any of the issues that cause emissions."[89]

Meanwhile, controversial plans to upgrade an oil refinery on Costa Rica's east coast with Chinese financing emerged in 2013. The plan is to upgrade RECOPE (Refinadora Costarricense de Petróleo), the national oil refinery in Moín, with $1.5 billion in Chinese funds to improve the quality of the refined fuel and more than triple production from 18,000 to 65,000 barrels per day.[90] Proponents of the refinery suggest that it will create jobs and lower petrol prices and that the use of fossil fuels will continue for decades anyway.[91] Former minister René Castro said that Costa Rica has the opportunity to develop its own capacity to refine oil instead of paying high prices to import it.[92]

The refinery has led to a public outcry in Costa Rica, and a state visit to Costa Rica in June 2013 by the Chinese president, Xi Jinping, led to a backlash against the refinery. Costa Rica's environmentalists and global groups were mystified that the government would risk undermining the country's pledge to become carbon neutral by building an oil refinery they deemed unnecessary at the expense of low-carbon and sustainable options.[93] The global campaigning group Climate Action Network asked, "How can an oil refinery fit in a carbon neutral economy, as carbon capture and storage is still a pipedream?" Mónica Araya, leader of the citizen action group Costa Rica Limpia (Clean Costa Rica), suggests that Costa Rica has a golden opportunity to redirect Chinese and Costa Rican relations toward low carbon growth.[94] Having openly criticized[95] the oil refinery, Araya, who was an adviser to the Costa Rican delegation at the UN climate negotiations, was dismissed in 2013,[96] suggesting a high level of sensitivity around Chinese cooperation and political pressures behind the refinery.

The boom in connections between Costa Rica and China poses a double-edged sword for the country and government. After Costa Rica broke diplomatic ties with Taiwan in 2007, cooperation with China accelerated. In 2011, the China–Costa Rica Free Trade Agreement entered into force, and China is now Costa Rica's second-largest trading partner, after the United States. These trade and commercial ties are flourishing even as Costa Rica took some leadership in AILAC and made bold commitments on emission reductions, which suggests that China is more focused on improving economic and commercial relations than in pressuring for alignment in the UN climate negotiations. The power disparity between China and Costa Rica is a concern for Costa Ricans who are critical of the new oil refinery, which they see as potentially undermining their country's independence and pioneering climate policies.[97] After protests and a series of disagreements, the project's future looked decidedly uncertain. A conflict of interest between a Chinese company and Costa Rica's RECOPE led to the project being put on hold, and RECOPE's executive president, Jorge Villalobos, resigned in June 2013.[98]

But the oil refinery question did go not away. President Solís was apparently under domestic and Chinese pressure to dust off the proposed upgrade. In July 2014, China accepted Costa Rica's request to renegotiate the project, with the aim of "resolving inconsistencies in the contract." Costa Rican unions that supported the president in the most recent election are in favor of the oil refinery upgrade and are threatening to strike if the project is abandoned. Patrick Johnson, a leader of the oil workers' union, the Sindicato de Trabajadores Petroleros Químicos y Afines, said, "We have always defended the construction of a refinery.... We want the confusion to be cleared up ... and if the project is beneficial, then it should go ahead because the country needs a refinery."[99] In November 2014, the Costa Rican government announced that it had reached an agreement to reactivate the oil refinery proposal with an upgrade that has lower emissions and includes the production of biofuels.[100]

Given China's interest in natural resources and energy access, Costa Rica's ability to persuade China to emphasize low-carbon cooperation will be a revealing challenge.[101] Politicians and diplomats praise Chinese and Costa Rican relations and their importance for economic growth,[102] but others worry that China is developing an aggressive energy diplomacy to guarantee access to those resources.[103] Bilateral cooperation on climate change and environmental protection feature in China's 2008 Policy Paper on Latin American and the Caribbean, but little if any action has so far materialized except for a growing number of investments in renewable energy.[104]

Meanwhile, some in Costa Rica's legislative branch have sought to advance the national climate agenda. Alfonso Pérez introduced a Framework Law on Climate Change in late 2013, which called for the creation of a national council, substantially increasing capacity on the issue, and the adoption of a National Climate Change Plan.[105] However, due to mounting opposition, the bill was sent back to be modified. At this writing, environmental organizations such as Costa Rica Limpia, left-leaning politicians, and even the minister of the environment all oppose the current draft of the bill.

Although it was recently an undisputed world leader on climate change, Costa Rica's image is less assured than before. The revelations that scant progress has been made on the carbon-neutral target coincide with a dramatic slippage of Costa Rica's environmental performance. Yale University's Environmental Performance Index shows that Costa Rica dropped from fifth to fifty-fourth out of 178 countries in its 2014 ranking.[106] The need for economic growth, the development of new trade and commercial ties, and its weak and inconsistent government leadership on climate change have led to a tarnishing of its green brand. Costa Rican civil society groups have reacted vocally against these policies in the hope of reversing Costa Rica's poor environmental performance by pressing for real progress on the carbon-neutral pledge and pushing for climate legislation. The pledge may currently be too ambitious to be achievable, and Costa Rica now seems out of sync with the lofty rhetoric of AILAC and its own position of just a few years ago.

Peru Walks the Tightrope

In June 2013, following the withdrawal of Venezuela's candidacy, the UN Group of Latin American and Caribbean States announced that Peru had been selected to host the December 2014 UN climate negotiations in Lima. Peru was seen as an exciting prospect for hosting the talks for several reasons.[107] Peru's foreign policy was regarded as pragmatic and moderate, and its foreign affairs ministry was respected internationally. Peru was considered a potential bridge builder between the global North and South because it participated in the Cartagena Dialogue alongside its AILAC partners (see above). It was highly vulnerable to climate impacts, which gave it a vested interest in pushing progress at the negotiations. In 2008, Peru also announced a voluntary emission-reduction pledge by offering to reduce the net deforestation of primary forests to zero by 2021. After losing its bid to Mexico to host the COP16 for 2010, by 2012 Peru felt it was again ready to put forward its candidacy to host COP20 in 2014. The Peruvian minister for the environment, Manuel Pulgar-Vidal, described what the event meant to Peru:

This is not only the largest international event in Peru's history, but also a milestone in the development of a Peruvian and regional position [regarding climate change action]. The COP represents a big episode for change, and also a great opportunity for Peru to position and bring international attention to the Amazon forest, water and glaciers, science, and sustainable cities.[108]

Peru's bid to host the COP20 was a reflection of its growing confidence due to its economic performance, moderate foreign policy, largely positive and well received role at the UNFCCC negotiations, growing sense of concern about climate impacts, and responsibility to reduce its own emissions. Peru's pre-COP20 slogan was bold: "Don't come to Peru if you don't want to change the world." On huge banners at the entrance to the venue for the negotiations read another: "COP20 Lima: The Place for Action."

In Durban in 2011, the year 2015 was set as the deadline by which countries would have to reach a new global climate change agreement. To ensure that sufficient progress was made, the 2014 UN climate conference in Lima was charged with delivering a draft version of that agreement. The example of Mexico's leadership in the Cancun round was raised on numerous occasions, adding to the pressures that Peru faced. An important difference was that Peru had to attempt both to facilitate the process and also to secure considerable progress on the substantive elements of the negotiations.

As we saw with the examples of Copenhagen and Cancun, presidents of the UN climate negotiations face relentless pressures. Leaders walk a tightrope as they attempt to guide over 190 countries toward consensus. They are criticized for being either overbearing or lackluster in their leadership. As was shown with Cancun, however, decisive leadership by a COP president can at least secure the support of enough countries to build progress.[109]

Four criteria define a successful COP for its hosts: setting appropriate levels of expectations for the conference, adeptly facilitating the process, demonstrating strong domestic climate action, and being a good host in terms of logistics. Peru was cautiously optimistic that Lima should produce a draft agreement for the text. The Peruvian minister of the environment, Manuel Pulgar-Vidal, said at a conference at Brown University in April 2014 that the COP20 needed to provide a solid basis for a strong agreement in Paris in 2015. Yet he warned against viewing the next two years of negotiations as a final push rather than as the beginning of a new chapter in global climate cooperation.[110] At the midyear negotiations in Bonn, Germany two months later, Pulgar-Vidal adopted a leadership role and attempted to shape expectations: "Eighteen months is not enough time to finish with all these discussions.... So probably in Lima what we're going to have is some very realistic narrative, to try to lift to Paris a draft agreement that could be signed by the end of 2015."[111]

Copenhagen showed that raising expectations too high can prove disastrous. The COP president facilitates the negotiation process before and during the COP, which usually falls into two categories—either a bold or a reluctant approach. Reluctant facilitators take a back seat and emphasize that the process is "Party-driven" and inclusive of all countries. A bold facilitator publicly recognizes that all countries need a seat at the table but acts assertively in addressing tough issues and finding compromises and solutions on the negotiating texts. This approach may focus on informal consultations between smaller groups of countries and the COP president and UNFCCC secretariat—an approach that has been discussed in the case of Mexico. The support of the major emitters and leaders of the other influential negotiating groups is required if the negotiations go into overtime and Peru needs to deal with dissenting countries that are blocking progress. With negotiators confronting a two-week marathon of sleep deprivation, the ability of the host nation to put on a well-managed and logistically sound event is essential.[112]

Pulgar-Vidal, his ministry of environment team, and diplomats from the ministry of foreign relations wasted no time in visiting a number of countries around the world.[113] During the preparatory stages of the Lima Conference, the ministry of environment made public efforts to include national and international civil society and indigenous peoples' groups.[114] In May 2014, the ministry of environment with Christiana Figueres held an event in Lima with Latin American civil society organizations. Minister Pulgar-Vidal said, "We want to see the voices of all reflected in this process and we believe that we are a country that can be open and listen to everyone."[115] Another innovation was that the Coordinator of Indigenous Organizations of the Amazon River Basin (Coordinadora de las Organizaciones Indígenas de la Cuenca Amazónica, COICA) was given support to lead the first indigenous pavilion at a COP.[116]

A few factors explain this enhanced public outreach by the Peruvian ministry for the environment to civil society. First, minister Pulgar-Vidal was formerly executive director of one of Peru's leading environmental organizations, the Peruvian Society for Environmental Law (Sociedad Peruana de Derecho Ambiental [SPDA]). Second, at the Warsaw Climate Conference in 2013, global civil society staged a symbolic walkout from the negotiations to protest the lack of real climate action taken by governments and their increasing marginalization in the process. In June 2014, organizations such as 350.org and Oxfam returned to the negotiation space with a declaration and a series of demands that called for global action by governments.[117] The Peruvian government attempted to engage these stakeholders to avoid a similar walkout in Lima because Warsaw generated some negative publicity for the Polish government. Third, Peru faced competition from the government of Venezuela to host COP20. Venezuela hosted the world's first "Social Pre-COP" (which is discussed in chapter 4) in November, and Peru did not want to be upstaged by its neighbor on openness to civil society.

Fourth, Peruvian civil society organizations also hosted a parallel People's Summit on Climate to coincide with the COP20. The People's Summit was an alternative event to share initiatives and proposals, define and coordinate agendas, and bring pressure to bear on the decision makers at COP20 to take account of the world's citizens and peoples.[118] As part of the activities, on December 10, tens of thousands took to the streets of Lima for the Global March in Defense of Mother Earth. The march was Latin America's largest climate march ever and drew between ten and thirty thousand people. Indigenous peoples, trade unionists, women's groups, students, and global activists came together to call for action on climate change and on the protection of environmental activists in regions that have faced harassment and violence.

Behind the scenes, the Peruvian COP20 presidency team actively engaged with civil society as it prepared to host the conference. It is an important reflection of how nonstate actors are engaging at a high level with government and how some governments are soliciting their input and support. During COP20 some of the wives of murdered indigenous leaders from Peru's Amazon held a demonstration and press conference demanding justice and more efforts by the government to protect their lands. *The Guardian* reported that the antilogging campaigner Edwin Chota and three other Ashéninka leaders were killed in Peru in September 2014 over territory they had being trying to secure for their community.[119] The Peruvian government has a sensitive relationship with indigenous groups following social protests over the past decade against extractive industries such as mining in the Peruvian Amazon, which saw hundreds of people killed.[120] Although Peru's Congress passed a law in 2011[121] that for the first time made it mandatory to seek indigenous peoples' consent before development projects are allowed to go ahead on their ancestral lands, tensions still abound. In April 2014, around five hundred Achuar indigenous protesters occupied Peru's largest oil field in the Amazon rainforest operated by Argentine Pluspetrol to demand the cleanup of decades of contamination from spilled oil.[122] The Peruvian government was facing a major backlash if it failed to include these groups and listen to their demands.

There is inconsistency between Peru's domestic development policies and climate policies and the high-ambition rhetoric it espouses at the UN climate negotiations. This exposes a lack of policy coherence between the various offices of state with the presidency, the ministry of finance, and the ministry of energy and mining, all seemingly at odds with the goals of the ministry of environment. The latter appears to have come out much worse in this policy tug of war. A central tenet of Peru's candidacy to host the conference in Lima in 2014 was its willingness to volunteer a domestic emission-reduction pledge in 2008. In 2011, a new planning project was launched (PlanCC) to study and analyze future national scenarios for climate change, and potential for sectoral greenhouse gas reductions. PlanCC set out to produce a plan for sectoral mitigation based on economic and social cobenefits.[123] The PlanCC process aims to generate a scientific evidence base to build greenhouse gas emission scenarios, evaluate mitigation options, and assess the implementation of mitigation measures.

The first phase, launched in July 2014, consists of a study on alternative development scenarios and their relationship to climate change mitigation and impacts up to 2050.[124] According to the study, the population of Peru will grow from its current 30 million inhabitants to as many as 46 million by 2050. If Peru does not take measures between now and 2050, it will have 8 tons of CO_2 emissions per capita—equal to roughly the per capita emissions of the EU today. Carbon dioxide emissions are currently around 5.7 tons per capita (according to 2010 figures), but if the country were to adopt sustainable mitigation measures, this figure could drop to 4.3 tons per capita by 2050.[125] The study presents seventy-seven options to mitigate climate change in six sectors—energy, transport, industry, waste, forestry, and agriculture.[126]

Although the release of this PlanCC report is an important step and keeps Peru ahead of most developing countries, climate change policies in general in Peru are insufficiently implemented. Climate policies are only weakly integrated or coordinated with other sectoral or macroeconomic policies. Although increasing attention is paid to climate issues, the topic is still in a marginal position on the domestic policy agenda.[127] Following a process of decentralization, regional governments in Peru have responsibility for managing the environment, but climate change legislation is driven at the national level. The decentralization process has been very complex, and the level of implementation of the National Plan of Reforestation, for example, has been very low.[128] As evidence of this problem, the Peruvian government recently admitted that deforestation in the Peruvian Amazon is rising, after expanding over more than 145,000 hectares (560 square miles) in 2013—an 80 percent jump from the start of the century.[129]

The implementation of Peru's climate policies remains a challenge, and some environmental laws appear to be in the process of being rolled back. Most stark have been reports that the Peruvian government was planning a new law that would weaken the social and environmental checks on companies exploring for oil and gas and thereby accelerate investment in the fossil fuel sectors.[130] The ministry of environment in a statement distanced itself from the energy minister and referred to concerns expressed by the citizenry about the proposed law.[131]

On July 4, 2014, the Peruvian Congress approved a series of reforms that sought to reactivate the economy following a downturn in economic performance.[132] Following approval of the reform package, President Ollanta Humala said, "I want to thank Congress, which approved a set of laws which we sent to promote investment and strengthen investor confidence in Peru."[133]

The minister for the environment, Pulgar-Vidal, voted against the reform package in a ministerial meeting and said that it was a major setback for the country's progress on environmental issues and weakened his ministry.[134] Pulgar-Vidal's decision to vote against the economic package was a bold yet calculated risk. The minister took confidence from the fact that because he has been very visible internationally since Peru won the COP presidency bid, he would not likely be fired by the president. Further, the minister had little choice but to vote against the package, given how much it weakened his own ministry and given his former position as executive director of one of Peru's most prestigious environmental NGOs, the Peruvian Society for Environmental Law. His former colleagues and their network would have branded him a traitor.

He also had support from his predecessors. Jose de Echave, a former deputy environment minister, said, "As far as Latin America goes, we are the country backpedaling the most."[135] Over a hundred civil society groups both in Peru and globally came out strongly against the reforms, saying that they reduced the audit capacities of the ministry of environment and its Body for Assessment and Audit (El Organismo de Evaluación y Fiscalización Ambiental,OEFA). The reforms are intended to promote fuel and oil extraction off the ocean coast and in Peru's Amazon region, raising fears that they will undermine Peru's COP20 leadership and as a result compromise the UN climate talks to be held in Lima.[136]

The isolation of the ministry of environment in the face of a lack of commitment from other ministries—especially finance, energy, and mining—was a serious concern. There was also a question about the commitment of Peru's president to push for an ambitious COP. President Humala had committed to attend the UN Secretary General Leaders' Summit on climate change in New York in September 2014, but his appearance seemed superficial. Given the president's commitment to secure the passing of the reform package that undermined key environmental legislation, Humala's interest in the climate change issue and COP20 seemed hollow to some observers.

Despite these problems, the COP was a diplomatic victory for Peru. The Peruvian presidency was widely credited for its hard work to ensure a successful outcome in Lima. It was thoroughly engaged throughout the buildup to and during the conference itself. In the end, countries avoided a serious breakdown, and a last-minute agreement was produced two days after the conference was scheduled to finish. So the results of the Lima climate conference are generally considered a success—albeit a limited one. The test of whether enough was accomplished in Lima will be the success or failure of the larger negotiations, which will culminate in Paris in December 2015, the deadline for producing a new agreement that is scheduled to come into force from 2020. The Lima Call for Climate Action was a step in the right direction, but most of the hard decisions were yet to be tackled.

According to Michael Jacobs, despite the weakness of the Lima deal, it managed to achieve its two primary goals while also representing a fundamental breakthrough for the global response to climate change. The meeting was charged with adopting an outline of a new text to be agreed to in Paris. A vast document was produced with a plethora of options that countries wished to see in the final agreement. Yet nothing was actually decided upon. The difficult decisions about what will stay and what will be scrapped will begin in 2015. The second goal was to reach agreement on how countries will devise and submit their intended nationally determined contributions (INDCs) for the 2015 agreement, which include information on how countries will reduce their greenhouse gas emissions and adapt to climate impacts. This was decided by taking an approach that could be described as countries reporting at a "lowest common denominator" level.

The major breakthrough was that all countries have to reduce their emissions, based on their "common but differentiated responsibilities and respective capabilities (CBDR+RC) in light of different national circumstances." This language is cumbersome, but each word turns out to be important because the phrase balances traditional agreements that the developed countries would "go first" in their emissions reductions (CBDR+RC) and a new universality that all countries will act (but according to national circumstances). This represents a significant shift because previously only developed countries had mandatory obligations and developing countries were required only to make voluntary efforts.[137]

The AILAC group and others have been pushing for this shift for some time, based on the idea that all countries need to act according to their different responsibilities and capabilities.[138] It is fitting that this major breakthrough occurred on the soil of one of those countries that together with its AILAC partners had been pushing for an end to the North-South firewall for a number of years; it was in Lima where this idea came of age.

Less Talk, More Action

This chapter has recounted a relatively new development in the climate negotiations—the rise of a group of middle-income countries that are eager to overcome the endless North-South fighting to achieve an adequate global deal on climate change. The formation of the informal Cartagena Dialogue crossed North and South lines, and Mexico's effective statesmanship rebuilt trust after the disaster in Copenhagen, facilitated the Cancun negotiations in 2010 through a year of shuttle diplomacy, careful choreography, and gaveled through the agreements despite Bolivia's opposition. We discussed whether Cancun can really be regarded as a success beyond the national-level climate diplomacy, after considering the marginalization of civil society voices and the legacy of the event for Mexico's domestic climate policies. The creation of AILAC was something that we witnessed firsthand with its launch in Doha in 2012. We then told of two troubling cases where AILAC members faced difficulties in keeping their domestic actions on climate consistent with the strong pledges and rhetoric they brought to the international community. Costa Rica faces criticism over an oil refinery project, and as it was preparing to host the COP20, the Peruvian government passed a reform package that could drastically roll back the ability of agencies to assess environmental impacts and control fossil fuel extraction.

Costa Rica's floundering on meeting its hugely ambitious climate target is important because it has been seen for decades as perhaps the greenest nation on earth. Peru's similar problems are also serious because it was selected to host the critical UN climate talks in Lima, where a new climate change agreement was to be drafted for completion and signature by 2015 in Paris.

The position of AILAC at the UN climate negotiation has sometimes put that group at odds with China, Venezuela, and the other members of the Like-Minded Developing Countries group. AILAC and these groups state that "common but differentiated responsibilities" are the fundamental principle of climate action under the UNFCCC, but their distinct interpretations are important. Again, AILAC has called on all emitters (especially China) to reduce their emissions to ensure that the goal of limiting global temperature increases to 2 degrees Celsius remains viable. Despite this difference, all members of the G77—including AILAC and China—have been able to articulate some common interests in maintaining the right to develop, and their demands for developed countries to provide financial and technological support to support developing countries' response to climate change.[139] Both AILAC and China emphasize that developed countries need to make drastic reductions in their emissions, but China emphasizes developed countries' historical responsibility to reduce emissions, and Costa Rica stresses that developed countries' "lack of ambition puts the brake on global ambition."[140] On climate finance, China and AILAC both stress that developed countries need to deliver on their promise to contribute $100 billion in funding by 2020 to developing countries per year.

AILAC and the Pacific Alliance were both created in 2012, and there is great overlap in membership. It is unclear whether the goals of the two groups are compatible, however, because booming international trade involves greater extraction, production, shipping, and consumption, which can all have serious climate and social impacts. It is also unclear what effect the formation of these groups has had on their members' domestic climate change policies. Two parallel currents appear to be underway here: trade and finance ministries pushed for and received membership in the Pacific Alliance, and environment and climate ministries have focused on forming

AILAC in the UNFCCC negotiations.[141] The allure of new commercial and investment opportunities from Asia and their own considerable natural resources endowment might inadvertently be pulling the Pacific Alliance members away from their climate goals. A major challenge will be to ensure coherence between the objectives of the Pacific Alliance with those of AILAC to ensure the transition to low-carbon, prosperous and inclusive economies. But they are not as plainly contradictory as, say, Venezuela's internal actions and its external positions on climate and energy, especially if these countries can leverage the Pacific Alliance for trade and investment in renewable energy.

It is perhaps reflective of the urgent and troubling situation facing the UN climate negotiation that AILAC's third way is garnering so much attention with hopes that it can work with others to achieve a breakthrough. As we assess the power of the middle to bridge the North-South divide and to inspire bold action that might avoid the worst impacts of climate change, we need to pay attention to this assertive group of countries on which such great expectations are placed. At the same time as they are advancing pioneering ideas and policies on climate change, AILAC's leaders are attempting to balance their need for economic growth and job creation. Sometimes the economy seems to be smothering concern for the climate, a pattern that is common everywhere. Their bold pledges and efforts to inspire action on climate change have had some impact, as is seen in the breakthrough in Lima, but there needs to be meaningful political and material support for these countries when they take such important leadership. Otherwise, backsliding is inevitable as the pressure for economic growth overwhelms interest in tackling climate change, which is easily seen as an additional cost and brake on development. AILAC was formed to refute that perspective. If other nations are to take up AILAC's challenge, they will need the support of the international community and especially rich countries to succeed. Our final chapter takes up this and the broader questions of the origins and sustainability of national and international climate policies across our case study nations.

6 Sustainable Action?

A Decisive Region?

At the United Nations General Assembly in September 2010, Colombian president Juan Manuel Santos exclaimed, "Latin America as a whole must be a decisive region in saving the planet."[1] The president argued that the region is united in overcoming poverty, improving living standards, participating in global markets, and protecting the environment. According to the president, Latin American nations are beginning to take on a global leadership role in economic, environmental, and development issues.

This book has attempted to shed light on and evaluate these assertions. We see Latin America as a pivotal region where climate change politics have been understudied. We present what we believe are fascinating but poorly understood cases of climate governance struggles, and of sustainability solutions. As a way to summarize some of the key substantive issues, we present six reasons why neglecting Latin America could prove irreversibly costly for global climate governance.

First, some *Latin American countries are a bellwether* for how humanity will square the desire and need for development while staying within the limits of planetary boundaries, including emissions that drive the climate system. The region offers some of the only places on earth where nations have achieved high levels of human development (as measured by life expectancy, literacy, and income) while emitting small amounts of greenhouse gas emissions. This is due mainly to the dominance of hydropower, which is an asset for the region, but the ongoing debate about big hydro's social and environmental impacts and contributions to greenhouse gas emissions should not be overlooked. Hydropower is also vulnerable to drought as rain patterns shift and become more unreliable under likely warming scenarios.

New low-carbon pathways of development which emphasize renewable energy such as solar, wind, tidal, wave, and geothermal desperately need to be developed in the region.

Second, the IPCC's Fifth Assessments Report confirms that Latin America is *highly vulnerable to climate impacts*. These impacts include the potential collapse of the Caribbean coral biome, the disappearance of glaciers, coastal erosion with the rise of sea-levels, the risk of dieback of the Amazon rainforests, and the intensification of extreme weather events such as tropical storms, floods, and droughts. This sobering list is beginning to register on the agendas of government planners, but adaptation efforts remain incipient. Climate change presents a risk to hard-earned development gains and could exacerbate the gap between rich and poor. In some cases, the region has built up a head start, given earlier efforts in areas such as forestry protection and urban sustainable transport networks (discussed in chapter 2).

Third, Latin American countries have *played a diverse and crucial role at the UN climate negotiations*. Brazil was instrumental in shaping the UNFCCC and the Kyoto Protocol and its Clean Development Mechanism. Mexico's presidency of the Cancun climate conference helped to rescue the multilateral climate process following the disaster in Copenhagen. Peru hosted the Lima round of negotiations in late 2014 and secured progress toward finalizing an agreement in Paris in 2015. The increasing prominence of the Independent Association of Latin America and the Caribbean (AILAC) has the potential to bridge the North-South divide given its focus on trying to enhance consensus and ambition. The call from the Bolivarian Alliance for the Peoples of Our America (ALBA) to respect UNFCCC procedures and its promotion of climate justice, the role played by civil society, and innovative proposals they brought into the process represent unique and important contributions.

Fourth, various Latin American countries are attempting to take *significant steps to confront climate change*. Mexico created a climate change law in 2012, with targets to reduce emissions by 30 percent below "business as usual" by 2020 and by 50 percent by 2050. Brazil has established a national greenhouse gas reduction target of roughly 36 percent below "business as usual" projected emissions by 2020, largely based on reducing deforestation rates. On adaptation to climate change, Colombia is developing new innovations in disaster preparation, and Cuba has long been the world leader in hurricane preparedness. Other countries, including Bolivia, Costa Rica,

Honduras, and Peru, have either passed laws or announced the intention to create legislation to reduce emissions and adapt to climate impacts.[2] By early 2014, at least nineteen countries in the region had renewable energy policies, and at least fourteen had renewable energy targets. As has been argued in previous chapters, however, there is the considerable challenge of implementing these policies and laws, which in some cases are being undermined by other policies or lack of implementation.

Fifth, Latin America has a *remarkable endowment of natural resources and energy* reserves, including 25 percent of the planet's arable land and 22 percent of the world's forest area, and is home to some of the largest fossil fuel reserves in the world. What happens to those fossil fuel reserves—whether they will stay underground or be burnt and their carbon launched into the atmosphere—will be determinative for Latin America's and the world's future. Our fate rests on the domestic politics of countries like Argentina, Brazil, Mexico, and Venezuela that lead them to control major fossil fuel reserves in a way that does not undermine those nations' sustainable development or consume a dangerous part of the global carbon budget. Nations buying these resources in Asia, Europe, and North America need to make drastic reductions in their consumption and support efforts to diversify Latin Americans economies that are reliant on fossil fuels.

Finally, sustained *economic growth is driving an increase in Latin America's emissions from energy generation, transport, and agriculture.* As the region continues to develop and grow, Latin America's ability to keep its emissions down presents a pressing challenge. The region needs to balance its development objectives while tackling climate change, and there are worrying examples that show the difficulties in implementing climate policies as discussed in the earlier chapters. The priority therefore must be to limit increases in emissions and reduce them to avoid becoming locked into high-carbon development pathways that involve the increased use of fossil fuels or a failure to consolidate important gains on protecting forests.

As we have said, real leadership on solving climate change will have to come from those countries that drive the global carbon cycle—China, Europe, and the United States. But major Latin American countries (such as Brazil and Mexico) can exert coleadership functions, while other nations (like Costa Rica) can lead the way by example, going carbon neutral or moving to low-carbon pathways of development to show that it can be done, even while creating high levels of human development. The region is deeply divided, and because there is little published literature in this area, we have focused on three major negotiating groups of nations, acknowledging that others in Central America, South America and the Caribbean also deserve the attention of researchers.

A Puzzle and Four Factors

In addition to shining some light on the importance of this region and the contrasting positions and inconsistent policies that Latin American nations have taken in the UN climate negotiations and in their climate policy and performance at home, we have sought to understand what explains them. Concern about climate change is widespread among Latin American citizens, climate negotiators, and politicians, but each faces direct and indirect pressures to act in ways that may not be fully in line with that concern. Citizens make decisions in a social system, not in a vacuum, and the choices are shaped by economic interests, cultural values, self-conceptions, and a healthy dose of self-preservation. Politicians are driven by the requirements of the political system by which they landed in power, and driving that system is a set of powerful economic interests that fund their campaigns and lobby their offices and bureaucracies. This is not a reductionist approach: we engaged with our questions with different kinds of explanations that fall into four categories of factors that we summarized as nature, development, foreign policy, and civil society.

Nature: Natural Resources and Vulnerability to Climate Impacts

By nature, we refer to the natural resource endowments that have shaped the societies and economies of Latin American nations. We repeatedly return to the difficulties and risks faced by "extractivist" economies that depend on the export of commodities and sold overseas at volatile prices. Although some Latin American countries emerged from the Great Recession of 2008 sooner and more strongly than other regions, they did so largely due to booming commodity prices and exports to China. Most dramatic and concerning are commodity-backed loans through which nations are taking capital upfront from China and are locked into selling fixed and increasing amounts of that oil back to it for decades. Targets for peaking and reducing emissions sharply are required by those scenarios that include a carbon budget that will keep us under dangerous levels of climate change, but it is difficult to imagine how those targets could be realized with a nation's fossil fuels reserves mortgaged into the future.

Also beyond international trade, there are domestic drivers that are placing Latin America's biodiversity under pressure. Due to a dearth of skills or lack of productivity, Latin American countries can at times be more dependent on exploiting their domestic natural resources to secure growth. In turn a reliance on these resources can undermine calls for improving productivity and the evolution of other sectors of the economy. Short-term election cycles and the populist draw of capitalizing on the immediate benefits of exploiting natural resources during election cycles also offer important reasons why governments may be less inclined to set and meet climate targets. President Correa's decision to wait until after the elections before pulling the plug on the popular Yasuní-ITT Initiative in order to exploit the oil reserves is indicative of the perils of short-term election cycles. Lastly, the lack of local awareness across Latin American societies on the importance of biodiversity further inhibits the shift toward more sustainable forms of development.

Second, we sought to understand the role played by vulnerability to climate impacts in the region and the ways that increasing vulnerability might act as an incentive for nations to take action on climate change and push for an ambitious and binding international agreement. As predicted by "ecofunctionalist" hypotheses,[2] in a number of our cases, political leaders and citizens are concerned about climate impacts in their countries that have led them to take action, especially at the UN climate negotiations. In both extractivism and vulnerability, the history of how societies interacted with the environment is a central factor shaping both some of the similarities and differences between Latin American countries today.

Development: Economic Growth and Competing Development Models

For development, we have focused on the unrelenting but varied pressures on government officials and leaders to generate economic growth and create jobs. Political economic theories expect these pressures to drive governments and firms to make environmentally destructive decisions,[3] which is often what we observed in our cases. These cases have demonstrated the importance of opening the black box of domestic politics, including understanding how subnational actors often drive national postures.[4] Political pragmatism often prioritizes economic growth over climate or environmental policies, but these are not necessarily at cross purposes. The emergence of AILAC, however, has revealed a new discourse that factors in the costs and risks of *not* incorporating climate change considerations, and results in an acknowledgment that it pays to try and be green. Some Latin American countries are seeing their already existing head starts with low-carbon energy sources (such as hydroelectricity-driven power grids), and forestry protection schemes give them an advantage under an aggressive climate regime. At the other end of the scale, some petrostates and semipetrostates in ALBA perhaps accurately believe that they have more to lose in a carbon-constrained future, despite the dominance of hydropower in their own energy matrices. Again, we hypothesize that the ongoing dependence on high-carbon exports would maintain or strengthen the balance of power in governments of ministries of mining, agriculture, or energy (what we call dirty ministries) over environment or climate change ministries and agencies.

The region is unified in demanding increased funding from the wealthy countries to pay for these efforts, but the ALBA countries and to a lesser extent Brazil have stated that they will not undertake any or further mitigation efforts until these funds materialize. Brazil's emphasizes the responsibility of wealthy countries to first meet their promises and obligations than its own need for funding in order for it to take further action. Alternatively, AILAC and Mexico have demanded the funding but have already begun to press ahead with emission reductions. Mexico's 2015 announcement of a pledge for the Paris negotiations included more ambitious "conditional" targets, and adequate climate finance was one of the key conditions for them to aim for this higher ambition. A few nations appear to be steering their nations' economy onto a new pathway of development, which can be seen in Costa Rica's pioneering carbon-neutral pledge and to a somewhat lesser extent Mexico's climate change law, which is tasked with reducing emissions and expanding clean energy. These countries' climate policies are very vulnerable to being undermined. Latin America's independent foreign policy is leading to the increasing presence of other actors in the region (notably China), whose impact on its environmental and climate policies is worrisome yet poorly understood.

Foreign Policy: Regional Integration, International Alliances, and Trade
Third, throughout the book we return repeatedly to how foreign policy and regional integration, international alliances, and trade have proven

formative in the climate change postures and coalitions of Latin American countries. In all three of our cases—Brazil, ALBA, and AILAC/Mexico—Latin American countries have been behaving more independently and assertively on their climate change policies. This reflects a trend toward a more autonomous foreign policy that involves stepping out from the United States' shadow. This contrasts with the days when the US could manipulate support in the region, which it tried to do after Copenhagen in 2009 by pledging foreign aid only if countries accepted the Accord that it supported.[4] US trade and commercial ties in the region are still strong, yet US political influence is not what it used to be. Most Latin American countries are developing closer ties to Asia, Russia, and India, with diplomatic agreements that complement substantial sales of raw materials to those countries, large volumes of imported products, and significant revenues for governments across the region.

This independence is also reflected in the splintering of these nations from the mainstream G77 positions in the climate negotiations exemplified by ALBA, AILAC, and AOSIS. The level of fragmentation in Latin America, as demonstrated by the region's numerous regional integration projects, also manifests itself at the UN climate negotiations. There is a correlation between Latin American countries' regional integration projects and their positions at the negotiations. ALBA and AILAC are groupings that lined up with trade blocs that are quite different in their natures and goals. But there are also differences within these groups. ALBA members differ in some of their positions at the UN climate negotiations, such as the use of markets and reducing emissions from deforestation and forest degradation (REDD+). Brazil is a Lone Ranger with its BASIC partners (South Africa, India, and China) and has few followers from Latin America and the Caribbean at the UN climate talks. Similarly, its attempts to lead the region through the Community of Latin American and Caribbean States (CELAC), for example, have shown poor results. Some Pacific Alliance countries also joined forces at the UNFCCC through AILAC. Their willingness to support carbon-trading mechanisms reflects their interest in free trade to promote their economic growth. AILAC's push for a legally-binding agreement for all countries is important. As left-wing nations in the region grow more dependent on trade and commercial deals and sending oil to China, it is difficult to untangle the role played by competing models of how to improve society and the ability to protect the climate in an extractivist economy.

Civil Society: The Gap between Climate Concern and Action

Our last theme addresses civil society organizations, which have attempted with some limited success to pressure governments to take more action to confront climate change. Although stronger on more traditional environmental issues, Latin American civil society has arrived relatively recently to the issue of climate change. At the national level, Brazilian civil society groups and businesses were able to influence the bill related to the National Policy on Climate Change prior to COP15. However, their lack of influence was exposed later when rural political elites successfully pushed through reforms to the Forest Code that civil groups were against. Ecuador's canceling of the Yasuní-ITT Initiative exposes the limitations of civil society action in the face of repressive states that are not interested in demands, even if they reflect those of a large portion of Ecuadorian society. Venezuela's Social Pre-COP aimed to promote civil society voices in the UNFCCC debate but shut out those groups that challenged Venezuela's own positions and policies. The oil refinery case in Costa Rica also reflects the power and influence of state actors and interests. Civil society groups and citizens strongly criticized the oil refinery deal, which they argue could undermine Costa Rica's carbon-neutral goal, but their concerns have largely been dismissed by the government.

Our cases reflect that civil society groups have been generally effective in generating increased media attention to climate change issues but have struggled to prevent governments from taking decisions that they are against. The 2010 World People's Conference on Climate Change in Cochabamba was regarded as a revolution in social mobilization around climate change, but the fact that the People's Agreement did not endure in any final drafts of the Cancun Agreements suggests limitations in the ability of civil society and climate justice advocates of all stations to influence the negotiations as they are currently structured. Despite the Peruvian COP20 presidency working with some NGO partners, the Lima outcome was severely criticized by various NGOs for its lack of ambition. This reflects the unwillingness of governments to incorporate nonstate actors in decision-making processes or, worse, the repression or stifling of civil society activities and demands. Latin American civil society is crucial for advancing the region's responses to climate change, but the mechanisms available to them to participate and coordinate with government are insufficient and require reform and expansion.

One Voice or Many?

All Latin American governments agree that climate change is a serious problem, and they are unified in viewing the UNFCCC as the principal vehicle to find a global solution. However, the region is largely fragmented on the details of how the issue should be addressed. Here we ask whether this diversity is a good or bad thing for the region at the talks.

The lack of a unified regional position at the UN negotiations is sometimes criticized as a weakness. During the Cancun climate conference, the Climate Action Network's publication *ECO* expressed its frustration:

Day after day *ECO* had a hard time hearing the Latin American region sharing either a whole integral vision or a truly active participation. Diverse groupings have formed in a continent with similar features and problems. But remaining differences have divided efforts and left the path open to stronger groups to block progress.... Latin American countries are not showing either the leadership or the needed consistency. COP16 is the opportunity for Latin America to express itself in a single voice.[5]

Supporting this idea, the former president of Chile, Ricardo Lagos, opined that "A region with many voices is not as listened to as one that speaks with one voice."[6] Lagos proposed that the region could present a common front on a number of issues, like the need for adequate financing, REDD+, and adaptation. Speaking of the region, the UNFCCC's executive secretary, Christiana Figueres, argued that "As regards climate change ... in the long term the countries of the continent have more shared interests than points of discord." She continued that "it is undeniable that the nature itself of climate change is such that no country can face it on its own. The problem can only be solved if all countries face it together."[7]

Latin American civil society organizations have emphasized some of the common areas between Latin American countries. The AVINA Foundation's Ramiro Fernández says, "Beyond ideological differences, Latin America shares a number of elements that could strengthen its global leadership to meet the challenges of climate change."[8] Antonio Hill, Executive Director of the Global Call for Climate Action, told the BBC that "We need to place more emphasis on the building of alliances in Latin America in areas of common interests, to ensure that Andean and Central American countries do not end up excluded from adaptation funds [due to their status (aside from Haiti) as middle-income countries and not Least Developed Countries]."[9] Andrew Hurrell and Sandeep Sengupta describe the stakes this way:

"Climate negotiations have now witnessed a role reversal of sorts, with greater unity within the developed world, centered on getting emerging countries to do more, and greater fragmentation within the South.... it is clear not only that climate coalitions today—by chance or by design—are in flux, but that traditional Southern coalitions are in particular disarray, with emerging powers finding it ever harder to rally support."[10]

These are some of the voices arguing that fragmentation is unhelpful. Others suggest that this lack of a common voice and divergences between countries help to maintain key issues on the negotiating table. By not adopting a single position, Latin American countries have had the flexibility to reach out to like-minded countries in other regions, which allows those countries to influence the international debate in a different way; and in some cases becoming influential actors rather than spectators, as is shown in earlier chapters.[11]

The G77 and China used to speak as one voice at the UNFCCC. Even the Small Island States, which face existential threats from rising seas, stuck with the G77 even as Saudi Arabia and other OPEC nations strongly influenced the group's position. The emergence of other groups listed in chapter 2 documents the fragmentation of the G77. The Alliance of Small Island States (AOSIS) was the first group to defy the G77's big players—China and India. But all of these countries stuck together because of shared colonial pasts and a shared view that the group was the only way to increase their leverage with the major players in the North, which they saw as attempting to pull up the ladder of development behind them and keep them poor.[12] Several groups have now emerged, including AILAC, ALBA, and AOSIS, and have challenged the G77's position. These divergent voices are also evidence that Latin American countries are embarking on more autonomous and assertive development and foreign policy priorities. These broader dynamics may limit the likelihood of greater cooperation on climate change, which usually remains well down the political agenda, compared to development and trade.

Political differences and diverse priorities explain why consensus is elusive. In Cancun in 2010, Latin American governments were vocal in their support of Mexico's presidency due to a strong collective commitment to safeguard the multilateral climate process. Although there is strong agreement across the region about the value of the Convention's core principles—including reducing the risk of dangerous climate change and the need for countries to act according to their common but differentiated responsibilities and capabilities—countries differ on how to proceed. If the region did negotiate with one voice—for instance, via the Community of Latin American and Caribbean States (CELAC)—powerful states could drown out the voices of weaker ones, as we have seen in the G77 of old. Taking into account some of the divergent positions, reaching a declaration that is agreeable to all probably would consist of a list of general goals and statements, which is not necessarily helpful for advancing the negotiations.

In an unprecedented intervention at COP20 in 2014, Costa Rica, as the rotating president of CELAC, made a statement on behalf of the community. The statement emphasized the need for adaptation to climate impacts, which is hardly a controversial topic. The statement was encouraging, however, given Latin American countries' shared vulnerability to climate impacts and the potential for countries to cooperate on adaptation. It also emphasized CELAC's commitment to the UNFCCC and its support for a legally binding agreement in 2015.

According to Waldemar Coutts, from Chile's Ministry of Foreign Affairs, the CELAC statement was the result of a diplomatic effort by Brazil and Chile, with the support of Peru as COP20 president and ECLAC. The Brazil-Chile initiative focuses on establishing dialogues between Latin American and Caribbean countries on climate change to build trust and understanding in order to strengthen the region´s contributions to the UN climate negotiations.[13] Yet despite the apparent value of this joint political statement by CELAC, the level of fragmentation within the region was on full display at COP20. As the draft texts made their way around the negotiations, there was a clear split between those Latin American countries in favor of the drafts (such as Brazil, Mexico, and AILAC) and those opposing it (such as El Salvador, Paraguay, and ALBA).

Our view is that nations' international positions depend largely on their own national experiences and contexts. This is not a new idea, but most of the focus has been on domestic politics in the main polluters (the US and China) with nearly no discussion of the national roots of positions in regions like Latin America, where positions were often assumed to be shared with other nations in the global South. The region's experiences are spilling over borders. Because of migrants and energy flows (pipelines, tanker trains and ships, and cross-boundary shared hydroelectric plants), climate impacts are increasingly regional and global, and trade and economies are becoming more globally connected. But national experiences are still very different. This idea of Latin America as a microcosm for the wider negotiations is relevant here. Many factors—including the diversity of its economies, disparities in nations' climate vulnerability and emissions, the diversity of ideological positions, differences in foreign policies and development models, and differences in shares of natural resources—are important to consider.

Taking into account the myriad regional integration projects, Latin American trade initiatives will continue to shape national and subregional climate agendas, as has been seen with the Pacific Alliance and ALBA. These regional projects follow their own logics, but that does not mean they cannot be complementary and beneficial overall to securing greater climate action. There will likely be limited Latin American integration on climate beyond some joint political statements, as happened in Lima. Although there are numerous areas for enhancing cooperation (adaptation strategies, promoting renewable energy, disaster risk reduction, and diversification away from natural resources) that could prove positive for the region's resilience, the likelihood of greater cooperation at the UNFCCC is currently low.

Outside of the negotiations, we believe that there would be great value in more regional cooperation and dialogue. The nine Amazonian countries (which straddle BASIC, AILAC, and ALBA) could come together more actively to share best practices and cooperate on forestry protection, inclusion of indigenous peoples, and small hydroelectric projects. Nations are already close to agreement on a series of issues, such as setting priorities for adapting to climate change, coordinating demands for and systems of deciding and tracking climate finance, building greater city-to-city sharing of solutions, strengthening agriculture (for example, through drought-resistant crops and soil carbon-sequestration methods), scaling up renewable energy, and building a regionwide grid that could improve energy efficiency and increase the use of renewable energy. Some of the fragmentation at the UN can be remedied by the kinds of national and concrete cooperative actions that would tend to create a convergence of norms and precedents for working together. Then more trust and collaborative spirit may prove beneficial when nations form up at the UNFCCC.

In terms of dialogue, there are several efforts to expand on, including the EU-funded EUROCLIMA capacity-building project or efforts by ECLAC and the Inter-American Development Bank (IDB) to produce studies on the economics of climate change. These will not magically unify the region, but they will continue to promote a convergence of scientific understanding and norms and promote a proactive regional climate change culture.

The Inter-American Development Bank says that to prevent irreversible damage to the earth, global emissions cannot exceed a yearly 20 gigatons of carbon dioxide equivalent ($GtCO_2e$), or 2 tons per capita, by 2050. Under the business-as-usual scenario, Latin America and the Caribbean will emit nearly 7 $GtCO_2e$ by 2050, when its per capita emissions will reach 9.3 tCO_2e. CELAC should discuss the merit of such an aspirational regional target for 2 tCO_2e per capita by 2050. This target can help countries get past some of their differences about how to respond to climate change by offering a common way forward for all. How countries decide to reach the target is up to them, but the extensive use of off-setting emissions through forestry would need to be closely scrutinized to ensure economy-wide emissions-reductions. To achieve this goal would require a worldwide transformation toward low-emission development and require substantial support from developed countries. The IDB presents some of the available pathways by which Latin America and the Caribbean could contribute to this global stabilization goal by 2050, including taking actions to stop deforestation, reducing emissions from agriculture, boosting energy efficiency, deploying renewable energy, and electrifying the transport sector. The probability of reaching this per capita emissions target by 2050 increases substantially if all countries in the region contribute.[14]

Finally, Latin American and Caribbean countries should work through CELAC to demand greater action on climate change and support for low-carbon development efforts in the region from their international partners, especially the US, EU, and China. CELAC countries regularly hold summits with the US and Canada (Summit of the Americas), with the EU (EU-CELAC Summit) and China (China-CELAC Forum). These meetings are an ideal space for CELAC to work collectively and present a common list of demands and areas for cooperation with their partners. Many of these opportunities are currently being missed.

Making a Mark in Lima

Compared to previous negotiations, the number and quality of official and outside events focusing on Latin America at COP20 in Lima were unprecedented, reflecting new levels of regional activity on climate change and of civil society's access to decision makers. The Global March in Defense of Mother Earth was Latin America's largest climate march ever, and it brought together indigenous peoples, trade unionists, women's groups, students, and global activists. With Manuel Pulgar-Vidal, the former head of one of Peru's leading environmental organizations, as COP20 president, it appeared that governments and UNFCCC officials were reaching out again for their input and support.

However, civil society groups and citizens working on climate change and environmental issues face dangers and difficulties due to Latin American governments' unwillingness to effectively incorporate nonstate actors in decision-making processes or repression of civil society activities and demands.[15] During the COP20, some of the wives of murdered indigenous leaders from Peru's Amazon held a demonstration and press conference demanding that the government do more to protect their lands.[16] Authorities in Ecuador repeatedly stopped a group of activists from the Yasunidos group on their way to the COP20 to protest against the decision to extract oil from reserves under Ecuador's Yasuní National Park.

As has been shown in the book's case studies, the ability of civil society organizations to influence government policy and orchestrate change depends largely on whether governments wish to open the space for dialogue. Compounding this problem is the lack of scientific and policy expertise and research capacity in the region, especially among some NGOs focusing on climate change. Although this is improving rapidly, for the most part, the majority of research comes from a handful of outlets in the region, including the regional offices of the World Bank, the Inter-American Development Bank, and ECLAC, rather than civil society organizations such as think tanks. We found that only 29 percent of the seventy-nine top think tanks from Latin America have programs, projects, or publications on climate change.[17] The Intergovernmental Panel on Climate Change's (IPCC) Fifth Assessment Report involved just eighty-four Latin American and Caribbean contributing authors, out of a total 833.[18]

A different problem is the isolation of climate expertise or the lack of outreach to mainstream areas of development and economics. At an event on Latin American and Caribbean think tanks at COP20, a small group of organizations discussed their views on the lead-up to Paris 2015. Only organizations that specialized in environmental or climate issues were represented, but not one of the Peruvian mainstream think tanks working on national economic or development issues was present. The participation of Latin American think tanks that are working on these core national issues is crucial for the climate debate in the region. These organizations have vital perspectives and ideas to contribute, especially on the political process, the policy process and budgeting, and national debates on development. These think tanks are needed to help develop effective domestic narratives that combine climate and development objectives.

Latin America's science funding is increasing as countries in the region show greater interest in the benefits of science for better policy. In the case of Brazil and Mexico, greater national science investment has helped develop and promote national policy agendas on climate change that are offering useful examples for other countries. Although some Latin American universities have formed networks with universities in Europe and North America or with their own governments, there seems to be only incipient attempts at regional collaboration.[19]

Although this is improving, one area that Latin American NGOs working on climate change may consider improving is their communication strategies. Current emphasis is placed on communicating news items and general reports on the UN climate process. Analysis of Latin American government positions is increasing but quite limited. There is duplication of efforts because some Latin American NGOs tend to publish similar news items on their website, but this falls short of the material required to set agendas, share new ideas, and create impactful narratives. A consequence of these current communication strategies is that NGOs are infrequently considered opinion setters or thought leaders, but rather are seen merely as conveyors of news items. Most Latin American NGOs working on climate change have not sufficiently emphasized the link between broader political and economic debates and decision-making processes with the UN climate negotiations and national climate action.[20]

With weak medium-term economic growth forecasts, Latin America is perhaps a more combustible region today than it has been in recent years because the public has grown used to relatively good economic times. The recent protests in Brazil, Mexico, Ecuador, Chile, and Venezuela are testimony to the discontent that is being felt by some citizens in the region.

Combined with the level of concern in the region about climate impacts, this represents an important moment for civil society groups to harness people power to generate more action on climate change.

Toward a New Research Agenda

As engaged researchers, we are attempting to provide information and analysis that are useful to promoting just climate solutions. Much of what we know about the political conditions shaping climate action in Latin America has been learned by our attempts to make positive differences in the negotiations and in international discussions about the issue more broadly. Although we have undertaken years of research for this volume, building on our enduring interest in the region, as outsiders our understanding is partial. Our aim in writing this book was to help make some sense of the complex divisions and positions of Latin American countries at the UNFCCC. The topic has been largely unexplored, and so our hope is that delegates, activists, analysts, and academics from inside and outside the region will find this contribution to be of sufficient interest to refute and improve its analysis. We have several suggestions for where research is needed on this book's core issues.

The majority of the materials on climate change in Latin America are technical and scientific. They describe the predicted impacts of global climate models in Latin America, potential mitigation actions, and particular vulnerabilities that will result. Very little discusses the politics and policy choices that nations face now, the issues that might shape their decisions, and the possible outcomes. Much of the existing literature has been led by ECLAC, the Inter-American Development Bank, and leading Latin American scientists who are involved with the Intergovernmental Panel on Climate Change. Latin American governments have published their national communications to the UNFCCC[21] and their national climate change strategies and plans. These publications focus on technical issues and greenhouse gas emissions inventories that float above the politics of daily life, parliaments, and presidential palaces. With few exceptions, they include very little work—in Portuguese, Spanish, or English—on theorizing issues of climate change in Latin America, especially in terms of international relations, comparative politics, or political economy. Further, there is sparse analysis of the relationship between Latin American countries' current economic models and little investigation of how an economywide shift to low-emission development could work. This is an exciting frontier of knowledge, and we hope that readers might open it up.[22]

Latin American civil society organizations, think tanks, and research institutes have come quite late to the issue, but they can fill this void.[23] There are some notable exceptions, including the Latin American Platform on Climate's study on the state and quality of climate change policies in a number of countries.[24] Much online reporting and analysis has responded to international studies (such as the IPCC) rather than national and regional climate debates. However, in 2014 at the COP20 in Lima, we noticed a marked increase in attention paid to national climate policies, especially in Peru and Costa Rica. Latin American newspapers still tend to relegate climate change and environmental issues to the back pages. Government officials and advisers with many years of experience working on the day-to-day details of both government policy and the UN climate negotiations have little time to write. Their knowledge and ideas need to be better captured and diffused beyond informal discussions at conferences and workshops.

The existing body of literature in the three main languages (Portuguese, Spanish, and English) needs to be translated and made available in each of the three languages. Brazilians are producing a growing body of technical and scientific knowledge in Portuguese that could be well used if translated into Spanish and English. Similarly, there is a lot of material in Spanish and English that could be translated into Portuguese. These efforts could support and encourage international collaboration and clarify what is at stake and which organizations are trying what actions. These are low-investment, high-return efforts and should be supported by national academies, disciplinary organizations, and science foundations.

We believe that strategically designed and implemented longitudinal case studies undertaken by international research teams in several nations in the hemisphere could have high value. A range of topics come to mind, but our own preference would be to see studies that link Latin American countries' national (and local) economies and politics with their governments' postures at the UN negotiations.

We need comparative histories that examine environmental action in Latin American countries and the actions of local grassroots citizen-led organizations. Reviews of the political economy of these countries should analyze how economic and commercial sectors drive the politics of climate action or inaction and what the competing interests between ministries and agencies are. It would be helpful to understand how negotiation teams from the region are formed, which ministries get sent, what roles they play, and how they operate. Understanding how negotiators receive instructions from their ministers and heads of state and how much latitude they have when they arrive at the UN climate negotiations also would be useful. Some negotiators appear to have far greater flexibility to interact with the media than their counterparts have. For example this appears to be the case with the Venezuelan delegation, which supports our argument that Venezuela's role at the UNFCCC is largely political and not technical or scientific. How these communications function on a day-to-day basis and in lower-visibility delegations needs to be studied.

A more in-depth understanding of how Latin American citizens' concerns about global warming and environmental issues interact with policy is urgently needed. A better grasp of the relevance of presidential interest and commitment on climate change and its implications for domestic and international climate policymaking would be helpful. Finally, research is needed on Latin American countries' relationships with older partners (such as the US and the EU) and the increasing presence of new actors (such as China, India and Russia). We need to understand how these countries interact on climate change at the UNFCCC and whether their interactions on trade and commercial ties may affect Latin American countries' climate politics and positions.

Building a Lead

Although Latin American countries have not had any binding limits on their greenhouse gas emissions, some are among the greenest on earth. However, emissions are rising in several countries as their economies expand, energy demand soars, exports increase, and their middle classes grow. As these trends continue, will governments be able to balance the demands of their citizens to build low-emission, climate-resilient, and prosperous nations?

Achieving this balance is critical for climate-friendly development strategies and for the political sustainability of those who propose and institute them. Mitigation and adaptation actions can be advanced simultaneously on many fronts, such as developing sustainable mass urban transport systems, promoting energy efficiency, scaling up renewable energy (such as wind, solar, and geothermal), implementing and strengthening existing climate policies, protecting biodiversity, and encouraging responsible consumerism. A greater task involves diversifying the region's development model away from extractivism. A boom in the international demand for natural resources may have been instrumental in enhancing Latin America's economic performance over the last decade, but diversification is needed to create national productive sectors that make these nations economically sound, ensure resilience in the face of climate and economic shocks, and improve investment in human capital.[25] Extractivism ultimately has a shelf life and is risky and destructive.

As discussed in chapter 2, the outlook for the region's economic performance over the next couple of years is modest. This presents a challenge for cash-strapped environmental ministries and for environmental and climate agendas more broadly. The concern is that the issue of climate change may slip to a lower position on the agenda at a time when it needs to be taken up by decision makers. The implementation of innovative climate and environmental laws and policies cannot be slowed or sacrificed in the interests of improving short-term economic growth. Rather, an economic slowdown for Latin America could present some useful opportunities, such as promoting low-carbon policies for building prosperity, and challenge the outdated discourse that tackling climate change slows development. Smart policy options such as reducing and eliminating fossil fuel subsidies and boosting energy efficiency and renewable energy should be prioritized. These can have important cobenefits, such as reducing urban air pollution, lowering health risks and costs, and improving productivity and innovation.

The adaptation agenda in Latin America is gaining momentum as the evidence of climate-related dangers grows and options for reducing climate-related impacts are identified and field-tested. Estimates for the region's exorbitant adaptation costs provide policy makers with a sobering reminder that work on adaptation and mitigation need to be accelerated to reduce the expected costs of climate impacts.[26] Latin America should incorporate vulnerability-assessment studies and joint mitigation-adaptation goals into medium- to long-term development planning and action plans.

Latin America is now regarded as one of the great frontiers for clean energy investment. The Inter-American Development Bank says that Latin America can meet its future energy needs through renewable-energy sources, including solar, wind, marine, geothermal, and biomass energy, which are estimated to be sufficient to cover its projected 2050 electricity needs twenty-two times over.[27] However, advancing clean energy faces a number of challenges, including fossil fuel subsidies and a lack of capital. Latin American countries' main trading partners—including China, the US, the EU, and the multilateral banks—can play a key role in accelerating the region's clean energy future, but only if there is a shift in the thinking of leaders and those in the private sector that the future requires clean energy and not fossil fuels.

As is discussed in chapter 5, the COP20 secured an important agreement on countries' intended nationally determined contributions (INDCs), which are what countries will pledge to do about reducing emissions, adapting to the impacts, and supporting developing countries' actions with funding, assistance, and technology transfer. The INDCs will be a central pillar of a new agreement in Paris. The World Resources Institute says that with sufficient review and assessment, the INDCs combine a bottom-up system (where countries put forward their contributions according to their national priorities, circumstances, and capabilities) with a top-down system (in which countries aim to bring down global emissions to limit the average global temperature rise to 2 degrees Celsius). Because INDCs could lead to significant changes across national economies, especially in carbon-intensive sectors, such climate contributions could be integrated with goals to reduce poverty and inequality while sending signals to the private sector to invest in these efforts.[28]

Developing INDCs has the potential to be a transformative process for increasing climate action from 2020 and ensuring progress along the way. Some Latin American countries are working on their pre-2020 voluntary emission reduction pledges, so they are not starting from scratch. The successful implementation of these policies between now and 2020 is crucial for creating the right conditions for ambitious targets in the next round, which are likely to be negotiated every five years. The INDCs present a considerable opportunity for Latin America. They can be used as a strategic tool to nudge countries on a path toward low-carbon sustainable development, while building resilience to climate impacts. The way in which governments define their plans will determine the level of political buy-in from citizens and business. The implementation of ambitious contributions is more likely if constituencies consider them beneficial and legitimate. Therefore, carefully managed public consultations are required to democratize the climate change debate in Latin America. Chile's decision to run a public consultation on its draft INDC from December 2014 through April 2015 was a laudable effort to receive observations and proposals from civil society, academia, and the private sector to improve its INDC proposal.[29]

To ensure real progress on climate change, can Latin American countries promote a new climate narrative? Costa Rica Limpia's Mónica Araya suggests that Latin America still lacks a convincing story on climate that works for mainstream politicians. The debate against the high-carbon economy cannot be won unless the battle for a low-carbon shift becomes a political battle that is fought at elections. The conversation can shift toward the protection of people, increased resilience in the face of climate-related disasters and economic shocks, and inclusiveness as the basis of any effort to become prosperous middle-income societies.[30]

After over twenty years of stalemate, skepticism abounds about the possibility of a radical change in direction in the UN negotiations, and it is easy to be dismissive about controlling global warming. However, the positive and negative feedback loops of an unpredictable climate suggest very different scenarios. The rise of climate disasters and an awareness of common vulnerability have the potential to turn nations quickly from infighting and factionalism to positions of cooperation in the face of a common threat. An important question is whether the UNFCCC will be the forum for a solution. Although Mexico managed to save the UNFCCC from collapse, the longevity of this regime despite its continued failure to reach an adequate international agreement suggests that alternative decision-making fora—such as the G7, the G20, the Major Economies Forum (MEF), and even the G2 (China and the US)—make take over.[31] Some of these exclude Latin America entirely. The MEF and G20 each include just Argentina, Brazil, and Mexico among the major polluter economies.

In the future, climate change, resource scarcity, and green growth could become the defining issues for Latin America's relationship with Europe, the US, and China. Whether the region will be left behind on climate finance (as funding flows largely to Asia or to Africa) also will be closely watched. South-South cooperation (such as Brazil's development investments in biofuels in Africa) is worth attention.

Brazil has accomplished impressive reductions in deforestation, but these advances are being eclipsed by rising emissions in other sectors. Rather than claiming that it already has done its part and playing a defensive game at the climate negotiations to avoid any binding commitments, Brazil could play an active role in building a regime that looks for the opportunities in a global low-carbon economy, especially on forestry and clean energy. A binding universal regime would speed up the transition to a low-carbon economy, which Brazil could capitalize on. Given that the UNFCCC has long since gone down a market-based mechanism path, there is value in creating a new class of actors who see aggressive climate policy as an economic interest. A more constructive position at the UNFCCC would enhance Brazil's case for inclusion at the UN Security Council instead of holding on to its current spoiler position.

During her second presidential administration, Dilma Rousseff should attempt to bolster Brazil's domestic climate policy. Maintaining sharply lower rates in deforestation will require more difficult steps.[32] Keeping the electricity sector from turning to fossil fuels will require active efforts to promote renewables and improve efficiency. Brazil needs to do more in Latin America to reach consensus or compromise on contentious issues of the UN climate negotiations. Brazil could promote climate and renewable energy goals as part of its efforts to lead the region, through the Union of South American Nations (UNASUR) and CELAC.

There is growing concern that ALBA's focus on extractivism is pushing these countries irrevocably onto a high-carbon development pathway, with serious implications for achieving sustainable development and social justice. The vulnerability of the ALBA countries to climate impacts makes it not in their long-term interests to participate in the Like-Minded Developing Countries group, which has tended to stall the negotiations and resist universal ambition. A more productive approach would have ALBA to improve dialogue and attempt to build alliances with other G77 members, such as the Least Developed Countries Group and AILAC.

We believe that AILAC's "revolt of the middle" offers the gridlocked UN negotiations a much-needed boost. AILAC's effort to bridge the North-South divide has positive implications for the value of multilateralism. However, the mismatch between ALBA's and AILAC's rhetoric at the UNFCCC and their members' domestic climate actions require urgent focus and harmonization. Finally, despite the success of COP16, recent energy reforms in Mexico are of considerable concern for the country's ability to implement its climate law and related emission-reduction targets.

Given the concerns that Latin American citizens have about climate change, civil society organizations in the region and globally should attempt to enhance their impact, which will require government support (without strings attached). Mechanisms for including citizens in decision making on climate change remain weak. Political leaders need to be forced to incorporate growing concerns over climate change into election platforms and national policy, with a focus on issues such as air pollution and sustainable mass urban transport systems. There are ways to explain the value of taking these steps, such as describing local cobenefits and resilience building, including improved air quality and job creation.

This democratic deficit in Latin American climate policy is of fundamental importance. The legislative approach to building action on climate change that has been demonstrated by Mexico and others is an important avenue to pursue, but only if the climate laws are sufficiently ambitious, actually implemented and are not undermined by other policies. Latin American countries need to lock in action on climate change through robust and adequate laws that attempt to confront and not exacerbate climate risks. Boosting citizen participation in the legislative processes at the national and subnational levels can strengthen countries' positions at the UN negotiations and facilitate the transition to low-emission, resilient, and prosperous economies. As a result, Latin America's responses on climate change could be transformative for its citizens and for us all.

Notes

Chapter 1: Paradoxes of a Neglected Region

1. Purvis 2010.

2. United Nations Partners on Climate Change n.d.

3. Painter 2010.

4. Araya 2011a, 2011b.

5. Ibid.

6. Eduardo Viola, personal communication, 2014.

7. Ibid.

8. Steinberger and Roberts 2010.

9. Arias and Edwards 2013.

10. Colom 2010.

11. Vergara 2011; Vergara et al. 2007.

12. Vergara et al. 2013b.

13. Magrin et al. 2007.

14. Frayssinet 2013.

15. Rabatel et al. 2013.

16. Colombia 2010; Perú Ministerio del Ambiente 2010.

17. Vergara et al. 2007.

18. Vergara et al. 2013b.

19. Edwards 2008.

20. Edwards 2009.

21. "Ecuador Energy Crisis" 2009.

22. Vergara et al. 2013b.

23. Lewis et al. 2011.

24. Caravani et al. 2011.

25. Githeko and Woodward 2003.

26. ECLAC 2011a.

27. Ibid.

28. Sistema de la Integración Centroamericana 2011.

29. Chávez 2011, 1

30. Vergara et al. 2013b.

31. Caribbean Catastrophe Risk Insurance Facility 2010.

32. UNDP 2007.

33. Mata and Nobre 2006.

34. Steven and Bujones 2013.

35. Buen Vivir is an old and new concept that is based on indigenous views about nature and the purposes of the economy. Buen Vivir means "reinforcing ways of life that promote healthy relationships and sustainability rather than participate in destructive economic activity." Madden 2014.

36. UNDP 2010.

37. Moseley and Layton 2013.

38. UNDP 2010.

39. World Bank 2009b.

40. These totals are per capita for 2011 estimates from the Food and Agriculture Organization of the UN Corporate Statistical Database (FAOSTAT) as compiled by the World Resources Institute's Climate Analysis Indicators Tool (CAIT) system, and they include emissions from land-use change and forestry. Fossil fuel data from the International Energy Agency 2014 shows a somewhat different picture: nearly fifteen tons of carbon per person in Argentina and Chile; nearly twenty-two tons in Venezuela; around 3.67 tons in Paraguay and Central America (except Panama, about nine tons); and about seven tons per person in Brazil, the Dominican Republic, and Ecuador. Figures are from IEA 2014a. Note that the IEA reports in tons of carbon and that WRI reports in CO_2; one ton of carbon makes 3.67 tons of CO_2.

41. ECLAC/IDB 2010.

42. Houghton 2005a. Data on tropical forest biomass are from Houghton 2005a and based on 2000 FAO data. Data on share in total forest biomass are from the FAO's 2005 *Global Forest Resource Assessment*.

43. International Energy Agency 2007.

44. Vergara et al. 2013b. Brazil's extensive efforts to reduce deforestation have led to a decline in land-use emissions, which have pushed down the land-use sector's contribution to Latin America and the Caribbean's total emissions from 47 percent to less than 35 percent in 2010. For more details, see Vergara et al. 2013.

45. Vergara et al. 2013b. In 2010, Latin America's primary energy mix included more oil (42 percent), hydropower (21 percent), and biomass (13.5 percent) than the global average mix (32 percent, 6.7 percent, and 8.7 percent, respectively).

46. Vergara et al. 2013b.

47. Tegel 2013.

48. Figueres 2011.

49. Garibaldi, Araya, and Edwards 2012.

50. Townshend and Matthews 2013.

51. Vergara et al. 2014.

52. SELA 2010; World Bank 2012a, 2010b.

53. By 2050, annual agricultural exports in Latin America could decline by around US$50 billion due to climate impacts on crop yields. By 2020, net export revenues could decline by US$8 to $11 billion because of regional reductions in maize, soybean, wheat, and rice yields. Alexandratos and Bruinsma 2012.

54. Fernandes et al. 2012.

55. IDB 2014.

56. WRI 2012.

57. WRI CAIT 2014.

58. Opio et al. 2013.

59. Vergara et al. 2013b.

60. Ibid.

61. Ibid.

62. International Energy Agency 2007.

63. Riahi et al. 2011.

64. Ibid.

65. Vergara et al. 2013b.

66. Harrison and Sundstrom 2007, 2010.

67. This approach can improve understanding of complex decision making and policy processes on climate change (and other issues), differences in governance structures, and the power relations mediating competing claims over resources. Tanner and Allouche 2011.

68. Carvalho 2007.

69. Roberts and Parks 2007.

70. Many studies could be cited here, but some starting places for documenting this include Wolf 1982; Cardoso and Faletto 1979; Galeano 1973; Frank 1969.

71. Rootes, Zito, and Barry 2012. Other key studies in this area include Harrison and Sundstrom 2007, 2010; Dolsak 2001; Hochstetler and Viola 2012; Bernauer 2013; Andonova, Betsill, and Bulkeley 2009; Stoett 2012; Desai 2002; Okereke 2007; Paterson 1996; Zahran et al. 2007; Javeline 2014; Andonova 2008; Keohane and Victor 2011; Hochstetler 2012.

72. E.g., Harrison and Sundstrom 2007, 2010; Hochstetler and Viola 2012; Putnam 1988.

73. E.g., Rootes, Zito, and Barry 2012; Andonova, Betsill, and Bulkeley 2009.

74. See, e.g., Cardoso and Faletto 1979; Galeano 1973; Edwards and Roberts 2014; Gudynas 2009.

75. Moreno 2011; BP 2008; FAO 2011.

76. Bovarnick, Alpizar, and Schnell 2010.

77. UNEP 2010.

78. See, e.g., Hicks et al. 2008; Waldron et al. 2013; Waldron et al. 2013.

79. This is using the IPCC's (2014) 2 degrees Celsius global average temperature rise above preindustrial levels. McGlade and Ekins 2015 adopt 1,100 gigatons to demonstrate their point about unburnable carbon, cited just below. They list 2,900 gigatons of known resources and reserves.

80. Watkins 2013.

81. McGlade and Ekins 2015. This is without carbon capture and storage, technology that is unproven and likely to be very expensive in energy and monetary terms.

82. Their study is a modeling and scenario-building exercise that uses a unified logic of burning only economically optimal fossil fuels to maximize social welfare, keeps the globe within the expected "carbon budget" to stay below two degrees, and does not include political factors in which regions must make such sacrifices. McGlade and Ekins 2015.

83. Vergara et al. 2013a.

84. "Climatescope 2014" 2014.

85. Flavin et al. 2014.

86. UNEP 2010.

87. Roberts and Thanos 2003; UNEP 2010; Silva 2012.

88. ECLAC 2014a.

89. Hicks et al. 2008. This was in the area of the allocation of environmental foreign assistance.

90. Extractivism (*Extractavismo*, in Spanish) refers to a capitalist economy in which the exploitation of natural resources is seen as key to the wealth of a nation. See, for example, Gudynas 2009; Bunker 1985; Cardoso and Faletto 1979; Padua 2002.

91. See, e.g., Roberts and Thanos 2003.

92. Sinnott, Nash, and de la Torre 2010.

93. World Bank 2010.

94. Moreno 2011; IMF 2010; ECLAC 2010b.

95. "Brazil Takes Off" 2009; "The Dragon Is in the Backyard" 2009.

96. Karl 1996.

97. ECLAC 2014a. See also Karl 1996.

98. ECLAC 2014a.

99. Edwards and Roberts 2014.

100. MacArthur Foundation 2011.

101. Gallagher et al. 2012.

102. UNEP 2010.

103. E.g., Schnaiberg and Gould 1994; Bunker 1985; O'Connor 1979; Rudel, Roberts, and Carmin 2011.

104. Donnelly 2008 describes several of the stereotypes often applied to realists, each with some truth but exaggerated for most acting realists.

105. Gardini and Lambert 2011.

106. Hurrell and Sengupta 2012.

107. E.g., Hochstetler 2012; Blaxekjær and Nielsen 2014.

108. Blaxekjær and Nielsen 2014, 12.

109. See also Roberts and Parks 2007; Najam 2005.

110. See, e.g., Najam 2005; Roberts and Parks 2007.

111. Hakim 2011.

112. Latin America's traditional partners—the US and the EU—have climate change initiatives in Latin America. The US has a (nominal) Energy and Climate Partnership of the Americas, and the EU has a program to build capacity across government agencies called EUROCLIMA. As of April 2015, China and Latin America have yet to establish a region-wide initiative on climate change.

113. ECLAC 2012.

114. Shixue n.d.

115. Putnam 1988.

116. Martins 2011.

117. UNEP 2010.

118. See, e.g., Roberts and Thanos 2003; Hochstetler and Keck 2007.

119. Harrison and Sundstrom 2007, 1–4; 2010.

120. Harrison and Sundstrom 2007, 2010.

121. Atiq Rahmin, cited in Roberts and Parks 2007.

122. DeSombre 2005.

123. Townshend and Matthews 2013, 1–5.

124. At COP20, ALBA was considerably less vocal. Bolivia offered a position paper on a mechanism for equity and development but did not block the consensus as the negotiations came to a close.

125. Brazil's emphasis has been placed more on the responsibility of wealthy countries to meet their promises and obligations than its own need for funding in order for it to take more action.

Chapter 2: Latin America's Emerging Leadership on Climate Change

1. Santos 2010.

2. Moreno 2011.

3. Ibid.

4. World Bank 2009a, 2009b, 2010.

5. IMF 2010; Moreno 2011; ECLAC 2010b.

6. Lagos and Rosales 2013.

7. "The Great Deceleration" 2014.

8. ECLAC 2014c.

9. Ocampo 2014.

10. "The Great Deceleration" 2014.

11. De la Torre et al. 2014.

12. Gardini and Lambert 2011.

13. Amaral 2011.

14. ECLAC 2014a.

15. Comments made by Ana Toni, CDL, NIVELA, NRDC side event, Lima, Peru, December 11, 2014.

16. Oppenheimer 2014.

17. See, e.g., Roberts 2011.

18. Steven and Bujones 2013.

19. ECLAC 2014a.

20. As DeSombre 2005 found for the US. Citing the example of reductions in deforestation prior to Brazil announcing its 2009 emissions reduction target, Kathryn Hochstetler commented to us in April 2015 that Brazil takes climate action at the global level once it has secured national progress on the issue.

21. G77 2015.

22. Garibaldi, Araya, and Edwards 2012.

23. OAS 2015.

24. Gardini 2011.

25. Shifter 2012.

26. Gardini 2009.

27. See, e.g., Roberts 2007.

28. Meadows, Dennis, and Behrens 1972.

29. Catton 1980.

30. Guimarães 1986.

31. Cardoso and Faletto 1979; Roberts and Thanos 2003.

32. Prebisch 1950; Frank 1969; Cardoso and Faletto 1979.

33. See review in Roberts, Bellone-Hite, and Chorev 2015.

34. Galeano 1994.

35. See, e.g., Viola 1995; Hochstetler and Keck 2007.

36. Hurrell and Sengupta 2012.

37. See Muller, Höhne, and Ellerman 2009.

38. An exception is perhaps Argentina, which had a large role growing out of its interest in the ozone regime. See Hochstetler 2002.

39. Cole and Liverman 2011.

40. Ott et al. 2005.

41. Dillon 2000; Roberts and Parks 2007.

42. Garibaldi 2014.

43. Hochstetler and Viola 2011.

44. Garibaldi 2009.

45. Marshall 2008.

46. Brazil 2008.

47. Gera 2008.

48. Ibid.

49. Ximenes 2008.

50. Garibaldi, Araya, and Edwards 2012.

51. IEA 2014a, 2014b.

52. Riahi et al. 2011.

53. Vergara et al. 2013a, 2013b.

54. Ibid.

55. Hirschfeld 2014.

56. Edwards 2008.

57. Buytaert et al. 2010.

58. Condo 2012.

59. Magrin and Marengo 2014.

60. Boccaletti 2013.

61. ECLAC 2012.

62. Klein 2014.

63. Fearnside 2011.

64. Fearnside 2002.

65. Reasons for omitting these emissions may be that they are considered controversial or uncertain or have no scientific consensus on their measurement or comparability with emissions from other sectors; other reasons may be the inconvenience of complex processes in calculating national carbon accounts.

66. Fearnside and Pueyo 2012.

67. Finer and Jenkins 2012.

68. Howard 2014.

69. "Chile's Energy Dilemma" 2014.

70. Howard 2014.

71. Craze 2014.

72. Climate Action Tracker 2014a, 2014b.

73. Shortell 2014.

74. See, e.g., Steinberger and Roberts 2010; Steinberger et al. 2012.

75. World Bank 2012a, 2010b.

76. IPEM-SP n.d.

77. Roberts and Thanos 2003.

78. "Road Space Rationing" 2015.

79. Eduardo Viola, personal communication, August 2014.

80. "Road Space Rationing" 2015.

81. This approach has also been adopted in a couple of Brazilian cities. In both cases, the problem arises when people who can afford to buy a second car, to drive on alternate days.

82. Tompkins 2005.

83. Hoyos et al. 2013.

84. Paula Caballero, personal communication, September 2012.

85. Bumpas and Liverman 2008.

86. Kirkland 2012.

87. E.g., Hochstetler and Keck 2007.

88. Friedman 2014.

89. Javier Gonzales Iwanciw, personal communication, July 2014.

90. Friedman 2014.

91. Lagos 2014.

92. Eduardo Viola, personal communication, August 2014.

93. Argentina and Saudi Arabia are the only countries in the G20 not to have filed a pledge under the Copenhagen Accord. Personal communication between Kathryn Hochstetler and the authors, January 2015.

94. Garibaldi, Araya, and Edwards 2012.

95. We discuss this issue at significant length in Ciplet, Roberts, and Khan 2015.

Chapter 3: Brazil: Climate Leader or Spoiler?

1. BBC 2009.

2. Gibson 2013.

3. Ibid.

4. "Copper Solution" 2013.

5. Davies 2014.

6. After the mayor of São Paulo announced bus and metro fare hikes, protests were organized and spread to over a hundred cities across Brazil, with more than a million people on the streets that month. Prada and Marcello 2013.

7. Dimenstein 2013.

8. See, for example, Reid 2014.

9. Da Silva 2009.

10. Ministério da Ciência, Tecnologia e Inovacão (MCTI), Secretaria de Políticas e Programas de Pesquisa e Desenvolvimento (SEPED), and Coordenação Geral de Mudanças Globais de Clima (CGMC) 2013.

11. La Rovere et al. 2013.

12. REN21 2014. See, for example, "Climatescope 2014" 2014. According to the Climatescope report in 2014, which ranks countries on their level of attractiveness for clean energy investment, Brazil ranked second only to China.

13. Brazil seeks to become one of the world's top oil producers for export. According to Mauricio Tolmasquim, president of the government's Energy Research Company, by 2023 Brazil will produce 5 million barrels per day with 30 percent for export, while maintaining a clean energy mix and growing renewable capacity at home. Ministério de Minas e Energia 2014.

14. Viola and Hochstetler 2014, 12.

15. On the impasse, see, e.g., Roberts and Parks 2007; Roberts 2011; Ciplet, Roberts, and Khan 2015; and Grasso and Roberts 2014. Brazil was not alone in creating this impasse, and many other countries and nonstate actors contributed to this difficult situation.

16. Roberts and Parks 2007.

17. See, e.g., Roberts 2011.

18. Viola and Hochstetler 2014.

19. Often cited in these situations was a 2011 paper by Kartha and Erickson. The authors make and support the point that developing countries were doing more than developed countries to reduce their emissions.

20. Toni 2014.

21. Teixeira 2014.

22. Ibid.

23. Rittl 2014.

24. EcoEquity.org. 2014.

25. Kirsch 2014.

26. See, e.g., Boyd et al. 2009.

27. E.g., ibid.

28. Pulver, Hultman, and Guimarães 2010; Hultman et al. 2012.

29. UNEP/DTU Partnership 2014.

30. The Science and Technology agency (CNPQ) struggled with the environment agency (IBAMA), the Ministry of Finance, and Ministry of External Relations.

31. Viola and Hochstetler 2014, 18.

32. Halding et al. 2011.

33. Masters 2012.

34. Hochstetler and Viola 2012; Viola and Hochstetler 2014.

35. Olsson et al. 2010.

36. Lagos 2014.

37. Masters 2012.

38. See Hallding et al. 2011; Rachman 2010; Ciplet, Roberts, and Khan 2015. At the end of the Doha negotiations, the US chief negotiator, Todd Stern, proclaimed victory in the Copenhangen/Cancun round by eroding the firewall between the global North with commitments and the South without.

39. "Brazil, South Africa, China, India (BASIC) and the Climate Change Conundrum: Round Table Discussions," Chatham House, February 2011, cited in Hallding et al. 2011.

40. Hallding et al. 2011.

41. We leave India off this list because its per capita emissions are so much lower than China's, Brazil's, and South Africa's. See PBL Netherland Environmental Assessment Agency 2013.

42. Hallding et al. 2011. The new BRICS bank will extend loans to developing countries from the contributions made by the BRICS nations.

43. Hochstetler 2012.

44. Hochstetler and Viola 2012.

45. Hallding et al. 2011.

46. Ibid.

47. Viola 2013.

48. EU delegate, interview with the authors, COP19, Warsaw, November 2013.

49. Viola and Hochstetler 2014, 16.

50. Roberts 2011.

51. Hurrell and Sengupta 2012, 463.

52. Lagos, Hounshell, and Dickinson 2012; Hakim 2011.

53. Cabral 2010.

54. Trinkunas 2014.

55. Lagos, Hounshell, and Dickinson 2012.

56. Trinkunas 2014, 5–6.

57. Alves de Carmo and Pecequilo 2012.

58. Trinkunas 2014.

59. Ibid.

60. Brand and Schewel 2012.

61. Hochstetler 2013.

62. Malamud 2011.

63. Trinkunas 2014.

64. Ibid.

65. Saraiva 2011.

66. UNASUR is still under construction. Its first budget proposal was approved in March 2012, and committees are drafting the general regulation for their operation. UNASUR has eight ministerial councils that cover topics from defense to health. Most of the councils are beginning to function, and the early initiatives show some of the regional priorities.

67. Saraiva 2011.

68. Burges 2013.

69. For further details on how Brazil is perceived by other developing countries and in this case India at the World Trade Organization, see Hopewell 2015.

70. Nepstad et al. 2014.

71. Hochstetler and Viola 2012.

72. UNEP and ACTO 2009.

73. Vergara et al. 2013a, 2013b.

74. Secretariat for Social Communication 2010.

75. We tell some of this history in Roberts and Thanos 2003, chapter 5, where there are more sources.

76. Lemos and Roberts. 2008.

77. Foweraker 1981; Pompermeyer 1984. See also Roberts and Thanos 2003.

78. Bunker 1985.

79. Lemos and Roberts 2008.

80. Eduardo Viola, personal communication, 2014.

81. Cardoso et al. 2012. See also Nepstad et al. 2014.

82. Eduardo Viola, interview with the authors, April 2013.

83. Nepstad et al. 2014; Brazilian Secretariat for Social Communication (SECOM) 2010.

84. UNEP and ACTO 2009.

85. Bovarnick, Alpizar, and Schnell 2010.

86. Eduardo Viola, personal communication, 2014.

87. The report is available online at http://www.greenpeace.org/international/Global/international/planet-2/report/2006/4/amazon-soya-crime-file.pdf.

88. "McDonald's Pledges" 2006.

89. Nepstad et al. 2014.

90. Macedo et al. 2012; VanWey et al. 2013.

91. Padua 2002.

92. Nepstad et al 2014.

93. Assunção et al. 2012.

94. Eduardo Viola, personal communication, 2014.

95. Tollefson 2013.

96. IEA 2014.

97. Tollefson 2013.

98. WRI 2012.

99. Brazilian Secretariat for Social Communication (SECOM) 2010; INPE 2010.

100. Viola, Franchini, and Ribeiro 2012.

101. Prada 2013.

102. Butler 2014a.

103. Cardoso et al. 2012.

104. "Brazil Takes Off" 2009.

105. "Has Brazil Blown It?" 2013.

106. World Bank 2014.

107. UNEP and ACTO 2009.

108. "Brazil President Makes Final Changes" 2012.

109. AOSIS 2012.

110. Leahy 2014.

111. Although deforestation rates were lower in 2010 than in 2000, Fearnside, Figueiredo, and Bonjour 2013 confirm that soybean-planted areas increased both exports and deforestation over this period.

112. Ibid.

113. Ibid.

114. Finally, the ABC (Agriculture for Low Carbon) Program is designed to help farmers take up techniques and technologies to reduce emissions from farming, but it is chronically underfunded. Cardoso et al. 2012.

115. This figure is based on the 2008 National Energy Balance produced by the Brazilian ministry of mines and energy, cited in World Bank 2012a, 2012b.

116. ECLAC 2007.

117. Marcio Pontual, interview with the authors, Brasilia, April 2013.

118. IEA 2014.

119. Nachmany et al. 2014; IEA 2014.

120. Plautz 2014. For information about the development of Brazil's wind and solar sectors see Hochstetler and Kostka, forthcoming.

121. Butler 2014a.

122. UNEP 2010.

123. REN21 2014.

124. IEA 2014.

125. Anderlini 2011.

126. US EIA 2013.

127. Ferreira et al. 2014.

128. Ibid.

129. Ibid.

130. Gardner 2014.

131. See, e.g., Hochstetler and Keck 2007.

132. Cardoso et al. 2012.

133. Trennepohl 2010.

134. Rittl 2014.

135. Teixeira 2014.

136. Larco 2012.

137. Watts 2014.

138. Romero 2015.

139. Trennepohl 2010.

140. Brazilian Secretariat for Social Communication (SECOM) 2010.

141. Hurrell and Sengupta 2012.

142. Viola 2013.

143. Viola, Franchini, and Riberio 2012.

144. Held, Roger, and Nag 2013.

145. Hochstetler and Viola 2012.

146. Burck, Bals, and Parker 2010.

147. Burck, Marten, and Bals 2014.

148. Climate Action Network 2014a, 2014b.

149. Sustainable Development Solutions Network (SDSN) and Institute for Sustainable Development and International Relations (IDDRI) 2014.

150. Amazon Fund 2014.

151. Kozloff 2011.

Chapter 4: "A Flea in the Ear"?

1. Salerno 2009.

2. Sudan and Tuvalu were the other two countries that voted against the Copenhagen Accord.

3. Espinosa 2009.

4. Vidal 2009.

5. Goldenberg 2010.

6. Goodman 2012.

7. Chávez 2009.

8. ALBA 2009.

9. Granizo, personal communication, August 1, 2012.

10. Andrés Flores, former director of research on climate change, National Institute of Ecology, Mexico, personal communication with the authors, December 2013.

11. Allan 2013.

12. Soto 2004; Gardini 2011.

13. Venezuela 2011; Gardini 2011.

14. Soto 2004.

15. Fuentes and Pereira 2011.

16. Heine 2012.

17. Gardini 2011.

18. Jácome 2011.

19. Glickhouse 2013.

20. ALBA-TCP 2009a.

21. Ibid.

22. ALBA-TCP 2009c. The summit also produced a Special Declaration for a Universal Declaration of Mother Earth Rights, stating that it is "impossible to achieve full human rights protection if at the same time we do not recognize and defend the rights of the planet earth and nature." ALBA-TCP 2009b.

23. "Cable sobre la pasividad del Gobierno de Bolivia" 2010.

24. In Copenhagen, ALBA leaders such as Chávez and Morales portrayed themselves as speaking on behalf of the people. In Copenhagen, thousands of protestors were on the streets demanding action on climate change. President Chávez said: "A spectre is haunting the streets of Copenhagen. Capitalism is the spectre.... It's capitalism, the people roar out there. Hear them." Socialist Voice 2010.

25. Other countries such as Mexico and AILAC members have also conducted similar meetings with civil society groups in the spirit of dialogue.

26. Edwards 2012.

27. ALBA's declarations on climate change by heads of state in 2009 provided important indications of its likely positions at COP15.

28. Kathryn Hochstetler, personal communication with the authors, November 22, 2011.

29. Luis Alfonso de Alba, personal communication with the authors, March 2013.

30. John Ashton, personal communication with the authors, September 2012.

31. Edwards 2010a, 2010b.

32. Goldenberg 2010.

33. Lee 2010.

34. Carrington 2010.

35. "Copenhagen Ends by Only 'Noting' an Accord" 2009. The former UK lead delegate and minister, Ed Milliband, according to the Third World Network, was also blunt about linking the funding of developing countries with accepting the Accord.

36. African Group, Least Developed Countries Group, and ALBA Group 2011a.

37. African Group, Least Developed Countries Group, and ALBA Group 2011b.

38. Interview with Bolivian delegate to the UNFCCC in COP17, December 2011; Fuentes 2011.

39. Stalley 2013. See also Hallding et al. 2011 and Roberts and Parks 2007.

40. E.g., Hallding et al. 2011; Roberts and Parks 2007.

41. E.g., Roberts 2011.

42. Allan and Edwards 2011.

43. Goodman 2009.

44. Aguirre and Cooper 2010.

45. Shultz 2010.

46. Morales 2010a, 2010b.

47. World People's Conference on Climate Change and the Rights of Mother Earth 2010.

48. Lee 2010.

49. Guachalla 2010.

50. ECLAC 2010d.

51. Shultz 2010; Balbus 2011a, 2011b.

52. According to the Conference website: "The People's Agreement stems from an integral vision of climate change, incorporating the issue of the structural causes of the climate crisis, the rupture of harmony with nature, the need to recognize the rights of Mother Earth in order to guarantee human rights and the importance of creating a Tribunal of Climate and Environmental Justice." World People's Conference on Climate Change and the Rights of Mother Earth 2010.

53. Balbus 2011a, 2011b.

54. Raman 2010.

55. "Climate Change Tops UN Chief's Talks" 2010.

56. "People's Agreement of Cochabamba" 2010.

57. Balbus 2011a, 2011b.

58. Ibid.

59. Aguirre and Cooper 2010.

60. Balbus 2011a, 2011b.

61. Another Bolivian senator said that Morales's climate change campaign is about enhancing his global stature, not about the environment. The senator said that there is a huge gap between Morales's proenvironmental rhetoric in international meetings and his domestic emphasis on industrialization. "Cable sobre la pasividad del Gobierno de Bolivia" 2010.

62. Solón mentioned Bolivia's disappointment at the text: "We expected a text with different options in order to negotiate them; not a text of what the Chair thinks is the consensus of a discussion that has not been a negotiation between the Parties. It is not for the Chair to say whether we have consensus or not. It is the role of the Chair to facilitate negotiations." Bolivia 2010.

63. Delegation of the Plurinational State of Bolivia 2010.

64. World People's Conference on Climate Change and the Rights of Mother Earth 2010.

65. Marien 2011.

66. Solón 2010a.

67. Estrada 2010.

68. Delegation of the Plurinational State of Bolivia 2010.

69. Butler 2010.

70. Chemnick and Friedman 2010.

71. Solón 2010b.

72. "Cancún" 2010.

73. Friedman 2010.

74. Randerson and Batty 2010.

75. Marien 2011.

76. Solón 2010b.

77. Sterk et al. 2011.

78. However, Salerno hailed the results of the conference as positive, particularly the creation of the Green Climate Fund. The Cuban negotiator, Orlando Rey, also expressed his satisfaction with the result and said that it helped everyone "regain confidence in the value of multilateralism." Cabezas 2010.

79. Friedman 2010; Chemnick and Friedman 2010.

80. Enciso 2010.

81. The road through the Isiboro Secure Indigenous Territory and National Park (Territorio Indígena y Parque Nacional Isiboro-Secure, TIPNIS) was designed to provide the first direct route between the city of Cochabamba and Beni Departments. Indigenous groups in TIPNIS stated their strong opposition and marched against the project. Opposition focused on the concern that deforestation in the park could rapidly increase if the road is built. In early October, the Plurinational Legislative Assembly passed legislation authored by the Movimiento al Socialismo (MAS – Movement for Socialism) authorizing the road following a consultation process, but indigenous deputies and the indigenous movement opposed the bill. At the opening of negotiations with the protesters on October 21, Morales announced that he would veto the legislation and support the text proposed by the indigenous deputies. This text was passed by the Assembly and signed into law on October 24, effectively ending the conflict. Law 180 of 2011 declares TIPNIS to be an untouchable zone and prohibits the construction of highways that cross it. "El Presidente promulga" 2011.

82. Solón 2011.

83. Nele Marien, former member of Bolivia's delegation to the UNFCCC, personal communication with the authors, October 2012.

84. Ibid.

85. Rene Orellana, personal communication with the authors, COP18, Doha, December 2012.

86. "Bolivia to Host People's Climate Change Summit Ahead of COP21" 2014.

87. Correa 2007.

88. Edwards 2010a, 2010b.

89. "Ecuador Pledges" 2010.

90. UNDP-Peru 2014.

91. Ecuador n.d.

92. Martin 2011; Madden 2014.

93. Edwards 2010a, 2010b.

94. In 2000, Alberto Acosta and Acción Ecológica, an Ecuadorian NGO, published a book entitled *El Ecuador Post-Petrolero*, which called for a moratorium on oil extraction in the Amazon and a move toward alternative energy sources for the country. Martin 2011.

95. "ITT Block Will Go" 2009.

96. "The Government Freezes Extraction from Yasuní" 2009.

97. Larrea 2012.

98. Ibid.

99. Martin 2011.

100. Correa 2013.

101. Araujo 2013.

102. Watts 2013.

103. Ibid.

104. "Tres propuestas" 2013.

105. Hill 2014b.

106. Jarrín 2014.

107. In May 2014, Yasunidos made an appeal to the National Electoral Council, but its appeal was rejected because it was not submitted in sufficient time. "Ecuador Rejects Vote" 2014. The Yasunidos collective lobbied the Inter-American Court of Human Rights to elicit a response about the situation in relation to the submission of the signatures to the National Electoral Council and also accusations that the Ecuadorian government is persecuting Yasunidos activists. "Yasunidos buscará respuesta" 2014.

108. Hance 2014.

109. "Yasunidos buscará respuesta" 2014.

110. Hill 2014a, 2014b, 2014c.

111. Gudynas 2014.

112. "Government of Ecuador Shuts Down Fundacion Pachamama" 2013. Then during the COP20, Ecuador police repeatedly stopped a group of activists who were on their way to the COP20 and eventually seized their bus. The activists from the Yasunidos group were en route to Lima to protest against the decision to extract oil from reserves under Ecuador's Yasuní National Park. According to the activists, they were stopped because President Correa sought to avoid any potentially embarrassing

incidences in Lima. Government officials in Ecuador say they stopped the bus because the driver had incorrect documentation. Collyns 2014b.

113. Chávez 2009.

114. Nachmany et al. 2014.

115. Venezuela 2012.

116. OPEC n.d.

117. Bull 2008.

118. Inter-American Dialogue 2013.

119. Crooks 2011.

120. Downs 2011.

121. Inter-American Dialogue 2013.

122. Petrocaribe has supplied its members with hundreds of thousands of barrels per day and has promised to contribute to the cost of developing and repairing refineries, but so far, repair of the Cienfuegos refinery in Cuba is the only project that has been completed. Cote 2011.

123. Jácome 2011.

124. Altmann 2011.

125. Jácome 2011.

126. Rojas 2011.

127. Trinkunas 2014.

128. Oppenheimer 2014.

129. Goodman 2012.

130. Venezuela 2005; WRI n.d.

131. Edwards and Mage 2012.

132. Nachmany et al. 2014.

133. "Oil Rich Venezuela Inks Plan" 2012.

134. "Climatescope 2013" 2013.

135. Venezuelan climate change scientist, personal communication with the authors, December 2012.

136. Mallett-Outtrim 2013.

137. Chávez 2013.

138. Edwards supported regional groups in the drafting and circulation of this declaration.

139. Edwards 2013b.

140. Goodman 2013.

141. Edwards, Murphy, and Eisner 2014.

142. Tong 2014.

143. "Changing the System Not the Climate" 2014.

144. Red ARA Venezuela 2014.

145. Yeo 2014.

146. Tong 2014.

147. Fernández 2014.

148. Villamizar and Edwards 2014.

149. McKibben 2012.

150. McGlade and Ekins 2015.

151. Garibaldi, Araya, and Edwards 2012.

152. Shifter 2012.

153. In late 2013, the Quito office of the Foundation Pachamama was closed by the Ecuadorian government. Alvaro 2013.

154. Shultz 2010.

155. Wallace 2013.

156. Gudynas 2014.

157. Gudynas 2012.

158. Lander 2010.

159. Richard Shackleton, UK Foreign Office, personal communication with the authors, June 2012; Tarsicio Granizo, Ecuadorian Ministry for Natural and Cultural Heritage, personal communication with the authors, July 2012.

Chapter 5: The Revolt of the Middle

1. "AILAC será un 'modelo'" 2013.

2. Although Chile is a member of the Organisation for Economic Co-operation and Development (OECD), it continues to negotiate with the G77 at the UNFCCC.

Mexico is an OECD country and therefore outside of the G77. It forms part of the Environmental Integrity Group, with Lichtenstein, Monaco, South Korea, and Switzerland. Mexico is part of the G20 and Major Economies Forum along with Argentina and Brazil from Latin America.

3. Gardini and Lambert 2011.

4. Ramírez 2013.

5. Gilberto Arias, former ambassador from Panama to the United Kingdom, personal communication with the authors, December 21, 2012.

6. Garibaldi et al. 2010.

7. Garibaldi et al. 2014.

8. Pineda 2012; Bowering 2012.

9. Cartagena Dialogue 2010; Araya 2011a, 2011b; Lynas 2011.

10. Garibaldi et al. 2012.

11. Pineda 2012.

12. Araya 2011a, 2011b.

13. Mark Lynas, personal communication with the authors, COP17, Durban, December 2011.

14. Bangladesh 2013.

15. Balbus 2010.

16. Ibid.

17. Balbus 2011a, 2011b.

18. Interview with Luis Alfonso de Alba, March 2013, and personal communication with the authors, April 2014.

19. Bialek 2010.

20. Luis Alfonso de Alba, personal communication with the authors, March 2013.

21. Rodolfo Godínez, member of Mexico's UNFCCC delegation, personal communication with the authors, Doha, December, 2012.

22. Luis Alfonso de Alba, personal communication with the authors, March 2013.

23. Park 2011.

24. Friedman 2010.

25. Park 2011.

26. Espinosa 2010a.

27. Espinosa 2010b.

28. Park 2011.

29. Benavides 2006.

30. De Alba was surprised at Solón's criticism after COP16 because he believed Bolivia had had plenty of time to put forward concerns. Luis Alfonso de Alba, personal communication with the authors, March 2013.

31. La Vina, Ang, and Dulce 2011.

32. Park 2011.

33. Nele Marien, former member of Bolivia's delegation, personal communication with the authors, October 2012.

34. Espinosa 2011.

35. Luis Alfonso de Alba, personal communication with the authors, March 2013.

36. Ibid.

37. Civil society mobilization and Mexico's worst drought in over seventy years during 2011 also galvanized support for the General Law on Climate Change.

38. Nachmany et al. 2014.

39. "Mexico's President Enacts Climate Change Legislation" 2012.

40. Black 2012.

41. "Mexico Awards 83% of Oil Reserves to State Firm Pemex" 2014.

42. US EIA 2014.

43. Sustainable Development Solutions Network (SDSN) and Institute for Sustainable Development and International Relations (ISDIR) 2014.

44. Centro Mexicano de Derecho Ambiental 2014.

45. Gabriela Niño, comments made at a CDL, NIVELA, NRDC side event, Lima, Peru, December 11, 2014.

46. Teixeira 2012.

47. "Mexican President Presents" 2013.

48. Smith 2014.

49. Höhne et al. 2012.

50. Garibaldi et al. 2014.

51. Ibid.

52. Garibaldi et al. 2012.

53. According to Jose Alberto Garibaldi, who was seminal in helping to create AILAC, the Peruvian case emerged from a growing awareness of what the country stood to gain and lose by being more or less ambitious in a high-ambition international coalition, taking into account mitigation, adaptation, and climate impacts. Garibaldi 2009; Garibaldi, Figari, and Gamio 2009.

54. Peru Ministerio del Ambiente 2009.

55. Painter 2008.

56. Marshall 2008.

57. Garibaldi et al. 2014.

58. IISD 2009.

59. Garibaldi 2009, 2014.

60. Colombia heard misleading information at the negotiations that the EU was not willing to reject the proposal of the South African COP presidency, despite the proposal not including references to commitments for all countries or strong language on the legal nature of the agreement. The Colombian delegation spoke to its minister about the situation. Frank Pearl, former Colombian minister of environment, gave the delegation authorization to reject the current package if necessary. The Colombian delegation then approached the former EU Climate Action Commissioner, Connie Hedegaard, about the weak text. Hedegaard responded that she did not know what the Colombia delegation was talking about and that the EU did actually want to reject the South African president's proposal given how weak it was. The EU made an intervention that called for the text to refer to commitments for all countries and strong language on the legal nature of the agreement, and Colombia intervened along similar lines. Colombia was a nonpermanent member of the UN Security Council from 2011 to 2012. Although Borda and Castillo (2011) suggest that Colombia was implementing a "highly pragmatic and non-aligned strategy," Colombia's potential decision to reject the Durban Package is also likely to have been based on the domestic context. From 2010 to 2011, Colombia was adversely affected by La Niña phenomenon, which caused severe flooding, hundreds of deaths, and over US$7 billion in damages.

61. Andrea García, former member of Colombia's UNFCCC delegation, October 2012.

62. Mabey 2012.

63. One of AILAC's principal positions has emphasized the importance of equity while promoting a flexible interpretation of CBDR+RC that encourages all countries

to commit to reducing their emissions. AILAC considers that all countries should contribute but that each country's differentiated capacities and responsibilities need to be reflected in the negotiations. Developed countries need to lead on this endeavor by making drastic reductions in their emissions, but all countries need to act to the best of their ability. AILAC says that developed countries have historic responsibilities for causing climate change but that this framing alone will not help make progress at the UNFCCC. AILAC focuses on the "Common" part of the concept of CBDR+RC. The "Respective Capabilities" element is looked at not as a barrier to action but as a gateway through which to generate it. AILAC does state that developed countries need to provide climate finance and technology transfer to developing countries, which is similar to broader G77 positions. Gilberto Arias, former ambassador from Panama to the UK, personal communication with the authors, December 21, 2012.

64. Méndez 2012.

65. Friedman 2013a, 2013b.

66. Ibid.

67. Castro and the Minister of Environment, Energy, and Telecommunications 2012.

68. Roberts and Edwards 2012.

69. Sarah Thacker, formerly UK Department of Energy and Climate Change, personal communication with the authors, February 2013.

70. With the exception of the COP20, which gave the Peruvian delegation a considerable boost.

71. Ryan 2012.

72. Manuel Rodríguez Becerra, personal communication with the authors, October 2012.

73. See, e.g., Roberts and Edwards 2012.

74. Costa Rica 2009.

75. Porras et al. 2012.

76. Costa Rica 2009.

77. Dobles 2008.

78. Costa Rica abolished its military in 1948, and Arias received the Nobel peace prize in 1987 for leading negotiations between rebels and governments in two of Central America's civil wars. Fletcher 2013.

79. Costa Rica 2009.

80. Or 30 percent if other nations also make commitments.

81. Marshall 2008.

82. Nachmany et al. 2014.

83. He lifted a ban on open-pit mining, which caused considerable criticism. Carlos Manuel Rodríguez from Conservation International called Arias "neither serious nor coherent on the issue of the environment." Roberto Jiménez, an activist who started the group co2neutral2021.org, said that Costa Rica's carbon output increased more during the first three years of Arias's presidency than it had in the previous ten years combined. Rogers 2009. See also Roberto Jiménez, press release, August 9, 2009, quoted in Fletcher 2013.

84. Fletcher 2013.

85. Ibid.

86. Although hydropower is generally considered a cleaner source of energy compared to fossil fuels, hydroelectric dams can produce emissions from methane produced by rotting vegetation submerged in reservoirs. These emissions are not measured or taken into account in calculating Costa Rica's carbon balance. Robert Fletcher argues that the inclusion of these emissions from hydroelectric dams in the country's carbon-neutral calculations would probably make it difficult for Costa Rica to ever achieve its goals. Fletcher 2010. Chapter 2 also addresses the double edge of big hydro.

87. To offset these emissions, the carbon-neutral plan stipulated that 20 to 25 percent of the country's transport would need to have switched to carbon-neutral alternatives by 2014, and according to Leiner Vargas, who advises the government on the pledge, this has not happened. Fendt 2014a, 2014b.

88. Dyer 2014.

89. Fendt 2014.

90. Cota 2013a, 2013b.

91. Cedeño 2013.

92. Ibid.

93. Friedman 2013a; Climate Action Network International 2013. Leiner Vargas at Costa Rica's National University argues that the new refinery could result in losses of up to US$300 million per year and would increase the price of petrol. Contreras 2013.

94. Araya 2013a, 2013b.

95. Rueda 2013.

96. Araya 2013a, 2013b.

97. There are also concerns that the new oil refinery could be a bridgehead for future oil and gas exploitation in the area. Alvarez 2013.

98. Due to a conflict of interest between a Chinese company and Costa Rica's RECOPE, the project was temporarily frozen, and RECOPE's Executive President Jorge Villalobos resigned in June 2013. Font 2013.

99. Arguedas 2014.

100. "Costa Rica y China" 2014.

101. Edwards 2013a, 2013b.

102. "Deals to Link Costa Rican Market" 2013.

103. Blázquez and Martín-Moreno 2012.

104. "Deals to Link Costa Rican Market" 2013.

105. Nachmany et al. 2014.

106. Yale University 2013. Conducted every other year, the EPI features new categories such as wastewater treatment, climate change, and energy.

107. This was not the first time that Peru had expressed interest in hosting the climate negotiations. Peru and Mexico competed to host the COP16. But Peru had insufficient space to hold the conference and provide hotel rooms for delegates. Luis Alfonso de Alba, personal communication with the authors, March 2013.

108. WWF 2013.

109. Edwards and Skovgaard 2014.

110. Pulgar-Vidal 2014.

111. Yeo 2014a, 2014b.

112. Edwards and Skovgaard 2014.

113. For example, the authors hosted Minister Pulgar-Vidal at Brown University for the conference they organized in April 2014 with AILAC delegates and former presidents Felipe Calderón and Ricardo Lagos from Mexico and Chile, respectively. The Peru delegation also attended the World Economic Forum in Panama and Forest Asia Summit in Indonesia and various other countries.

114. The inclusiveness of these efforts is unclear. We participated in two such events oriented toward academia. The delegation participated in our conference at Brown University in April 2014, and the Peruvian delegation initiated an event at NYU Law School in September 2014 at which Roberts was invited to present. Neither can be described as broadly inclusive.

115. Peru Ministerio del Ambiente 2013.

116. UNDP-Peru 2014.

117. Climate Action Network 2014a, 2014b.

118. Grupo Peru 2014.

119. Collyns 2014c.

120. Cabitza 2012.

121. Amnesty International 2011.

122. Collyns 2014d.

123. Nachmany et al. 2014.

124. MAPS 2014.

125. Constantine 2014.

126. Villanueva 2014.

127. Ryan 2012.

128. Felandro and Araujo 2012.

129. "Peru Says Deforestation on the Rise" 2014.

130. The current law states that companies must research and write environmental impact assessments (EIAs) of proposed operations before submitting them to the government for approval and beginning exploration. Energy minister Eleodoro Mayorga announced that oil and gas companies that plan to explore by conducting seismic tests will be exempt from the EIA process. A report by a Peruvian newspaper *Gestión* stated that the new law, according to Mayorga, is intended to weaken protections and speed investment. Peruvian journalist Claudia Cisneros said that Mayorga's announcement is evidence of a government "subjugated by the extractive industries' big lobbyists to the detriment of the environment, social harmony, and those without a voice." Hill 2014c.

131. Ibid.

132. "Congreso peruano" 2014.

133. Presidency of Peru 2014.

134. Collyns 2014a; Cruz 2014.

135. "Peruvian Government Guts Power" 2014.

136. Bell 2014.

137. Jacobs 2014.

138. Garibaldi et al. 2012.

139. Hochstetler 2012.

140. Castro and the Minister of Environment, Energy, and Telecommunications 2012.

141. In Lima, the presidents of the Pacific Alliance presented the Declaration of the Pacific Alliance on Climate Change. The declaration emphasizes that climate change is one of the greatest global challenges that requires concrete actions by all countries. This is significant given it is the first time that leaders of the Pacific Alliance have made such a statement on the issue, but it lacks specifics.

Chapter 6: Sustainable Action?

1. Santos 2010.

2. Hicks et al. 2008.

3. Schnaiberg and Gould 1997.

4. Harrison and Sundstrom 2007, 2010; Tanner and Allouche 2011; Rootes, Zito, and Barry 2012.

5. CAN-International 2010, 4.

6. Muñoz 2010.

7. Figueres 2011.

8. Roberts et al. 2014.

9. Painter 2009.

10. Hurrell and Sengupta 2012.

11. See also Garibaldi et al. 2012.

12. See, e.g., Agrawal, Narain, and Sharma 1999; Najam 2004; Roberts and Parks 2007; Roberts 2011.

13. Waldemar Coutts, personal communication with the authors, Lima, Peru, December 2014.

14. Vergara et al. 2013b.

15. The public consultation carried out by the Chilean government from December 2014 through April 2015 on the design of its Intended Nationally Determined Contribution for the Paris climate conference is a notable exception.

16. *The Guardian* reported that the antilogging campaigner Edwin Chota and three other Ashéninka leaders were killed in Peru in September 2014 over land disputes.

17. The ranking is based on a list produced by the University of Pennsylvania and quoted in Edwards and Mage 2013.

18. Although the total number of Latin American contributing authors has increased since 2007, the percentage of authors from the region has actually decreased. In 2007, Latin American authors represented 12 percent of the total 620 contributing authors to the IPCC's Fourth Assessment Report. Now they represent just over 10 percent of the total. Latin America's limited scientific impact can be attributed to funding shortages because countries invest a little more than 0.6 percent of their GDP in research and development—well below the global average. Edwards, Elmore, and Lee 2012.

19. For example, the Regional Centre for Climate Change and Decision Making (Centro Regional de Cambio Climático y Toma de Decisiones), which was launched in 2013, is an alliance between the AVINA Foundation and UNESCO and includes the participation of various Latin American universities in Brazil, Uruguay, Paraguay, Argentina, and Chile.

20. We would like to highlight examples from Peru such as the organization DAR (Derecho, Ambiente y Recursos Naturales /Law, Environment and Natural Resources) and Costa Rica Limpia (Clean Costa Rica), which are particularly active in engaging in national debates linking economic and development policy with climate change.

21. Mexico has published five, but most countries in the region have produced around two or three.

22. The Mitigation Action Plans and Scenarios (MAPS) Program, which is a collaboration amongst developing countries including South Africa, Peru, Colombia, Chile, and Brazil, to establish the evidence base for long-term transition to robust economies that are both carbon efficient and climate resilient, is a notable exception that should be expanded throughout Latin America and other regions.

23. Edwards and Mage 2013.

24. Ryan 2012.

25. ECLAC 2014b.

26. Ibid.

27. Vergara, Alatorre, and Alves 2013a.

28. World Resources Institute n.d.

29. Chile Ministry of Environment 2014.

30. Araya 2013a, 2013b.

31. See, e.g., Grasso and Roberts 2014.

32. Nepstad et al. 2014.

33. Friedman 2014.

34. We discuss this issue further in chapter 4.

References

African Group, Least Developed Countries Group, and ALBA Group. 2011a. "African, Least Developed and Latin American Countries Forge New Alliance to Save Climate Regime and Ensure Success in Durban." Press release, October 7. http://climate-justice.info/wp-content/uploads/2011/11/AGN-LDC-ALBA-Panma-PR.pdf.

African Group, Least Developed Countries Group, and ALBA Group. 2011b. "Statement of Common Position: African Group, Group of Least Developed Countries and ALBA Group." http://climate-justice.info/wp-content/uploads/2011/11/Statement-of-Common-Positions-Afr-LDC-ALBA-FINAL.pdf.

Agrawal, Anil, Sunita Narain, and A. Sharma, eds. 1999. *Green Politics: Global Environmental Negotiation. 1, Green Politics*. New Delhi: Centre for Science and Environment.

Aguirre, Jessica Camille, and Elizabeth Sonia Cooper. 2010. "Evo Morales, Climate Change, and the Paradoxes of a Social-Movement Presidency." *Latin American Perspectives* 37: 238.

"AILAC será un 'modelo' de desarrollo y en mitigar los efectos del calentamiento global." 2013. Agencia Peruana de Noticias, August 28. http://www.andina.com.pe/agencia/noticia-ailac-sera-un-modelo-desarrollo-y-mitigar-los-efectos-del-calentamiento-global-472283.aspx#.U7WoidygMhE.

ALBA (Bolivarian Alliance of Latin America and the Caribbean). 2009. "ALBA Declaration on Copenhagen Climate Summit." Venezuelanalysis.com, December 18. http://venezuelanalysis.com/analysis/5038.

ALBA-TCP (Bolivarian Alliance of Latin America and the Caribbean–People's Trade Treaty). 2009a. "VII Summit–Cochabamba, Bolivia–October 17: ALBA–People's Trade Treaty." http://alba-tcp.org/en/contenido/joint-declaration-vii-summit.

ALBA-TCP (Bolivarian Alliance of Latin America and the Caribbean–People's Trade Treaty). 2009b. "VII Summit–Cochabamba, Bolivia–October 17: Special Declaration for a Universal Declaration of Mother Earth Rights." http://alba-tcp.org/en/contenido/special-declaration-universal-declaration-mother-earth-rights.

ALBA-TCP (Bolivarian Alliance of Latin America and the Caribbean–People's Trade Treaty). 2009c."VII Summit–Cochabamba, Bolivia–October 17: Special Declaration on Climate Change of ALBA-TCP towards the XV Copenhagen Conference." http:// alba-tcp.org/en/contenido/special-declaration-climate-change-alba-tcp-vii-summit-towards-xv-copenhagen-conference.

Alexandratos, N., and J. Bruinsma. 2012. "World Agriculture towards 2030/2050: The 2012 Revision." ESA Working Paper No. 12-03. UN Food and Agriculture Organization, Rome.

Allan, Laurence. 2013. IHS—Senior Risk Analyst—Latin America—January. Personal communication.

Allan, Laurence, and Guy Edwards. 2011. "UK-Latin American Relations: Rearranging the Deckchairs." *World Today* 67 (3).

Alliance of Small Island States (AOSIS). 2012. "Nationally Appropriate Mitigation Actions: The Importance of Common Accounting Rules." Session workshop, Ad Hoc Working Group on Long-Term Cooperative Action (AWGLCA), United Nations Framework Convention on Climate Change, Bonn, Germany, May 18.

Altmann, Josette. 2011. "El Alba como propuesta de integración regional." In *Alba: ¿Una nueva forma de integración regional?*, ed. Josette Altmann. San José, Costa Rica: Teseo/Oirla/ Fundación Carolina/Flacso.

Alvarez, Mauricio. 2013. "Opinión: la refinería es el señuelo para explotar gas y petróleo." CRHoy, June 4. http://www.crhoy.com/opinion-la-refineria-es-el-senuelo -para-explotar-gas-y-petroleo.

Alvaro, Mercedes. 2013. "Ecuador Shuts Down Environmental NGO." *Wall Street Journal*, December 4.

Alves do Carmo, Corival, and Cristina Soreanu Pecequilo. 2012. "The Dynamics of Crisis: Brazil, the BRICs and the G-20." *OIKOS* 11 (2): 306–325.

Amaral, Sergio. 2011. "US-Latin America Relations Over the Last Decade." In *A Decade Of Change Political, Economic, and Social Developments in Western Hemisphere Affairs*, ed. Inter-American Dialogue. Washington, DC: Inter-American Dialogue.

Amat y León, Carlos, et al. 2008. *El Cambio Climático no tiene fronteras: Impacto del Cambio Climático en la Comunidad Andina*. Lima: Secretaria General de la Comunidad Andina y la Facultad de Economía de la Universidad del Pacífico.

Amazon Fund. 2014. "Amazon Fund: Projects." http://www.amazonfund.gov.br/ FundoAmazonia/fam/site_en/Esquerdo/Projetos.

Anderlini, Jamil. 2011. "CDB: Lender with a Global Reach." *Financial Times*, May 20.

Andonova, Liliana B. 2008. "The Climate Regime and Domestic Politics: The Case of Russia." *Cambridge Review of International Affairs* 21 (4):483–504.

Andonova, Liliana B., Michele M. Betsill, and Harriet Bulkeley. 2009. "Transnational Climate Governance." *Global Environmental Politics* 9 (2): 52–73.

Araujo, Alberto. 2013. "Arranca explotación petrolera del Yasuní ITT." *El Comercio* (Ecuador), August 16.

Araya, Mónica. 2011a. "The Cartagena Dialogue: A Sui Generis Alliance in the Climate Negotiations." *Intercambio Climático*, February 2. http://intercambioclimatico .com/en/home/item/286-85the-cartagena-dialogue-a-sui-generis-alliance-in-the -climate-negotiations.html.

Araya, Mónica. 2011b. "The Squeezed Middle: Why Latin America Matters in Climate Politics." *Intercambio Climático*, April 13. http://www.intercambioclimatico.com/ en/2011/04/13/the-squeezed-middle-why-latin-america-matters-in-climate-politics.

Araya, Mónica. 2013a. "China y el clima: un momento decisivo." *La Nacion* (Costa Rica), June 7.

Araya, Mónica. 2013b. "Open Letter to René Castro, Minister of Environment of Costa Rica." June 18. http://www.monica-araya.com/refinery.html.

Arguedas, Diego Ortiz. 2014. "Oil Alliance between China and Costa Rica Comes to Life Again." IPS-Inter Press Service, July 30.

Arias, Gilberto, and Guy Edwards. 2013. "Latin American Climate Change Policy and Sustainable Growth." Paper presented at "Report on the Americas 2013: Economies in Flux," conference held at University College London, Institute of the Americas (UCL-IA), London, June 14.

Assunção, Juliano, Clarissa C. Gandour, and Rudi Rocha. 2012. "Deforestation Slowdown in the Brazilian Amazon: Prices or Policies?" Executive Summary, Climate Policy Initiative Rio de Janeiro Núcleo de Avaliação de Políticas Climáticas, PUC-Rio, January.

Balbus, Arielle. 2010. "Climate Justice Movement Increases Potency in Cancun." *Intercambio Climático*, December 21. http://intercambioclimatico.com/en/2010/12/ 21/climate-justice-movement-increases-potency-in-cancun.

Balbus, Arielle. 2011b. "¿Pachamama, o Muerte? Climate Change, Globalization, and the Politics of Indigeneity." Dissertation, Brown University, Providence, RI.

Balbus, Arielle. 2011b. "Reflections on Climate Justice at COP-16." *Intercambio Climático*, January 10.

Balbus, Arielle, and Guy Edwards. 2010. "Civil Society Organisations Look to Build on Cochabamba Success in Cancun." *Intercambio Climático*, November 1. http:// intercambioclimatico.com/en/2010/11/01/civil-society-organisations-look-to -build-on-cochabamba-success-in-cancun.

Bangladesh. 2013. Intervention by Bangladesh on Behalf of the Cartagena Dialogue for Progressive Action, Bonn, Germany, June 4.

Bell, Edward. 2014. "Sign the Petition: Peru Should Withdraw Anti-environmental Legislation." The Global Call for Climate Action 2013, July 1. http://tcktcktck.org/2014/07/sign-petition-ask-peruvian-government-withdraw-legislative-initiative-environmental-standards/63137.

Benavides, Carlos. 2006. "Se hará política exterior de Estado: Patricia Espinosa." El Universal, November 29.

Bernauer, Thomas. 2013. "Climate Change Politics." Annual Review of Political Science 16: 421–448.

Bialek, Dean. 2010. "How Trust Was Restored at Cancún." The Guardian, December 16.

Black, Richard. 2012. "Inside Mexico's Climate Revolution." BBC News, April 20.

Blaxekjær, Lau Øfjord, and Tobias Dan Nielsen. 2014. "Mapping the Narrative Positions of New Political Groups under the UNFCCC." Climate Policy (October 17): 1–14.

Blázquez, Jorge, and José María Martín-Moreno. 2012. "Emerging Economies and the New Energy Security Agenda." Real Instituto Elcano, April 27.

Boccaletti, Giulio. 2013. "It's a Mistake for NGOs Not to Engage with Hydropower Companies." Guardian Professional, August 19.

Bolivia. 2010. "Press Conference by Permanent Representative of Bolivia on Climate Change Talks." Department of Public Information, News and Media Division, New York, June 16. http://www.un.org/News/briefings/docs//2010/100616_Bolivia.doc.htm.

"Bolivia to Host People's Climate Change Summit Ahead of COP 21." 2014. La Nueva Televisión del Sur C.A., December 29.

Borda, Sandra, and Carlos Castillo. 2011. "Colombia in the UN Security Council." Friedrich-Ebert-Stiftung, Berlin, December.

Bovarnick, A., F. Alpizar, and C. Schnell, eds. 2010. The Importance of Biodiversity and Ecosystems in Economic Growth and Equity in Latin America and the Caribbean: An Economic Valuation of Ecosystems. New York: United Nations Development Programme.

Bowering, Ethan. 2012. "The Cartagena Dialogue and the Future of the Climate Regime." Australian Institute of International Affairs, Deakin, ACT. http://www.aiia.asn.au/qa/924-the-cartagena-dialogue-and-the-future-of-the-climate-regime#_ftn28.

Boyd, Emily, Nate Hultman, J. Timmons Roberts, Esteve Corbera, John Cole, Alex Bozmoski, and Johannes Ebeling. 2009. "Reforming the CDM for Sustainable

Development: Lessons Learned and Policy Futures." *Environmental Science and Policy* 12 (7): 820–831.

BP. 2008. *Statistical Review of World Energy, 2008*. London: BP.

Brand, Erik, and Matthew Schewel. 2012. "Energy Policy and Twenty-first-Century Globalization: The Responses of Brazil and Venezuela, and Opportunities for Renewable Energy Development in the Americas." In *Latin America in the Globalization Age: Hopes and Fears*, ed. Manuela Nilsson and Jan Gustafsson. London: Palgrave Macmillan.

Brauch, Hans Günter, and Jürgen Scheffran. 2012. "Introduction: Climate Change, Human Security, and Violent Conflict in the Anthropocene." In *Climate Change, Human Security and Violent Conflict: Challenges for Societal Stability*, ed. Jürgen Scheffran, Michael Brzoska, Hans Günter Brauch, Peter Michael Link, and Janpeter Schilling, 3–40. Berlin: Springer.

Brazil, Government of. 2008. "National Plan on Climate Change: Executive Summary." Brasília, December.

Brazilian Secretariat for Social Communication Presidency of the Federative Republic of Brazil (SECOM). 2010. "Climate Change and Biodiversity in Brazil: Key Facts and Figures." SECOM, November.

"Brazil President Makes Final Changes to Forestry Law." 2012. *Phys.org*. Agence France-Press, October 18.

"Brazil Takes Off." 2009. *The Economist*, November 12.

Bull, Warren. 2008. "Venezuela Signs Chinese Oil Deal." *BBC News*, September 25.

Bumpus, Adam G., and Diana M. Liverman. 2008. "Accumulation by Decarbonization and the Governance of Carbon Offsets." *Economic Geography* 84 (2): 127–155.

Bunker, Stephen. 1985. *Underdeveloping the Amazon: Extraction, Unequal Exchange, and the Failure of the Modern State*. Champaign-Urbana: University of Illinois Press.

Burck, Jan, Christoph Bals, and Lindsay Parker. 2010. "The Climate Change Performance Index Results 2011." *Germanwatch and Climate Action Network Europe*, December.

Burck, Jan, Lukas Hermwille and Laura Krings. 2012. "The Climate Change Performance Index Results 2013." *Germanwatch and Climate Action Network Europe*, November.

Burck, Jan, Franziska Marten, and Christoph Bals. 2014. "The Climate Change Performance Index Results 2015." *Germanwatch and Climate Action Network Europe*, December.

Burges, Sean W. 2013. "Brazil as a Bridge between Old and New Powers?" *International Affairs* 89 (3): 577–594.

Butler, Rhett A. 2014a. "Brazil's Planned Tapajós Dams Would Increase Amazon Deforestation by 1M ha," September 14. http://news.mongabay.com/2014/0915 -tapajos-dam-deforestation.html.

Butler, Rhett A. 2014b. "In Cutting Deforestation, Brazil Leads World in Reducing Emissions." *Mongabay*, June 5. http://news.mongabay.com/2014/0605-brazil -emissions-reductions-amazon.html.

Buytaert, W., M. Vuille, A. Dewulf, R. Urrutia, A. Karmalkar, and R. Célleri. 2010. "Uncertainties in Climate Change Projections and Regional Downscaling in the Tropical Andes: Implications for Water Resources Management." *Hydrology and Earth System Sciences Discussions* 14 (7): 1821–1848.

Caballero, Paula. 2012. Senior Director Environment & Natural Resources, World Bank and former head of Colombia's delegation to the UNFCCC, September. Interview with the authors in Doha, Qatar.

Cabezas, Alberto. 2010. "Bolivia Fought for Ambitious Goals at Cancun Summit, Ended Up Isolated." *Latin American Herald Tribune*, December 13. http://laht.com/ article.asp?CategoryId=12394&ArticleId=381315.

Cabitza, Mattia. 2012. "Peru's Indigenous People: from García to Humala Their Battle Goes On." *The Guardian*, June 5. http://www.theguardian.com/global-development/ poverty-matters/2012/jun/05/peru-indigenous-people-garcia-humala.

"Cable sobre la pasividad del Gobierno de Bolivia." 2010. *El País*, March 12. http://internacional.elpais.com/internacional/2010/12/03/actualidad/1291330 830_850215.html.

Cabral, L. 2010. "Brazil: An Emerging Aid Player." Briefing Paper 64. Overseas Development Institute, London.

"Calculating Deforestation Figures for the Amazon." 2014. *Mongabay*. http:// rainforests.mongabay.com/amazon/deforestation_calculations.html.

"Cancún: Cumbre logra pacto de 193 países." 2010. *Los Tiempos*, December 12. http://www.lostiempos.com/diario/actualidad/nacional/20101212/cancun-cumbre -logra-pacto-de-193-paises_103485_201858.html. (Author's translation)

Caravani, Alice, Smita Nakhooda, Neil Bird, and Liane Schalatek. 2011. "Climate Finance Fundamentals, Regional Briefing: Latin America." Brief 6. Heinrich-Böll-Stiftung and Overseas Development Institute, Berlin, November.

Cardoso, Denilson, Rachel Bidermann, Luciana Betiol, and Laura Valente. 2012. "Informe sobre o estado e qualidade das politicas públicas sobre mudanças climáticas e desenvolvimento no Brasil. Um panorama geral, com destaque ao setor de agricultura, florestas e outros usos do solo." Sociedade de Pesquisa em Vida Selvagem e Educacao Ambiental.

Cardoso, Fernando H., and Enzo Faletto. 1979. *Dependency and Development in Latin America*. Berkeley: University of California Press.

Caribbean Catastrophe Risk Insurance Facility (CCRIF). 2010. "Enhancing the Climate Risk and Adaptation Fact Base for the Caribbean: Preliminary Results of the ECA Study." Caribbean Catastrophe Risk Insurance Facility, Grand Cayman, Cayman Islands. http://www.ccrif.org/sites/default/files/publications/ECABrochure FinalAugust182010.pdf.

Carrington, Damian. 2010. "WikiLeaks Cables Reveal How US Manipulated Climate Accord." *The Guardian*, December, 3. http://www.theguardian.com/ environment/2010/dec/03/wikileaks-us-manipulated-climate-accord.

Cartagena Dialogue. 2010. "Chairman's Statement." Third Meeting of the Cartagena Dialogue for Progressive Action, San Jose, Costa Rica, October 31–November 2. http://switchboard.nrdc.org/blogs/sclefkowitz/Cartagena/Chairman's_Statement_ COSTA_RICA%20Nov%202010.pdf.

Carvalho, A. 2007. "Ideological Cultures and Media Discourses on Scientific Knowl- edge: Re-reading News on Climate Change." *Public Understanding of Science* 16 (2): 223–243.

Castro, René, and the Minister of Environment, Energy and Telecommunications. 2012. Speech presented during a High-Level Segment, Eighteenth Conference of the Parties (COP18), Doha, Qatar, December 5, http://unfccc.int/resource/docs/cop18 _cmp8_hl_statements/Statement%20by%20Costa%20Rica%20%28COP%29.pdf.

Catton, Bruce. 1980. *Overshoot: The Ecological Basis of Revolutionary Change*. Cham- paign-Urbana: University of Illinois Press.

Cedeño, Silvana. 2013. "Refinería y carbono neutralidad batallan en Costa Rica." *Revista Mercados y Tendencias*, June 5. http://revistamyt.com/2013/06/refineria-y-carbono -neutralidad-batallan-en-costa-rica.

Cedeño, Silvana. 2013 "Derecho de respuesta del ministro de Ambiente y Energía, René Castro." *Amelia Rueda*. http://www.ameliarueda.com/derecho-de-respuesta-del -ministro-de-ambiente-y-energia-rene-castro-salazar/.

Centro Mexicano de Derecho Ambiental (CEMDA). n.d. *Postura ante la reforma ener- gética CEMDA*. http://www.cemda.org.mx/postura-ante-la-reforma-energetica.

"Changing the System, Not the Climate." 2014. *Social PreCOP*, November 1. http:// www.precopsocial.org/en.

Chávez, Herman Rosa. 2011. "Speech by the Minister of the Environment of El Sal- vador for the Central American Commission for the Environment and Development

(CCAD)." Seventeenth Conference of the Parties (COP17) / Seventh Meeting of the Parties (MOP7), Durban, South Africa, December 9.

Chávez, Hugo. 2009. "Statement." Presented at the Fifteenth Conference of the Parties (COP15), Copenhagen, Denmark, December 18. Speech available on Youtube at http://www.youtube.com/watch?v=Cp90gNCDaNw&feature=player_embedded.

Chávez, Hugo. 2013. "Second Socialist Plan 2013–2019." Translation. Caracas, Venezuela.

Chemnick, Jean, and Lisa Friedman. 2010. "Deal in Cancun Restores Faith in U.N. Climate Process but Many Questions Remain." *ClimateWire*, December 13.

Chile Ministry of Environment. 2014. "Ministro de Medio Ambiente da inicio a proceso de participacion ciudadana para definir contribucion nacional frente a cambio climatico." *Ministro de Medio Ambiente*, December 17. http://portal.mma.gob.cl/ ministro-de-medio-ambiente-da-inicio-a-proceso-de-participacion-ciudadana-para -definir-contribucion-nacional-frente-a-cambio-climatico.

"Chile's Energy Dilemma after Ditching Megaproject." 2014. *BBC News Online*, June 10. http://www.bbc.com/news/world-latin-america-27780937.

Ciplet, David, J. Timmons Roberts, and Mizan Khan. 2015. *Power in a Warming World: The New Geopolitics of Climate Change*. Cambridge, MA: MIT Press.

Climate Action Network (CAN). 2014a. "CAN Intervention: Volveremos Civil Society Intervention and Declaration with CAN, CJN and YOUNGO in ADP High-Level Ministerial." June 7. http://www.climatenetwork.org/publication/ can-intervention-volveremos-civil-society-intervention-and-declaration-can-cjn-and.

Climate Action Network (CAN). 2014b. "Will Brazil Win?" *CAN Blog*, June 13. http:// www.climatenetwork.org/blog/will-brazil-win.

Climate Action Network (CAN) International. 2010. "Latin America Needs a Voice!" *ECO* 127 (7). http://climatenetwork.org/sites/default/files/ECO_7_COP_16_English_ version.pdf.

Climate Action Network (CAN) International. 2013. "Costa Rica Carbon Neutral for 2020 … Really?" *Climate Action Network International* (blog), June 14. http://www .climatenetwork.org/blog/costa-rica-carbon-neutral-2020really.

"Climate Change and Financial Instability Seen as Top Global Threats." 2013. *Pew Research Center*, June 24. http://www.pewglobal.org/2013/06/24/climate-change -and-financial-instability-seen-as-top-global-threats.

"Climate Change Tops UN Chief's Talks with Bolivian President." 2010. *United Nations News Centre*, May 7. http://www.un.org/apps/news/story.asp?NewsID=34634 &Cr=climate+change&Cr1.

"Climatescope 2013: Assessing the Climate for Climate Investing in Latin America and the Caribbean." 2013. Multilateral Investment Fund and Bloomberg New Energy Finance.

"Climatescope 2014: Mapping the Global Frontiers for Clean Energy Investment." 2014. Multilateral Investment Fund and Bloomberg New Energy Finance.

Cole, John C., and Diana M. Liverman. 2011. "Brazil's Clean Development Mechanism Governance in the Context of Brazil's Historical Environment: Development Discourses. *Carbon Management* 2 (2): 145–160.

Collyns, Dan. 2013. "Why Climate Change Threatens Peru's Poverty Reduction Mission." *The Guardian*, December 13. http://www.theguardian.com/global-development/poverty-matters/2013/dec/13/undp-climate-change-peru-poverty-reduction.

Collyns, Dan. 2014a. "Economic Reforms Spark Environmental Worries." *Yachay Productions*, July 3.

Collyns, Dan. 2014b. "Green Activists from Ecuador Harassed by Police on Way to Climate Summit." *The Guardian*, December 3.

Collyns, Dan. 2014c. "Illegal Loggers Blamed for Murder of Peru Forest Campaigner." *The Guardian*, September 8.

Collyns, Dan. 2014d. "Indigenous Protesters Occupy Peru's Biggest Amazon Oil Field." *The Guardian*, April 25.

Colom, Álvaro. 2010. "Statement of the Former Guatemalan President." Presented at the Sixteenth Conference of the Parties (COP16), Cancun, Mexico, December 7. http://unfccc.int/files/meetings/cop_16/statements/application/pdf/101207_cop16_hls_guatemala.pdf.

Colombia, República de. 2010. *Primera comunicación nacional ante la Convención Marco de las naciones unidas sobre el cambio climático*. Bogotá: República de Colombia and Ministerio del Ambiente.

Condo, Lissette. 2012. "Ecuador busca exportar energía limpia." 12. *Infosurhoy*, December 12. http://www.canalazul24.com/?p=19134.

"Congreso peruano aprueba paquete de medidas del Gobierno para reactivar economía." 2014. *Reuters*, July 4.

Constantine, Giles. 2014. "Peru Unveils 2050 Climate Change Strategy Amid Fracking Plans." *Eye on Latin America* (blog), July 18. http://eyeonlatinamerica.wordpress.com/2014/07/18/peru-2050-climate-change-plans-fracking.

Contreras, Gabriela. 2013. "Ticos tendrían que pagar hasta ¢30 más por litro de combustibles con nueva refinería, dice analista." *CRHoy*, May 27. http://www.crhoy

.com/ticos-tendrian-que-pagar-hasta-%C2%A230-mas-por-litro-de-combustibles-con-nueva-refineria-dice-analista.

"Copenhagen Ends by Only 'Noting' an Accord after Much Wrangling." 2009. *Third World Network*, December 20. http://www.twnside.org.sg/title2/climate/copenhagen.up.01.htm.

"Copper Solution." 2013. *The Economist*, April 27. http://www.pucp.edu.pe/climadecambios/index.php?tmpl=articulo&id=1669.

Correa, Rafael. 2007. "Speech of the President of Ecuador." Presented at the High-Level Dialogue on Climate Change of the Sixty-second Period of Sessions of the General Assembly of the United Nations, September 24. http://www.ecuador.org/bulletin_board/relative_docs/letter_climatechange.pdf.

Correa, Rafael. 2013. "Cadena Nacional sobre iniciativa Yasuní ITT." August 21. http://www.youtube.com/watch?v=315v8QPAqQg.

Costa Rica. 2009. Second National Communication to the United Nations Framework Convention on Climate Change (UNFCCC). http://unfccc.int/resource/docs/natc/cornc2.pdf.

"Costa Rica y China reactivarán plan de refinería de $1.300 millones." 2014. *El Financiero*, November 27. http://www.elfinancierocr.com/m/economia-y-politica/Costa-Rica-China-reactivaran-refineria_0_636536348.html.

Cota, Isabella. 2013a. "China Lends Costa Rica $400 Million on Xi Visit." *Reuters*, June 3.

Cota, Isabella. 2013b. "Costa Rica Halts Chinese-Backed Plan for Refinery Upgrade." *Reuters*, June 20.

Cote, Chris. 2011. "PetroCaribe: Welcome Relief for an Energy-Poor Region." *Hemisphere* 20 (Spring): 34.

Craze, Matt. 2014. "Chile Attracts $7 Billion in Renewable Energy Investment." *Bloomberg*, August 26.

Crooks, Nathan. 2011. "Venezuela to Invest $5 Billion in Orinoco Oil Belt, Chavez Says." *Bloomberg*, December 31.

Cruz, Alejandra. 2014. "El paquete reactivador le corta los brazos al Minam." *Grupo La República Digital*, June 18.

Da Silva, Luiz Inácio. 2009. Lula speech at the Fifteenth Conference of the Parties (COP15). United Nations Framework Conference on Climate Change (UNFCCC). Copenhagen, December.

Davies, Wyre. 2014. "Brazil and Its 'Relatively Simple' World Cup Delays." *BBC News Online*, January 24.

"Deals to Link Costa Rican Market." 2013. *China Daily*, June 5.

de la Torre, Augusto, Eduardo Levy Yeyati, Guillermo Beylis, Tatiana Didier, Carlos Rodríguez Castelán, and Sergio Schmukler. 2014. "Inequality in a Lower-Growth Latin America." LAC Semiannual Report (October). World Bank, Washington DC.

Delegation of the Plurinational State of Bolivia. 2010. Press Briefing. UN Climate Change Conference, Bonn, Germany, August 6. http://unfccc2.meta-fusion.com/kongresse/100802_AWG/templ/play.php?id_kongresssession=2959&theme=unfccc.

Desai, Uday. 2002. "Institutional Profiles and Policy Performance: Summary and Conclusion." In *Environmental Politics and Policy in Industrialized Countries*, ed. Uday Desai, 357–382. Cambridge, MA: MIT Press.

DeSombre, Elizabeth. 2005. "Understanding United States Unilateralism: Domestic Sources of US International Environmental Policy." In *The Global Environment: Institutions, Law, and Policy*, ed. Regina S. Axelrod, David Leonard Downie, and Norman J. Vig. Washington, DC: CQ Press.

Dillon, J. 2000. "Deuda ecológica. El Sur dice al Norte: 'es hora de pagar.'" *Ecología Política* 20.

Dimenstein, Gilberto. 2013. "Acordem: R$ 0,20 são apenas um detalhe." *Folha de São Paulo*, June 14.

Dobles, Roberto. 2008. "Summary of the National Climate Change Strategy." February. Ministry of the Environment, San Jose, Costa Rica.

Dolsak, Nives. 2001. "Mitigating Global Climate Change: Why Are Some Countries Doing More Than Others?" *Policy Studies Journal: The Journal of the Policy Studies Organization* 29 (3): 414–436.

Donnelly, Jack. 2008. "The Ethics of Realism." In *The Oxford Handbook of International Relations*, ed. Christian Reus-Smit and Duncan Snidal, 150–162. New York: Oxford University Press.

Downs, Erica. 2011. *Inside China, Inc.: China Development Bank's Cross-Border Energy Deals*. John L. Thornton China Center Monograph Series, Number 3, March. Brookings Institution, Washington, DC.

"The Dragon in the Backyard." 2009. *The Economist*, August 13.

Dyer, Zach. 2014. "President Solís Reaffirms Carbon Neutrality Goal in UN Climate Summit Address." *Tico Times*, September 23. http://www.ticotimes.net/2014/09/23/president-solis-reaffirms-carbon-neutrality-goal-in-un-climate-summit-address.

EcoEquity.org. 2014. "Climate Equity Reference Calculator." http://www.gdrights.org/calculator.

Economic Commission for Latin America and the Caribbean (ECLAC). 2007. "Estadísticas de recursos naturales y del medio ambiente." In *Anuario estadístico de América Latina y el Caribe.* Santiago, Chile: UN ECLAC.

Economic Commission for Latin America and the Caribbean (ECLAC). 2010a. "Economics of Climate Change in Latin America and the Caribbean: Summary." Santiago, Chile: UN ECLAC.

Economic Commission for Latin America and the Caribbean (ECLAC). 2010b. *Foreign Direct Investment in Latin America and the Caribbean.* Santiago, Chile: UN ECLAC.

Economic Commission for Latin America and the Caribbean (ECLAC). 2010c. "La Hora de la Igualdad: Brechas por cerrar, caminos por abrir." Report of the Thirtieth Session of UN ECLAC. http://www.eclac.cl/publicaciones/xml/0/39710/100604_2010 -114-SES.33-3_La_hora_de_la_igualdad_doc_completo.pdf.

Economic Commission for Latin America and the Caribbean (ECLAC). 2010d. "UN Seeks Inclusion and Transparency in Discussion over Climate Change." Press Release, UN ECLAC, April 20.

Economic Commission for Latin America and the Caribbean (ECLAC). 2011a. *En busca de una asociación renovada entre América Latina y el Caribe y la Unión Europea.* Santiago, Chile: UN ECLAC.

Economic Commission for Latin America and the Caribbean (ECLAC). 2011b. *Natural Disaster Prevention and Response in the Americas and Financing and Proposals.* Santiago, Chile: UN ECLAC.

Economic Commission for Latin America and the Caribbean (ECLAC). 2011c. *People's Republic of China and Latin America and the Caribbean: Ushering in a New Era in the Economic and Trade Relationship.* Santiago, Chile: UN ECLAC.

Economic Commission for Latin America and the Caribbean (ECLAC). 2011d. *The United States and Latin America and the Caribbean: Highlights of Economics and Trade.* Santiago, Chile: UN ECLAC.

Economic Commission for Latin America and the Caribbean (ECLAC). 2012. "Sustainable Development Twenty Years on from the Earth Summit: Progress, Gaps and Strategic Guidelines for Latin America and the Caribbean." Santiago, Chile: UN ECLAC.

Economic Commission for Latin America and the Caribbean (ECLAC). 2014a. *Compacts for Equality: Towards a Sustainable Future,* Santiago, Chile: UN ECLAC.

Economic Commission for Latin America and the Caribbean (ECLAC). 2014b. *The Economics of Climate Change in Latin America and the Caribbean: Paradoxes and Challenges.* Santiago, Chile: UN ECLAC.

Economic Commission for Latin America and the Caribbean (ECLAC). 2014c. "Preliminary Overview of the Economies of Latin America and the Caribbean." Santiago, Chile: UN ECLAC.

Economic Commission for Latin America and the Caribbean (ECLAC). 2014d. "Updated Economic Overview of Latin America and the Caribbean." Santiago, Chile, UN ECLAC.

Economic Commission for Latin America and the Caribbean/Inter-American Development Bank (ECLAC/IDB). 2010. *Climate Change: A Regional Perspective*. Santiago, Chile: UN ECLAC.

"Ecuador Energy Crisis Cripples Production, Disrupts Cities." 2009. *United Press International*, November 17. http://www.upi.com/Science_News/Resource-Wars/2009/11/17/Ecuador-energy-crisis-cripples-production-disrupts-cities/UPI-91091258489130.

Ecuador, Government of. n.d. "Yasuni-ITT Initiative Fact Sheet." Quito.

"Ecuador Pledges No Oil Drilling in Amazon Reserve." 2010. *BBC*, August 3. http://www.bbc.com/news/world-latin-america-10861415.

"Ecuador Rejects Vote on Amazon Oil Drilling in Yasuni Park." 2014. *BBC News*, May 6. http://www.bbc.com/news/world-latin-america-27303717.

Edwards, Guy. 2008. "Andes Face Glacial Meltdown." *The Guardian*, July 10. http://www.guardian.co.uk/commentisfree/2008/jul/13/climatechange.colombia.

Edwards, Guy. 2009. "Ecuador's Energy Supply Runs Dry." *Intercambio Climático*, November 11.

Edwards, Guy. 2010a. "Ecuador's Yasuní Initiative Shakes Up the Climate-Development Agenda." *Intercambio Climático*, August 16. http://intercambioclimatico.com/en/2010/08/16/ecuador%E2%80%99s-yasuni-initiative-shakes-up-the-climate-development-agenda.

Edwards, Guy. 2010b. "US Special Envoy Makes Stern Remarks on ALBA's Ideological Posturing." *Intercambio Climático*, July 16. http://intercambioclimatico.com/en/2010/07/16/u-s-special-envoy-makes-stern-remarks-on-albas-ideological-posturing.

Edwards, Guy. 2012. "Latin American Governments and Civil Society Combine Forces at COP17." *Intercambio Climático*, January 20. http://intercambioclimatico.com/en/2012/01/20/latin-american-governments-and-civil-society-combine-forces-at-cop17.

Edwards, Guy. 2013a. "Chinese Loan for Oil Refinery Clashes with Costa Rica's Climate Policies." *Intercambio Climático*, June 20. http://www.intercambioclimatico.com/en/2013/06/20/chinese-loan-for-oil-refinery-clashes-with-costa-ricas-climate-policies.

Edwards, Guy. 2013b. "Latin American Civil Society Organizations Back Peru's Bid to Host COP20." *Intercambio Climático*, June 5. http://intercambioclimatico.com/ en/2013/06/05/latin-american-civil-society-organizations-back-perus-bid-to-host -cop20.

Edwards, Guy, Victoria Elmore, and Jin Hyung Lee. 2012. "Latin American Scientists Can Play a Greater Role in Promoting Robust Climate Policies." *Intercambio Climático*, May 9. http://intercambioclimatico.com/en/2012/05/09/latin-american -scientists-can-play-a-greater-role-in-promoting-robust-climate-policies.

Edwards, Guy and Susanna Mage. 2012. "Could Ecuador Play a More Pivotal Role on Climate Change within ALBA?" *Intercambio Climático*, September 4.

Edwards, Guy, and Susanna Mage. 2013. "Think Tanks in Latin America Have Major Role to Play on Climate Change." *Intercambio Climático*, June 20. http:// intercambioclimatico.com/en/2013/06/20/think-tanks-in-latin-america-have -major-role-to-play-on-climate-change.

Edwards, Guy, Michael Murphy, and Paola Eisner. 2014. "Venezuela's 2014 Climate Summit Faces Credibility Crisis." *Responding to Climate Change*, March 11.

Edwards, Guy, and Timmons Roberts. 2014. "High Carbon Partnership? Chinese-Latin American Relations in a Carbon Constrained World." Working Paper 72. Brookings Institution, March.

Edwards, Guy, and Jakob Skovgaard. 2014. "Can Peru Deliver a Successful UN Climate Summit?" *Responding to Climate Change*, May 19. http://www.rtcc .org/2014/05/19/can-peru-deliver-a-successful-un-climate-summit.

"El Presidente promulga la ley corta del Tipnis." 2011. *Los Tiempos*, October 25.

Enciso, Angélica L. 2010. "Posición de la Alianza Bolivariana, más política que ambiental: Espinosa." *La Jornada*, December 3. http://www.jornada.unam.mx/2010/12/03/ index.php?section=sociedad&article=048n1soc.

Ministério de Minas e Energia. 2014. "PDE 2023: Brasil será grande produtor de petróleo mantendo matriz energética limpa." Ministério de Minas e Energia, September 10. http://www.epe.gov.br/Estudos/Paginas/PlanoDecenaldeEnergia-PDE/ MMEcolocaPlanoDecenal.aspx.

Espinosa, María Fernanda. 2009. ALBA Press Conference, December 19. http://www .youtube.com/watch?v=gKCLPB4orvg&feature=relmfu.

Espinosa, Patricia. 2010a. "Statement by Her Excellency, Mrs. Patricia Espinosa, COP 16/CMP 6 President." Informal meeting of the president, December 5.

Espinosa, Patricia. 2010b. "Statement by Her Excellency, Mrs. Patricia Espinosa, COP 16/CMP 6 President." Informal stocktaking plenary, December 8.

Espinosa, Patricia. 2011. "From Cancun to Durban: Implications for Climate and Multilateral Diplomacy." Speech made by Patricia Espinosa, Secretary of Foreign Affairs, Mexico, Chatham House, London, June 30.

Estrada, Daniela. 2010. "Climate Justice Treks from Cochabamba to Cancun." Inter Press Service, September 21. http://www.ipsnews.net/2010/09/climate-justice-treks-from-cochabamba-to-cancun.

"Ethics Tribunal: Ecuador Violated Rights: Tribunal Marked One-Year Anniversary of Decision to Drill Yasuní." 2014. El Universo, August. http://sitio.yasunidos.org/en/press/blog/28-prensa/blog-english/119-ethics-tribunal-ecuador-violated-rights-tribunal-marked-one-year-anniversary-of-decision-to-drill-yasuni.html.

Fearnside, Philip M. 2002. "Greenhouse Gas Emissions from a Hydroelectric Reservoir (Brazil's Tucuruí Dam) and the Energy Policy Implications." Water, Air, and Soil Pollution 133 (1–4): 69–96.

Fearnside, Philip M. 2011. "Greenhouse Gas Emissions from Hydroelectric Dams in Tropical Forests." In The Encyclopedia of Energy. New York: Wiley. http://philip.inpa.gov.br/publ_livres/Preprints/2011/Fearnside-Greenhouse%20gas%20Emissions%20from%20Dams-Wiley.pdf.

Fearnside, Philip M., Adriano M. R. Figueiredo, and Sandra C. M. Bonjour. 2013. "Amazonian Forest Loss and the Long Reach of China's Influence." Environment, Development and Sustainability 15 (2): 325–338.

Fearnside, Philip M., and Salvador Pueyo. 2012. "Greenhouse-Gas Emissions from Tropical Dams." Nature Climate Change 2: 382–384.

Felandro, Isabel, and Jean Pierre Araujo. 2012. Informe sobre el estado y calidad de las politicas públicas sobre cambio climático y desarrollo en El Perú – sector agropecuario y forestal. Lima, Peru: Sociedad Peruana de Derecho Ambiental (SPDA).

Fendt, Lindsay. 2014a. "Carbon Neutrality Won't Solve Everything, Environmentalists Say." Tico Times, September 25. http://www.ticotimes.net/2014/09/25/carbon-neutrality-wont-solve-everything-environmentalists-say.

Fendt, Lindsay. 2014b. "Solís to Suspend Costa Rica's Carbon Neutrality Goal." Tico Times, March 8. http://www.ticotimes.net/2014/03/08/solis-to-suspend-carbon-neutrality-goal.

Fernandes, E. C. M., A. Soliman, R. Confalonieri, M. Donatelli, and F. Tubiello. 2012. Climate Change and Agriculture in Latin America, 2020–2050: Projected Impacts and Response to Adaptation Strategies. Washington, DC: World Bank.

Fernández, Mauro. 2014. "Estuvimos en la PreCOP Social en Venezuela: Más que una declaración sobre la mesa." November 4. http://www.greenpeace.org.ar/blog/termino-la-precop-social-en-venezuela-con-resultados-poco-alentadores-para-luchar-contra-el-cambio-climatico/12911.

Figueres, Christiana. 2011. "'Decisive Opportunities' in Facing Climate Change." Comments Made at the OAS Conference Highlights, Organization of American States (OAS), May 13. http://www.oas.org/en/media_center/press_release .asp?sCodigo=E-664/11.

Finer, M., and C. N. Jenkins. 2012. "Proliferation of Hydroelectric Dams in the Andean Amazon and Implications for Andes-Amazon Connectivity." *PLoS ONE* 7 (4): 1–9.

Fletcher, R. 2010. "When Environmental Issues Collide: Climate Change and the Shifting Political Ecology of Hydroelectric Power." *Peace and Conflict Review* 5(1): 1–15.

Fletcher, Robert. 2013. "Making 'Peace with Nature': Costa Rica's Campaign for Climate Neutrality." In *Climate Governance in the Developing World*, ed. David Held, Charles Roger, and Eva-Maria Nag. London: Polity Press.

Font, Alberto. 2013. "National Oil Refinery President Resigns in Dispute over China-Backed Refinery." *Tico Times*, June 21. http://www.ticotimes.net/More-news/ News-Briefs/National-Oil-Refinery-president-resigns-in-dispute-over-China-backed-refinery_Friday-June-21-2013.

Foweraker, Joe. 1981. *The Struggle for Land: A Political Economy of the Pioneer Frontier in Brazil from 1930 to the Present Day*. Cambridge: Cambridge University Press.

Frank, Andre Gunder. 1969. *Latin America: Underdevelopment or Revolution?* New York: Monthly Review Press.

Frank, Gunter Andre. 1972. *Lumpenproletariat: Lumpenbourgiosie—Dependency, Class, and Politics in Latin America*. New York: Monthly Review Press.

Frayssinet, Fabiana. 2013. "Climate Change Threatens Crop Yields in Brazil." *Inter Press Service (IPS) News*, September 17. http://www.ipsnews.net/2013/09/ climate-change-threatens-crop-yields-in-brazil.

Friedman, Lisa. 2010. "A Near-Consensus Decision Keeps U.N. Climate Process Alive and Moving Ahead." *ClimateWire*, December 13.

Friedman, Lisa. 2013a. "China's Friendship with Costa Rica May Conflict with Its Green Goals." *ClimateWire*, June 20.

Friedman, Lisa. 2013b. "New Alliance Attempts to Bridge North-South Gap in U.N. Climate Talks." *ClimateWire*, January 22.

Friedman, Lisa. 2014. "Latin Americans Forge Ahead with CO_2 Reduction Plans." *ClimateWire*, June 9.

Ferreira, Joice, L. Aragão, J. Barlow, P. Barreto, E. Berenguer, M. Bustamante, T. A. Gardner, A. C. Lees, A. Lima, J. Louzada, R. Pardini, L. Parry, C. A. Peres, P. S. Pompeu, M. Tabarelli, and J. Zuanon. 2014. "Brazil's Environmental Leadership at Risk." *Science* 346 (6210): 706–707.

Flavin, Christopher, Milena Gonzalez, Ana Maria Majano, Alexander Ochs, Maria da Rocha , and Philipp Tagwerker. 2014. "Study on the Development of the Renewable Energy Market in Latin America and the Caribbean." Inter-American Development Bank, Washington, DC.

Fuentes, Federico. 2011. "ALBA Nations Prepare to Fight for Humanity at Durban Climate Summit." *Climate and Capitalism*, November 23. http://climateandcapitalism .com/2011/11/23/alba-nations-prepare-to-fight-for-humanity-at-durban -climate-summit.

Fuentes, Federico, and Ruben Pereira. 2011. "ALBA Giving Hope and Solidarity to Latin America." *Green Left Weekly*, November 28. https://www.greenleft.org.au/ node/49622.

Galeano, Eduardo. 1973. *The Open Veins of Latin America: Five Centuries of the Pillage of a Continent*. New York: Monthly Review Press.

Galeano, Eduardo. 1994. *Úselo y tírelo*. Barcelona: Planeta.

Gallagher, Kevin P., Amos Irwin, Katherine Koleski. 2012. "The New Banks in Town: Chinese Finance in Latin America." Inter-American Dialogue, Washington, DC, March.

Gardini, Gian Luca. 2009. *L'America Latina nel XXI Secolo*. Rome: Carocci.

Gardini, Gian Luca. 2011. "Unity and Diversity in Latin American Visions of Regional Integration." In *Latin American Foreign Policies: Between Ideology and Pragmatism*, ed. Gian Luca Gardini and Peter Lambert. London: Palgrave Macmillan.

Gardini, Gian Luca, and Peter Lambert, eds. 2011. *Latin American Foreign Policies: Between Ideology and Pragmatism*. London: Palgrave Macmillan.

Gardner, Toby. "Brazil's Environmental Record Hangs in the Balance." 2014. Thomson Reuters Foundation, November 6. http://www.trust.org/item/20141106175100 -fugqj/?source=fiBlogs.

Garibaldi J. A. 2009. "The Economics of Boldness: Equity Outcomes for This and Future Generations." Energeia, London.

Garibaldi J. A. 2014. "The Economics of Boldness: Equity, Action, and Hope." *Climate Policy* 14 (1): 82–101.

Garibaldi, Jose Alberto, Mónica Araya, and Guy Edwards. 2012. "Shaping the Durban Platform: Latin America and the Caribbean in a Future High Ambition Deal." CDKN Policy Brief. Climate and Development Knowledge Network, March.

Garibaldi, Jose Alberto, Gilberto Arias, Manuel Estrada, Louallalen Alejandra Lopez Romain, and Guy Edwards. 2014. "Tying the Knot: Why Linking Domestic Mitigation Action and the International Climate Regime Is Paramount to Building Progress towards 2015." Unpublished paper, Energeia, London, January.

Garibaldi, J. A, M. P. Cigarán, M. Estrada, and Murray Ward. 2010. *Scaling Up Responses in Latin America: Large-Scale Nested Strategic Program Approaches*. London: Energeia.

Garibaldi, J. A., A. Figari, and P. Gamio. 2009. "Propuesta Nacional de Estrategia de Mitigacion: documento preparado para el MINAM (National Proposal for Mitigation, Document prepared for the Environment Ministry)." Keplel Consulting, Energeia, London, July.

Garibaldi, Jose Alberto, Harald Winkler, Emilio Lebre la Rovere, Angela Cadena, Rodrigo Palma, José Eduardo Sanhueza, Emily Tyler, and Marta Torres Gunfaus. 2013. "Comparative Analysis of Five Case Studies: Commonalities and Differences in Approaches to Mitigation Actions in Five Developing Countries." *Climate and Development Knowledge Network*, July.

Gera, Vanessa. 2008. "Mexico Vows to Cut Carbon Gas Emissions 50 Percent below 2002 Levels by 2050." *Carbon Offsets Daily*, December 12. http://www.carbonoffsetsdaily.com/news-channels/global/mexico-vows-to-cut-carbon-gas-emissions-50-percent-below-2002-levels-by-2050-3015.htm.

Gibson, Owen. 2013. "Brazil's World Cup Race against Time Leaves More Questions Than Answers." *The Guardian*, December 5.

Githeko, A., and A. Woodward. 2003. "International Consensus on the Science of Climate and Health: The IPCC Third Assessment Report." In *Climate Change and Human Health: Risks and Responses*, ed. A. J. Michael, D. H. Campbell-Lendrum, C. F. Corvalán, K. L. Ebi, A. Githeko, J. D. Scheraga, and A. Woodward, 43–60. Geneva: WHO/WMO/UNEP.

Glickhouse, Rachel. 2013. "What Is Petrocaribe?" *Americas Society Council of the Americas*, May 10. http://www.as-coa.org/articles/explainer-what-petrocaribe.

Goldenberg, Suzanne. 2010. "US Denies Climate Aid to Countries Opposing Copenhagen Accord." *The Guardian*, April 9. http://www.theguardian.com/environment/2010/apr/09/us-climate-aid.

Goodman, Amy. 2009. "Indigenous Leaders at the Frontline of Climate Change." *DemocracyNow!*, December 14.

Goodman, Amy. 2012. "*Democracy Now* Interview with Claudia Salerno in Doha." *DemocracyNow!* http://www.youtube.com/watch?v=fu4xDIaBhFI.

Goodman, Amy. 2013. "As Poor Countries Walk Out of Climate Talks, Venezuela Calls on Industrial Nations to Take Action." *DemocracyNow!*, November 20. http://www.democracynow.org/2013/11/20/as_poor_countries_walk_out_of.

"The Government Freezes Extraction from Yasuní." 2009. *El Comercio*, February 14.

"Government of Ecuador Shuts Down Fundacion Pachamama." 2013. *Pachamama Alliance*, December 4. http://www.pachamama.org/news/government-of-ecuador-shuts-down-fundacion-pachamama.

Grasso, Marco, and Timmons Roberts. 2014. "A Compromise to Break the Climate Impasse." *Nature Climate Change* 4 (7): 543–549.

"The Great Deceleration." 2014. *The Economist*, November 22.

Group of 77 (G77). 2015. "The Member States of the Group of 77." http://www.g77.org/doc/members.html.

Grupo Peru. 2014. "Conforman equipo negociador de Relaciones Exteriores para la #COP20." http://grupoperucop20.org.pe/index.php?option=com_k2&view=item&id=19:conforman-equipo-negociador-de-relaciones-exteriores-para-la-cop20&Itemid=227.

Grupo Peru. 2014. "Peoples' Summit on Climate Change." Twentieth Conference of the Parties (COP20). http://grupoperucop20.org.pe/index.php?option=com_content&view=article&id=67&Itemid=255.

Guachalla, Laura. 2010. "Bolivian Alternative Climate Conference Begins." *SciDev.Net*, April 19. http://www.scidev.net/en/news/bolivian-alternative-climate-conference-begins-1.html.

Gudynas, Eduardo. 2009. "Diez tesis urgentes sobre el nuevo extractavismo." *Centro Latino American de Ecologia Social (CLAES)*, July.

Gudynas, Eduardo. 2012. "La izquierda marrón." *Le Centre Tricontinental (CETRI)*. http://www.cetri.be/spip.php?article2552&lang=es.

Gudynas, Eduardo. 2014. "Yasuní en la coyuntura: economía, control y contra-dicciones." *Plan V: sociedad historias*, May 7. http://www.planv.com.ec/historias/sociedad/yasuni-la-coyuntura-economia-control-y-contradicciones.

Guimarães, Roberto P. 1986. *Ecopolitics in the Third World: An Institutional Analysis of Environmental Management in Brazil*. Storrs: University of Connecticut Press.

Hakim, Peter. 2012. "The Incredibly Shrinking Vision: US Policy in Latin America." *Política Exterior*, July 5. http://www.politicaexterior.com.

Hallding, Karl, Marie Olsson, Aaron Atteridge, Antto Vihma, Marcus Carson, and Mikael Román. 2011. *Together Alone: BASIC Countries and the Climate Change Conundrum*. Tema Nord 2011:530. Nordic Council of Ministers, Copenhagen.

Hance, Jeremy. 2014. "After Throwing Out Referendum, Ecuador Approves Oil Drilling in Yasuní's Embattled Heart." *Mongabay*, June 2. http://news.mongabay.com/2014/0602-hance-yasuni-oil-permits.html.

Harrison, Kathryn, and Lisa McIntosh Sundstrom. 2007. "Introduction: The Comparative Politics of Climate Change." *Global Environmental Politics* 7 (4): 1–18.

Harrison, Kathryn, and Lisa McIntosh Sundstrom, eds. 2010. *Global Commons, Domestic Decisions: The Comparative Politics of Climate Change*. Cambridge, MA: MIT Press.

"Has Brazil Blown It?" 2013. *The Economist*, September 28.

Heine, Jorge. 2012. "Regional Integration and Political Cooperation in Latin America." *Latin American Research Review* 47 (3): 209–217.

Held, David, Charles Roger, and Eva-Maria Nag. 2013. "Editors' Introduction: Climate Governance in the Developing World." In *Climate Governance in the Developing World*, ed. David Held, Charles Roger, and Eva-Maria Nag. Cambridge, MA: Polity.

Hicks, Robert L., and Bradley C. Parks. J. Timmons Roberts, and Michael J. Tierney. 2008. *Greening Aid? Understanding the Environmental Impact of Development Assistance*. New York: Oxford University Press.

Hill, David. 2014a. "Ecuador Pursued China Oil Deal While Pledging to Protect Yasuní, Papers Show." *The Guardian*, February 19.

Hill, David. 2014b. "Leaked Documents Cast Doubt on Ecuador's Commitment to Forest Plan." *The Guardian*, July 2.

Hill, David. 2014c. "Peru to 'Eliminate' Key Environmental Rule for Oil and Gas Firms, Says Minister." *The Guardian*, March 8.

Hirschfeld, Daniela. 2014. "Hydropower Needs 'New Climate Knowledge.'" *SciDev. Net*, March 25. http://www.scidev.net/global/energy/scidev-net-at-large/hydropower -needs-new-climate-knowledge.html.

Hochstetler, Kathryn. 2002. "After the Boomerang: Environmental Movements and Politics in the La Plata River Basin." *Global Environmental Politics* 2 (4): 35–57.

Hochstetler, Kathryn. 2012. "The G-77, BASIC, and Global Climate Governance: A New Era in Multilateral Environmental Negotiations. *Revista Brasileira de Política Internacional* 55 (special edition): 53–69.

Hochstetler, Kathyrn. 2013. *The Changing Face of Brazil as an International Donor— From Lula to Dilma Rousseff*. Waterloo, ON: The Centre for International Governance Innovation. https://www.cigionline.org/publications/2013/12/changing-face-of-brazil -international-donor-%E2%80%94-lula-dilma-rousseff.

Hochstetler, Kathryn, and Margaret E. Keck. 2007. *Greening Brazil: Environmental Activism in State and Society*. Durham, NC: Duke University Press.

Hochstetler, Kathryn, and Genia Kostka. Forthcoming. "Wind and Solar Sectors in Brazil and China: Interests, State-Business Relations, and Policy Outcomes." *Global Environmental Politics*.

Hochstetler, Kathryn, and Eduardo Viola. 2011. "Brazil and the Multiscalar Politics of Climate Change." Paper presented at the Colorado Conference on Earth Systems Governance, May 17–20.

Hochstetler, Kathryn, and Eduardo Viola. 2012. "Brazil and the Politics of Climate Change: Beyond the Global Commons." *Environmental Politics* 21 (5): 753–771.

Höhne, Niklas, Nadine Braun, Hanna Fekete, Ruut Brandsma, Julia Larkin, Michel den Elzen, Mark Roelfsema, Andries Hof, and Hannes Böttcher. 2012. "Greenhouse Gas Emission Reduction Proposals and National Climate Policies of Major Economies." PBL Netherlands Environmental Assessment Agency, The Hague/Bilthoven, November.

Hopewell, Kristen. 2015. "Different Paths to Power: The Rise of Brazil, India, and China at the World Trade Organization." *Review of International Political Economy* 22 (2): 311–338.

Houghton, R. A. 2005. "Above-Ground Forest Biomass and the Global Carbon Balance." *Global Change Biology* 11: 945–958.

Howard, Brian Clark. 2014. "Chile Scraps Huge Patagonia Dam Project after Years of Controversy." *National Geographic*, June 10.

Hoyos, N., J. Escobar, J. C. Restrepo, A. M. Arango, and J. C. Ortiz. 2013. "Impact of the 2010–2011 La Niña Phenomenon in Colombia, South America: The Human Toll of an Extreme Weather Event." *Applied Geography* 39: 16–25.

Hultman, Nathan E., Simone Pulver, Leticia Guimarães, Ranjit Deshmukh, and Jennifer Kane. 2012. "Carbon Market Risks and Rewards: Firm Perceptions of CDM Investment Decisions in Brazil and India." *Energy Policy* 40: 90–102.

Hurrell, Andrew, and Sandeep Sengupta. 2012. "Emerging Powers, North-South Relations and Global Climate Politics." *International Affairs* 88 (3): 463–484.

INPE (Brazilian National Institute for Space Research). 2010. "Desmatemento Cai." *INPE.* http://www.inpe.br/ingles/index.php.

INPE (Brazilian National Institute for Space Research). 2014a. "Monitoramento da Floresta Amazônica Brasileira por Satélite." *INPE.* http://www.obt.inpe.br/prodes/index.php.

INPE (Brazilian National Institute for Space Research). 2014b. "Taxas anuais do desmatamento: 1988 até 2013." *INPE.* http://www.obt.inpe.br/prodes/prodes_1988_2013.htm. Instituto de Pesos e Medidas do Estado de Sao Paol (IPEM-SP). N.d. "Botijão de Gás – Parte Um – Como tudo começou." *IPEMSP.* https://ipemsp.wordpress.com/botijao-de-gas.

Inter-American Development Bank (IDB). 2014. "The Next Global Breadbasket: How Latin America Can Feed the World: A Call to Action for Addressing Challenges and Developing Solutions." Inter-American Development Bank, Washington, DC.

Inter-American Dialogue. 2012. "Remaking the Relationship: The United States and Latin America." A Report of the Sol M. Linowitz Forum. Inter-American Dialogue, Washington, DC, April.

Inter-American Dialogue. 2013. "Was Maduro's Recent Trip to China a Success?" *Latin America Adviser*, September.

International Energy Agency (IEA). 2007. *World Energy Outlook 2007.* http://www .worldenergyoutlook.org/media/weowebsite/2008-1994/weo_2007.pdf.

International Energy Agency (IEA). 2012. "CO_2 Emissions from Fuel Combustion Highlights." OECD/IEA, Paris.

International Energy Agency. 2014. *World Energy Outlook 2014.* http://www .worldenergyoutlook.org/resources/energydevelopment/energyaccessdatabase.

International Institute for Sustainable Development (IISD). 2009. "ENB on the Side: A Special Report on Selected Side Events at the Fifteenth Conference of the Parties to the UN Framework Convention on Climate Change (UNFCCC) and Fifth Meeting of the Parties to the Kyoto Protocol (COP 15 and COP/MOP 5)." Copenhagen, Denmark, December 7–18. http://www.iisd.ca/climate/cop15/enbots/8dece.html.

International Monetary Fund (IMF). 2010. "World Economic Outlook: Rebalancing Growth." IMF, Washington, DC.

IPCC. 2014. "Working Group II, Fifth Assessment Report." Inter-governmental Panel on Climate Change.

"ITT Block Will Go for International Bidding." 2009. *Diario Hoy,* January 9.

Jacobs, Michael. 2014. "The Real Lima Deal." *Project Syndicate,* December 15. http:// www.project-syndicate.org/commentary/lima-global-climate-change-agreement -by-michael-jacobs-2014-12.

Jácome, Francine. 2011. "Petrocaribe: The Current Phase of Venezuela's Oil Diplomacy in the Caribbean." Policy Paper 40, Friedrich Ebert Stiftung, November.

Jarrín, Sofía. 2014. "Ecuador: ¡Lo Logramos! Despite All Odds, Activists Present Signatures Needed to Save Yasuní." *Upside Down World,* April 14. http://upsidedownworld .org/main/ecuador-archives-49/4794-ilo-logramos-despite-all-odds-activists-present -signatures-needed-to-save-yasuni.

Javeline, Debra. 2014. "The Most Important Topic Political Scientists Are Not Studying: Adapting to Climate Change." *Perspectives on Politics* 12 (2): 420–434.

Karl, Terri. 1996. *The Paradox of Plenty: Booms and Petro-States.* Berkeley: University of California Press.

Kartha, Sivan, and Peter Erickson. 2011. "Comparison of Annex 1 and Non-Annex 1 Pledges under the Cancun Agreements." SEI Working Paper 2011-06.

Keohane, Robert, and David Victor. 2011. "The Regime Complex for Climate Change." *Perspectives on Politics* 9 (1): 7–23.

Kirkland, Emily. 2012. "Indigenous Knowledge 'Invaluable' for Andean Adaptation." Thomson Reuters Foundation, July 11.

Kirsch, Alison. 2014. "Comparing Latin American Energy Policies on Climate Change: Toward an Ambitious and Equitable International Climate Agreement." Brown University, November.

Klein, Peter. 2014. "Flooded with Meaning: Contested Development and Brazil's Belo Monte Dam." Draft PhD thesis, Brown University.

Kozloff, Nikolas. 2011. "Time for a New Geopolitical Climate Bloc: Part 1." *Al Jazeera*, December 12. http://www.aljazeera.com/indepth/opinion/2011/12/201112121312 4688507.html.

Lagos, Ricardo. 2014. "Latin America's Climate Vanguard." *Project Syndicate*, November 3.

Lagos, Ricardo. 2014. Presentation at April 2014 conference at the Watson Institute, Brown University.

Lagos, Ricardo, Blake Hounshell, and Elizabeth Dickinson. 2012. *The Southern Tiger: Chile's Fight for a Democratic and Prosperous Future*. London: Palgrave Macmillan.

Lagos, Ricardo, and Osvaldo Rosales. 2013. "Globalization and Development Options." *Brown Journal of World Affairs* 19 (2): 11.

Lander, Edgardo. 2010. "Reflections on the Cochabamba Climate Summit." *Transnational Institute*, April 29. http://www.tni.org/article/reflections-cochabamba -climate-summit.

Larco, Pablo. 2012. "Climate Change Policies Struggle to Break into Development Plans in Latin America." *Intercambio Climático*.http://intercambioclimatico.com/ en/2012/07/25/climate-change-policies-struggle-to-break-into-development-plans -in-latin-america/#sthash.8LjPEYtA.dpuf.

La Rovere, E. L., C. B. S. Dubeux, A. O. Pereira, Jr., and W. Wills. 2013. "Brazil beyond 2020: From Deforestation to the Energy Challenge." *Climate Policy* 13 (suppl. 1): 71–86.

Larrea, Carlos. 2012. "Ecuador's Yasuní-ITT Initiative: A Critical Assessment." Paper presented at the Environmental Governance in Latin America and the Caribbean (ENGOV) Project Conference, Brasilia, June 13 and 16.

La Vina, Antonio G.M., Lawrence Ang & Joanne Dulce. 2011. "The Cancun Agreements: Do They Advance Global Cooperation on Climate Change?" Foundation for International Environmental Law and Development (FIELD). http://www.field.org .uk/files/the_cancun_agreements__lavina_ang_dulce_0.pdf.

Leahy, Joe. 2014. "Women of 2014: Marina Silva, Presidential Candidate." *Financial Times*, December 12.

Lee, Phil. 2010. "World Peoples Climate Change Summit Ends." *Friends of the Earth International*, April 24. http://www.foei.org/en/blog/world-peoples-climate-change-summit-ends.

Lemos, Maria Carmen, and J. Timmons Roberts. 2008. "Environmental Policymaking Networks and the Future of the Amazon." *Philosophical Transactions of the Academy of the Royal Society* 363 (1498): 1897–1902.

Lewis, Simon L., Paulo M. Brando, Oliver L. Phillips, Geertje M. F. van der Heijden, and Daniel Nepstad. 2011. "The 2010 Amazon Drought." *Science* 331 (6017): 554.

Lovgren, Stefan. 2008. "Costa Rica Aims to Be First Carbon-Neutral Country." *National Geographic* 7 (March). http://news.nationalgeographic.com/news/2008/03/080307-costa-rica.html.

Lynas, Mark. 2011. "Thirty 'Cartagena Dialogue' Countries Work to Bridge Kyoto Gap." *Mark Lynas*. http://www.marklynas.org/2011/03/thirty-cartagena-dialogue-countries-work-to-bridge-kyoto-gap.

Mabey, Nick. 2012. "Understanding Europe's Unexpected Durban Success." *E!Sharp*, January 2012. http://esharp.eu/big-debates/the-green-economy/16-understanding-europe-s-unexpected-durban-success.

MacArthur Foundation. 2011. "Conservation and Sustainable Development: International Programs, Strategic Framework 2011–2020." Chicago, March.

Macedo, Marcia N., Ruth S. DeFries, Douglas C. Morton, Claudia M. Stickler, Gillian L. Galford, and Yosio E. Shimabukuro. 2012. "Decoupling of Deforestation and Soy Production in the Southern Amazon during the Late 2000s." *Proceedings of the National Academy of Sciences of the United States of America* 109 (4): 1341–1346.

Madden, Keith W. 2014. "The Promise and Purpose of the Rights of Nature." Thesis, Brown University. *MAPS*. http://www.mapsprogramme.org/projects/peru-projects/plancc-overview.

Magrin, G., C. Gay García, D. Cruz Choque, J. C. Giménez, A. R. Moreno, G. J. Nagy, C. Nobre, and A. Villamizar. 2007: "Latin America." In *Climate Change 2007: Impacts, Adaptation and Vulnerability. Contribution of Working Group II to the Fourth Assessment Report of the Intergovernmental Panel on Climate Change*, ed. M. L. Parry, O. F. Canziani, J. P. Palutikof, P. J. van der Linden, and C. E. Hanson, 581–615. Cambridge: Cambridge University Press.

Magrin, Graciela, and José Marengo, coordinating lead authors. 2014. "Central and South America." In *Intergovernmental Panel on Climate Change (IPCC), Working Group 2 (WGII), Fifth Assessment Report (AR5)*, chapter 27. IPCC, March.

Malamud, Andrés. 2011. "A Leader without Followers? The Growing Divergence between the Regional and Global Performance of Brazilian Foreign Policy." *Latin American Politics and Society* 53 (3): 1–24.

Mallett-Outtrim, Ryan. 2013. "Venezuela's National Assembly Votes to Make Chavez's Six-Year-Plan Law." *Venezuelanalysis.com*, December 4. http://venezuel analysis.com/news/10214.

Marien, Nele. 2011. "Making Durban Climate Negotiations Understandable. Part 2, LCA or the Implementation of the Convention." World People's Conference on Climate Change and the Rights of Mother Earth, December 4. http://pwccc.wordpress. com/2011/12/04/making-durban-climate-negotiations-understandable-part-2-lca-or-the-implementation-of-the-convention.

Marshall, Claire. 2008. "Costa Rica Bids to Go Carbon Neutral." *BBC News*, August 11. http://news.bbc.co.uk/1/hi/world/americas/7508107.stm.

Martin, Pamela L. 2011. "Global Governance from the Amazon: Leaving Oil Underground in Yasuní National Park, Ecuador." *Global Environmental Politics* 11 (4): 22–42.

Martins, Alejandra. 2011. "América Latina, 'la menos escéptica sobre el cambio climático.'" *BBC Mundo*, November 16. http://www.bbc.co.uk/mundo/noticias/ 2011/11/111115_clima_escepticismo_am.shtml.

Masters, Lesley. 2012. "What Future for BASIC? The Emerging Powers Dimension in the International Politics of Climate Change Negotiations." *Institute for Global Dialogue* 95: 1–5.

Mata, Luis Jose, and Carlos Nobre. 2006. *Background Paper: Impacts, Vulnerability and Adaptation to Climate Change in Latin America*. Bonn: United Nations Framework Convention on Climate Change.

"McDonald's Pledges to Help Protect the Amazon." 2006. *Greenpeace*. http://www .greenpeace.org/usa/en/news-and-blogs/news/mcvictory.

McGlade, Christophe, and Paul Ekins. 2015. "The Geographical Distribution of Fossil Fuels Unused When Limiting Global Warming to 2°C." *Nature* 517: 187–190.

McKibben, Bill. 2012. "Global Warming's Terrifying New Math." *Rolling Stone*, July 19.

Meadows, Donella, Jorgen Randers Dennis, and William Behrens. 1972. *Limits to Growth*. New York: Signet.

Méndez, Rafael. 2012. "La tercera vía latinoamericana en la negociación del clima." *El País*, December 5. http://sociedad.elpais.com/sociedad/2012/12/05/ actualidad/1354699047_259945.html.

"Mexican President Presents National Climate Change Strategy." 2013. *OOSKAnews*, June 6. https://www.ooskanews.com/story/2013/06/mexican-president-presents-national-climate-change-strategy_156296.

"Mexico's President Enacts Climate Change Legislation." 2012. *BBC News*, June 6. http://www.bbc.com/news/world-latin-america-18345079.

Ministério da Ciência, Tecnologia e Inovacão (MCTI), Secretaria de Políticas e Programas de Pesquisa e Desenvolvimento (SEPED), and Coordenação Geral de Mudanças Globais de Clima (CGMC). 2013. "Estimativas anuais de emissões de gases de efeito estufa no Brasil." República Federativa do Brasil.

Ministério de Minas e Energia. 2014. "PDE 2023: Brasil será grande produtor de petróleo mantendo matriz energética limpa." Ministério de Minas e Energia, September 10. http://www.epe.gov.br/Estudos/Paginas/PlanoDecenaldeEnergia-PDE/MMEcolocaPlanoDecenal.aspx.

Morales, Evo. 2010a. "Potencias deben pagar deuda ecológica: Evo Morales." *TeleSur TV*, December 9. http://www.youtube.com/watch?v=LyAxny2kCGA&feature=related.

Morales, Evo. 2010b. "Convoca Evo Morales a cumbre climática de pueblos." Presidential invitation, January 7. http://www.youtube.com/watch?v=iN8JnXm3WM8.

Moreno, Luis Alberto. 2011. "The Decade of Latin America and the Caribbean: A Real Opportunity." Remarks by the president of the Inter-American Development Bank (IDB) at the book launch of *The Decade of Latin America and the Caribbean: A Real Opportunity*, Buenos Aires, Argentina, May 27.

Moseley, Mason, and Matthew Layton. 2013. "Prosperity and Protest in Brazil: The Wave of the Future for Latin America?" AmericasBarometer *Insights: 2013*, number 93. Latin American Public Opinion Project, Vanderbilt University, Nashville. http://www.vanderbilt.edu/lapop/insights/IO893en.pdf.

Müller, Benito, Niklas Höhne, and Christian Ellermann. 2009. "Differentiating (Historic) Responsibilities for Climate Change." *Climate Policy* 9 (6): 593–611.

Muñoz, Alain. 2010. "La Conferencia Climática de Cancún según Ricardo Lagos." *Intercambio Climático*, December 6. http://www.intercambioclimatico.com/2010/12/06/la-conferencia-climatica-de-cancun-segun-ricardo-lagos/http://www.intercambioclimatico.com/2010/12/06/la-conferencia-climatica-de-cancun-segun-ricardo-lagos.

Nachmany, M., S. Fankhauser, T. Townshend, M. Collins, T. Landesman, A. Matthews, C. Pavese, K. Rietig, P. Schleifer, and J. Setzer. 2014. *The GLOBE Climate Legislation Study: A Review of Climate Change Legislation in 66 Countries*. 4th ed. London: GLOBE International and the Grantham Research Institute, London School of Economics.

Najam, Adil. 2004. "The View from the South: Developing Countries in Global Environmental Politics." In *The Global Environment: Institutions, Law, and Policy.* 2nd ed., ed. Regina Axelrod, David Downie, and Norman Vig, 225–243. Washington, DC: CQ Press.

Najam, Adil. 2005. "Developing Countries and Global Environmental Governance: From Contestation to Participation to Engagement." *International Environmental Agreement: Politics, Law and Economics* 5 (3): 303–321.

Nepstad, Daniel, David McGrath, Claudia Stickler, Ane Alencar, Andrea Azevedo, Briana Swette, Tathiana Bezerra, Maria DiGiano, João Shimada, Ronald Seroa da Motta, Eric Armijo, Leandro Castello, Paulo Brando, Matt C. Hansen, Max McGrath-Horn, Oswaldo Carvalho, and Laura Hess. 2014. Slowing Amazon Deforestation through Public Policy and Interventions in Beef and Soy Supply Chains. *Science* 344 (6188): 1118–1123.

Ocampo, José Antonio. 2014."The Return of Slow Economic Growth." *World Bank* (blog), May 15. http://blogs.worldbank.org/latinamerica/return-slow-economic-growth.

O'Connor, James. 1979. *The Fiscal Crisis of the State.* Piscataway, NJ: Transaction.

"Oil-Rich Venezuela Inks Plans to Curb Spiraling Emissions." 2012. *Point Carbon,* August 17.

Okereke, Chuks. 2007. *Global Politics of the Environment.* Routledge.

Olsson, Marie, Aaron Atteridge, Karl Hallding, and Joakim Hellberg. 2010. "Together Alone? Brazil, South Africa, India, China (BASIC) and the Climate Change Conundrum." Policy Brief, Stockholm Environment Institute.

Opio, C., P. Gerber, A. Mottet, A. Falcucci, G. Tempio, M. MacLeod, T. Vellinga, B. Henderson, and H. Steinfeld. 2013. "Greenhouse Gas Emissions from Ruminant Supply Chains: A Global Life Cycle Assessment." UN Food and Agriculture Organization, Rome.

Oppenheimer, Andres. 2014. "Latin America 2015: A Leaderless Region." *Miami Herald,* December 31.

Organization of American States (OAS). 2015. "Member States of the OAS." *OAS.* http://www.oas.org/en/member_states/default.asp#Cuba.

Organization of Petroleum Exporting Countries (OPEC). 2011. *Development Cooperation Report 2011.* Paris: OPEC.

Organization of Petroleum Exporting Countries (OPEC). n.d. "Venezuela Facts and Figures." *OPEC.* http://www.opec.org/opec_web/en/about_us/171.htm.

Ortiz, Diego Arguedas. 2014. "Climate Change Legislation Faltering in Costa Rica." *IPS News,* May 21.

Ott, Hermann E., Bernd Brouns, Wolfgang Sterk, and Bettina Wittneben. 2005. "It Takes Two to Tango: Climate Policy at COP10 in Buenos Aires and Beyond." *Journal for European Environmental and Planning Law* 2 (2): 84–91.

Pádua, José Augusto. 2002. *Um sopro de destruição: pensamento politico e critica ambiental no Brasil escratista (1786–1888)*. Rio de Janeiro: Jorge Zahar.

Painter, James. 2008. "Peru Aims for Zero Deforestation." *BBC News*, December 7. http://news.bbc.co.uk/2/hi/7768226.stm.

Painter, James. 2009. "¿Escuchan a Latinoamérica en Copenhague?" *BBC Mundo*, December 10. http://www.bbc.co.uk/mundo/ciencia_tecnologia/2009/12/091130 _1457_copenhague_latam_gtg.shtml.

Painter, James. 2010. "Reflexiones bajo el sol de Cancun." *BBC Mundo*, December 10. http://www.bbc.co.uk/mundo/noticias/2010/12/101206_james_painter_blog_ cancun_wbm.shtml.

Park, Siwon. 2011. "The Power of Presidency in UN Climate Change Negotiations: Comparison between Denmark and Mexico." Working Paper No. 12-01, Korea Environment Institute, Seoul, August.

Paterson, Matthew. 1996. *Global Warming and Global Politics*. London: Routledge. PBL Netherland Environmental Assessment Agency. 2013. "Trends in Global CO_2 Emissions: 2013 Report." The Hague. http://edgar.jrc.ec.europa.eu/news_docs/pbl -2013-trends-in-global-co2-emissions-2013-report-1148.pdf.

"People's Agreement of Cochabamba." 2010. World People's Conference on Climate Change and the Rights of Mother Earth, Cochabamba, Bolivia, April 22. https:// pwccc.wordpress.com/2010/04/24/peoples-agreement.

Peru Ministerio del Ambiente. 2009. "Posición del Perú: XV Cumbre Mundial de Cambio Climático 2009." Lima, October 30.

Peru Ministerio del Ambiente. 2010. *El Perú y el Cambio Climático. Segunda Comunicación Nacional del Perú ante la Convención Marco de las Naciones Unidas sobre Cambio Climático 2010*. Lima: Ministerio del Ambiente.

Peru Ministerio del Ambiente. 2013. "Christiana Figueres y ministro Pulgar-Vidal participaron en Diálogos con la Sociedad Civil Latinoamericana camino a la COP20." Peru Ministry for the Environment, May 14. http://www.minam.gob.pe/notas-de -prensa/christiana-figueres-y-ministro-pulgar-vidal-participaron-en-dialogos-con -la-sociedad-civil-latinoamericana-camino-a-la-cop20.

"Peru Says Deforestation on the Rise, up 80 Percent from 2001." 2014. *Reuters*, December 3.

"Peruvian Government Guts Power of Its Environmental Ministry, Amid Protests." 2014. *ClimateWire*, July 22.

Pineda, Cecilia. 2012. "The Cartagena Dialogue for Progressive Action: A Bridge to the North-South Divide." Thesis, Brown University.

Plautz, Jason. 2014. "Brazil's Dangerous Climate Spiral." *National Journal*, October 31. http://www.nationaljournal.com/energy/brazil-s-dangerous-climate-spiral-20141031.

Pompermeyer, Malori J. 1984. "Strategies of Private Capital in the Brazilian Amazon." In *Frontier Expansion in Amazonia*, ed. M. Schmink and C. Wood, 419–428. Gainesville: University of Florida Press.

Porras, I., M. Miranda, D. Barton, and A. Chacón-Cascante. 2012. *De Rio a Rio+: Lecciones de 20 años de experiencia en servicios ambientales en Costa Rica*. London: International Institute for Environment and Development.

Prada, Paolo. 2013. "Brazil Government Figures Confirm Spike in Amazon Deforestation." *Reuters*, November 14.

Prada, Paulo, and Maria Carolina Marcello. 2013. "One Million March across Brazil in Biggest Protests Yet." *Reuters*, June 20.

Prebisch, Raul. 1950. *The Economic Development of Latin America andIits Principal Problems*. New York: United Nations.

Presidency of Peru. 2014. "Medidas presentadas por el Ejecutivo y aprobadas por el Congreso fortalecerán liderazgo del Perú destaca mandatario." *Presidencia*. http://www.presidencia.gob.pe/medidas-presentadas-por-el-ejecutivo-y-aprobadas-por-el-congreso-fortaleceran-liderazgo-del-peru-destaca-mandatario.

Pulgar-Vidal, Manuel. 2014. "Minister of Environment of Peru and COP20 President's talk at Brown University." *YouTube*, July 16. https://www.youtube.com/watch?v=OTnI42opLNg.

Pulver, Simone, Nathan Hultman, and Leticia Guimarães. 2010. "Carbon Market Participation by Sugar Mills in Brazil." *Climate and Development* 2 (3): 248–262.

Purvis, Nigel. 2010. "Cancun and the End of Climate Diplomacy." *GMF Blog. German Marshall Fund of the United States*, November 22. http://blog.gmfus.org/2010/11/22/cancun-and-the-end-of-climate-diplomacy.

Putnam, Robert D. 1988. "Diplomacy and Domestic Politics: The Logic of Two-Level Games." *International Organization* 42 (3): 427–460.

Rabatel, A., B. Francou, A. Soruco, J. Gomez, B. Cáceres, J. L. Ceballos, R. Basantes, et al. 2013. "The Current State of Glaciers in the Tropical Andes: A Multi-century Perspective on Glacier Evolution and Climate Change." *Cryosphere Discuss.* 6: 2477–2536.

Rachman, Gideon. 2010. "America Is Losing the Free World." *Financial Times*, January 4.

Raman, Meena. 2010. "Bolivia Submits Cochabamba Conference Outcome to UNFCCC." *World People's Conference on Climate Change and the Rights of Mother Earth (PWCCC)*, April 30. http://pwccc.wordpress.com/2010/04/30/bolivia-submits -cochabamba-conference-outcome-to-unfccc.

Ramírez, Socorro. 2013. "Regionalism: The Pacific Alliance." *Americas Quarterly* 7 (2). http://www.americasquarterly.org/content/regionalism-pacific-alliance.

Randerson, James, and David Batty. 2010. "Cancún Climate Change Summit: The Deal as It Happened." *The Guardian*, December 11. http://www.guardian. co.uk/environment/blog/2010/dec/11/cancun-climate-change-conference -2010-global-climate-talks.

"La Red ARA reitera su posición sobre la preCOP social y el compromiso del estado venezolano con el cambio climático." 2014. *Red ARA Venezuela*, November 2. http:// red-ara-venezuela.blogspot.com/2014/11/la-red-ara-reitera-su-posicion-sobre-la .html.

Reid, Michael. 2014. *Brazil: The Troubled Rise of a Global Power*. New Haven, CT: Yale University Press.

Renewable Energy Policy Network for the Twenty-first Century (REN21). 2014. *Renewables 2014 Global Status Report*. Paris: REN21 Secretariat.

Riahi, K., F. Dentener, D. Gielen, A. Grubler, J. Jewell, Z. Klimont, V. Krey, et al. 2011. "Energy Pathways for Sustainable Development." In *Global Energy Assessment: Toward a Sustainable Future*, ed. L. Gomez-Echeverri, T. B. Johansson, N. Nakicenovic, and A. Patwardhan. Laxenburg: International Institute for Applied Systems Analysis (IIASA); New York: Cambridge University Press.

"Rio to Stage 2016 Olympic Games." 2009. *BBC Sport*, October 2.

Rittl, Carlos. 2014. "Brazil Should Take Lead on Climate, Not Just Broker Talks." *The Guardian*, December 4. "Road Space Rationing." 2015. *Wikipedia*. http:// en.wikipedia.org/wiki/Road_space_rationing.

Roberts, J. Timmons. 2007. "Globalization: The Environment and Development Debate." *The Politics of the Environment*. , ed. Chukwumerije Okereke, 3–18. London: Routledge.

Roberts, J. Timmons. 2011. "Multipolarity and the New World (Dis)order: US Hegemonic Decline and the Fragmentation of the Global Climate Regime." *Global Environmental Change* 21 (3): 776–784.

Roberts, J. Timmons, Amy Bellone-Hite, and Nitsan Chorev. 2015. *The Globalization and Development Reader*. 2nd ed. London: Wiley/Blackwell.

Roberts, J. Timmons, and Guy Edwards. 2012. "A New Latin American Climate Negotiating Group: The Greenest Shoots in the Doha Desert." *The Brookings*

Institution, December 12. http://www.brookings.edu/blogs/up-front/posts/2012/12/12-latin-america-climate-roberts.

Roberts, J. Timmons, and Bradley C. Parks. 2007. *A Climate of Injustice: Global Inequality, North-South Politics, and Climate Policy.* Cambridge, MA: MIT Press.

Roberts, J. Timmons, and Nikki Demetria Thanos. 2003. *Trouble in Paradise: Globalization and Environmental Crises in Latin America.* London: Routledge.

Roberts, Timmons, Lisa Viscidi, Milena Gonzalez, Ramiro Fernández, and Ana R. Ríos. 2014. "What Will COP20 Mean for Climate Change and Energy?" Latin American Advisor, Inter-American Dialogue, July. http://www.thedialogue.org/page.cfm?pageID=32&pubID=3645.

Rogers, Tim. 2009. "Costa Rica's President: It's Not Easy Staying Green." *Time,* October 10.

Rojas, Andrés 2011. "Petrocaribe genera pérdidas y Pdvsa reduce regalías." *El Nacional* (Caracas), July 29, 4.

Romero, Simon. 2008. "Venezuela: Russian Navy Arrives for Joint Exercises." *New York Times,* November 26.

Romero, Simon. 2015. "Climatologists Balk as Brazil Picks Skeptic for Key Post." *New York Times,* January 6. http://www.nytimes.com/2015/01/07/world/americas/climatologists-balk-as-brazil-picks-skeptic-for-key-post.html?smid=pl-share.

Rootes, Christopher, Anthony Zito, and John Barry. 2012. "Climate Change, National Politics and Grassroots Action: An Introduction." *Environmental Politics* 21 (5): 677–690.

Rosales, Osvaldo, and Sebastián Herreros. 2013. "Trade and Trade Policy in Latin America and the Caribbean: Recent Trends, Emerging Challenges." *Journal of International Affairs* 66 (2): 31.

Rudel, Thomas K., J. Timmons Roberts, and JoAnn Carmin. "Political Economy of the Environment." *Annual Review of Sociology* 37: 221–238.

Rueda, Amelia. 2013. "Gobierno separa a asesora en cambio climático que criticó nueva refinería." June 11. http://www.ameliarueda.com/gobierno-separa-a-asesora-en-cambio-climatico-que-critico-nueva-refineria-en-nuestra-voz.

Ryan, D. 2012. "Informe sobre el Estado y Calidad de las Políticas Públicas sobre Cambio Climático y Desarrollo en América Latina: Sector Agropecuario y Forestal. Plataforma Climática Latinoamericana." http://intercambioclimatico.com/wp-content/uploads/Informe-regionalfinal-oct.pdf.

Salerno, Claudia. 2009. "Delegación de Venezuela en Copenhague no acepta documento del COP15." *TeleSur en Vivo.* http://www.youtube.com/watch?v=CPKCoeROnUg.

Santos Calderón, Juan Manuel. 2010. Speech delivered at the Sixty-fifth Session of the United Nations General Assembly, General Debate, New York, September 24.

Saraiva, Miriam Gomes. 2011. "Brazilian Foreign Policy: Causal Beliefs in Formulation and Pragmatism in Practice." In *Latin American Foreign Policies Between Ideology and Pragmatism*, ed. Gian Luca Gardini and Peter Lambert. New York: Palgrave Macmillan.

Schnaiberg, Allan, and Kenneth Alan Gould. 1994. *Environment and Society: The Enduring Conflict*. New York: St. Martin's Press.

Shifter, Michael. 2012. "The Shifting Landscape of Latin American Regionalism." *Journal of Current History* 111 (742): 56–61.

Shixue, Jiang, personal communication with the authors, January, 2014.

Shortell, Paul. 2014. "China's Hydropower Development in Latin America." *Inter-American Dialogue*, June 24. http://chinaandlatinamerica.com/2014/06/24/chinas-hydropower-development-in-latin-america.

Shultz, Jim. 2010. "Latin America Finds a Voice on Climate Change: With What Impact?" *North American Congress on Latin America*, July–August.

Silva, Eduardo. 2012. "Environment and Sustainable Development." In *Routledge Handbook of Latin American Politics*, ed. Peter Kingstone and Deborah J. Yashar. London: Routledge.

Sinnott, Emily, John Nash, and Augusto de la Torre. 2010. *Natural Resources in Latin America and the Caribbean: Beyond Booms and Busts*. Washington, DC: World Bank.

Sistema de la Integración Centroamericana (SICA). 2011. "Declaración de Comalapa Adoptada en la Cumbre Extraordinaria de Jefes de Estado y de Gobierno de los Países del Sistema Interamericano de la Integración Centroamericana." *SICA*, October 25.

Sistema Economica Latinoamericano y del Caribe (SELA). 2010. "Latin American and Caribbean Economic System, Food Security and Food Prices in Latin America and the Caribbean: Current Situation and Prospects." Thirty-sixth Regular Meeting of the Latin American Council, Caracas, Venezuelan, October.

Smith, Tierney. 2014. "Mexico Unveils Plans for 33 Percent Renewable Energy by 2018." *The Global Call for Climate Action*, May 22. http://tcktcktck.org/2014/05/mexico-unveils-plans-33-renewable-energy-2018/62176.

Socialist Voice. 2010. If the Climate Were a Bank, It Would Already Have Been Saved: Latin America vs. Imperialism at the Copenhagen Climate Summit. Chippendale, Australia: Socialist Alliance.

Solón, Pablo. 2010a. "Intervention of Pablo Solon in the COP16." Cancun, Mexico, December 11.

Solón, Pablo. 2010b. "Why Bolivia Stood Alone in Opposing the Cancún Climate Agreement." *The Guardian*, December 21. http://www.guardian.co.uk/environment/cif-green/2010/dec/21/bolivia-oppose-cancun-climate-agreement.

Solón, Pablo. 2011. "There Must Be Coherence between What We Do and What We Say." *Hoy es Todavía*, September 29. http://pablosolon.wordpress.com/2011/09/29/there-must-be-coherence-between-what-we-do-and-what-we-say.

Soto, Nayllivis N. N. 2004. "Alternativa Bolivariana para las Américas: Una propuesta histórico política al ALCA." *Geoenseñanza* 9 (1): 57–73.

Stalley, Phillip. 2013. "Principled Strategy: The Role of Equity Norms in China's Climate Change Diplomacy." *Global Environmental Politics* 13 (1): 1–8.

Steinberger, J. K., and J. T. Roberts. 2010. "From Constraint to Sufficiency: The Decoupling of Energy and Carbon from Human Needs, 1975–2005." *Ecological Economics* 70 (2): 425–433.

Steinberger, Julia K., J. Timmons Roberts, Glen P. Peters, and Giovanni Baiocchi. 2012. "Pathways of Human Development and Carbon Emissions Embodied in Trade. "*Nature Climate Change* 2 (2): 81–85.

Sterk, Wolfgang Christof Arens, Urda Eichhorst, Florian Mersmann, and Hanna Wang-Helmreich. 2011. "Processed, Refried: Little Substance Added, Cancún Climate Conference Keeps United Nations Process Alive but Raises More Questions Than It Answers." *Wuppertal Institute*, March. http://www.wupperinst.org/uploads/tx_wibeitrag/COP16-report.pdf.

Steve, David, and Alejandra Kubitschek Bujones. 2013. "A Laboratory for Sustainable Development? Latin America, the Caribbean, and the Post-2015 Development Agenda." Center on International Cooperation, New York University.

Stoett, Peter. 2012. *Global Ecopolitics: Crisis, Governance, and Justice*. Toronto: University of Toronto Press.

Sustainable Development Solutions Network (SDSN) and Institute for Sustainable Development and International Relations (IDDRI). 2014. *Pathways to Deep Decarbonization*. Paris: SDSN and IDDRI.

Tanner, Thomas, and Jeremy Allouche. 2011. "Towards a New Political Economy of Climate Change and Development." *IDS Bulletin* 42 (3): 1–14.

Tegel, Simeon. 2013. "Latin America's Oil Rush Means More Climate Change." *GlobalPost*, November 13. http://www.globalpost.com/dispatch/news/regions/americas/131112/latin-american-oil-carbon-emissions-climate-change.

Teixeira, Izabella. 2014. "Speech at the Twentieth Conference of the Parties (COP20)." United Nations Framework [LA1] Conference on Climate Change (UNFCCC). Lima, Peru, December.

Teixeira, Marcelo. 2012. "Mexico's Climate Law to Face Challenge under New President." *Reuters*, July 24. http://www.reuters.com/article/2012/07/24/us-mexico -climate-policy-idUSBRE86N0A220120724.

Teixeira, Marcelo. 2014. "Brazil Carbon Emissions Rise for the First Time Since 2004: Report." *Reuters*, November 19. http://www.reuters.com/article/2014/11/19/ brazil-carbon-rising-idUSL6N0T93SL20141119.

Tollefson, Jeff. 2013. "Brazil Reports Sharp Drop in Greenhouse Emissions." *Nature*, June 5. Nature Publishing Group. http://www.nature.com/news/brazil-reports -sharp-drop-in-greenhouse-emissions-1.13121.

Tompkins, Emma L. 2005. "Planning for Climate Change in Small Islands: Insights from National Hurricane Preparedness in the Cayman Islands." *Global Environmental Change* 15 (2): 139–149.

Tong, David. 2014. "Five Key Take-Aways from Last Week's Social PreCOP." *Global Call for Climate Action*, November 13. http://tcktcktck.org/2014/11/david-tong-five -key-take-aways-last-weeks-social-precop/65273.

Toni, Ana. 2014. "Dilma Speech at the UN Climate Summit: More of the Same." *Nivela*, September 24.

Trennepohl, Natascha. 2010. "Brazil's Policy on Climate Change: Recent legislation and Challenges to Implementation." In *Carbon and Climate Law Review, CCLR 3/2010*, ed. Michael Mehling, 271–277. Berlin: Lexxion.

"Tres propuestas para consulta popular por Yasuní." 2013. *El Universo*, August 22. http://www.elcomercio.com/actualidad/tcel-nego-apelacion-yasunidos.html.

Trinkunas, Harold. 2014. "Changing Energy Dynamics in the Western Hemisphere: Impacts on Central America and the Caribbean." Policy Brief. Brookings Institution, Washington, DC, April.

United Nations Development Programme (UNDP). 2007. *Human Development Report 2007/2008: Fighting Climate Change: Human Solidarity in a Divided World*. Basingstoke: Palgrave Macmillan.

United Nations Development Programme (UNDP). 2010. *Regional Human Development Report for Latin America and the Caribbean 2010: Acting on the Future—Breaking the Intergenerational Transmission of Inequality*. New York: United Nations.

United Nations Development Program–Peru (UNDP-Peru). 2014. "Por primera vez, los pueblos indígenas estarán presentes en la COP." *UNDP-Peru*, July 4. http://www.pe.undp.org/content/peru/es/home/presscenter/articles/2014/07/04/ por-primera-vez-los-pueblos-ind-genas-estar-n-presentes-en-la-cop.

United Nations Environment Programme (UNEP). 2010. *Latin America and the Caribbean: Environmental Outlook, GEO LAC 3*. Panama City: UNEP. *Gateway to the UN's*

System Work on Climate Change. http://visit.un.org/wcm/content/site/climatechange/lang/en/pages/gateway/the-negotiations.

United Nations Environmental Program (UNEP) and Technical University of Denmark (DTU). 2014. "CDM Projects by Host Region." *UNEP/DTU.* http://cdmpipeline.org/cdm-projects-region.htm

United Nations Environment Programme (UNEP) and Amazon Cooperation Treaty Organization (ACTO). 2009. *Environment Outlook in Amazonia: GEO Amazonia.* Nairobi: UNEP and ACTO.

United Nations Food and Agriculture Organization (FAO). 2005. *Global Forest Resource Assessment.* Rome: FAO.

United Nations Food and Agriculture Organization (FAO). 2011. *State of the World's Forest.* Rome: FAO.

United Nations Partners on Climate Change (UNPCC). n.d. "The Negotiations." *Gateway to the UN's System Work on Climate Change.* Web. http://visit.un.org/wcm/content/site/climatechange/lang/en/pages/gateway/the-negotiations.

United States Energy Information Administration (EIA). 2013. "Overview: Brazil Is the Eighth-Largest Total Energy Consumer and Tenth-Largest Producer in the World." *EIA.* http://www.eia.gov/countries/cab.cfm?fips=BR.

United States Energy Information Administration (EIA). 2014. "Energy Reform Could Increase Mexico's Long-term Oil Production by 75%." *Today in Energy.* http://www.eia.gov/todayinenergy/detail.cfm?id=17691.

VanWey, Leah K., et al. 2013. "Socioeconomic Development and Agricultural Intensification in Mato Grosso." *Philosophical Transactions of the Royal Society B: Biological Sciences* 368 (1619): 20120168.

Venezuela, Government of. 2005. "Primera comunicación nacional en cambio climático de Venezuela." *Caracas, Venezuela.* http://unfccc.int/resource/docs/natc/vennc01.pdf.

Venezuela, Government of. 2012. "Views from Venezuela on Area (A) of the Work Programme in Accordance with Decision 8/CP.17, Paragraph 1, Sharing of Information and Expertise, Including Reporting and Promoting Understanding of Positive and Negative Impacts of Response Measures." People's Ministry of Oil and Mining, Venezuela, Presentation and Submission made to COP18, November.

Venezuela, Ministerio de Relaciones Exteriores de la República Bolivariana de. 2011. "Boletin." Oficina de Coordinación de Prensa, Caracas.

Vergara, Walter. 2011. "The Economic and Financial Costs of Climate Change in Regional Economies in Latin America." Paper presented at the Seventeenth Conference of the Parties (COP17) on the Economic and Financial Costs of Climate

Change in Regional Economies in Latin America and the Caribbean Event, Durban, South Africa, December 7.

Vergara, Walter, Claudio Alatorre, and Leandro Alves. 2013a. "Rethinking Our Energy Future: A White Paper on Renewable Energy for the 3GFLAC Regional Forum." Discussion Paper 292. Washington DC: Inter-American Development Bank, June.

Vergara, Walter, A. M. Deeb, A. M. Valencia, R. S. Bradley, B. Francou, A. Zarzar, A. Grünwaldt, and S. M. Haeussling. 2007. "Economic Impacts of Rapid Glacier Retreat in the Andes." *EOS* 88 (25): 261–268.

Vergara, Walter, Hiroki Kondo, Edgar Pérez Pérez, Matías Méndez Pérez Juan, Victor Magaña Rueda, Constanza Martínez Arango María, Franklyn Ruíz Murcia José, Jesús Avalos Roldán Grinia, and Enrique Palacios. 2007. "Visualizing Future Climate in Latin America: Results from the Application of the Earth Simulator." Latin America and Caribbean Region Sustainable Development Working Paper 30. Washington, DC: World Bank.

Vergara, Walter, Ana R. Rios, Luis M. Galindo, Pablo Gutman, Paul Isbell, Paul H. Suding, and Joseluis Samaniego. 2013b. *The Climate and Development Challenge for Latin America and the Caribbean: Options for Climate Resilient Low Carbon Development.* Washington, DC: Inter-American Development Bank.

Vergara, Walter, Ana R. Rios, Paul Trapido, and Hector Malarín. 2014. "Agriculture and Future Climate in Latin America and the Caribbean: Systemic Impacts and Potential Responses." Discussion Paper No. IDB-DP-329. Washington, DC: Inter-American Development Bank.

Vidal, John. 2009. "Rich and Poor Countries Blame Each Other for Failure of Copenhagen Deal." *The Guardian*, December 18.

Villamizar, Alicia, and Guy Edwards. 2014. "Venezuela Needs Low-Carbon Action—Not Greenwash." *Thomson Reuters Foundation*, August 26. http://www.trust.org/item/20140826095421-gopl5.

Villanueva, Jorge. 2014. "NEWS: The Road to Low-Emissions Development—Peru's PlanCC Identifies More Than Seventy Mitigation Options." *Climate and Development Knowledge Network*, July 23. http://cdkn.org/2014/07/news-the-road-to-low-emission-development-project-plancc-identified-more-than-70-mitigation-options-for-peru.

Viola, Eduardo. 1995. *Meio Ambiente, Desenvolvimento e Cidadania: Desafios para as Ciencias Socias.* São Paulo: Cortez.

Viola, Eduardo. 2013. "Brazilian Climate Policy since 2005: Continuity, Change and Prospective." Centre for European Policy Studies Working Document No. 373. February.

Viola, Eduardo, Matias Franchini, and Thais Lemos Ribeiro. 2012. *Sistema internacional de hegemonia conservadora: Governanca global e democracia na era da crise climática.* Brasilia: Universidade de Brasília.

Viola, Eduardo J., and Kathryn Hochstetler. 2015. "Brazil in Global Climate Governance." In *Research Handbook on Climate Governance,* ed. Karin Bäckstrand and Eva Lövbrand, Cheltenham: Edward Elgar.

Waldron, Anthony W., Arne O. Mooers, Daniel C. Miller, Nate Nibbelink, David Redding, Tyler S. Kuhn, J. Timmons Roberts, and John L. Gittleman. 2013. "Targeting Global Conservation Funding to Limit Immediate Biodiversity Declines." *Proceedings of the National Academy of Sciences of the United States of America* 110 (29): 12144–12148. www.pnas.org/cgi/doi/10.1073/pnas.1221370110.

Wallace, Scott. 2013. "Ecuador Scraps Plan to Block Rain Forest Oil Drilling." *National Geographic,* August. http://news.nationalgeographic.com/news/2013/08/130819 -ecuador-yasuni-rain-forest-oil-drilling-environment-science.

Watkins, Kevin. 2013. "This Gamble on Carbon and the Climate Could Trigger a New Financial Crisis." *The Guardian,* August 2. http://www.theguardian.com/ business/2013/aug/02/carbon-tax-investment-market-timebomb.

Watts, Jonathan. 2013. "Ecuador Approves Yasuní National Park Oil Drilling in Amazon Rainforest." *The Guardian,* August 16.

Watts, Jonathan. 2014. "Brazil's 'Chainsaw Queen' Appointed New Agriculture Minister." *The Guardian,* December 24. http://www.theguardian.com/world/2014/ dec/24/brazil-agriculture-katia-abreu-climate-change.

Wolf, Eric R. 1982. *Europe and the People without History.* Berkeley: University of California Press.

World Bank. 2009a. "Fast-Track Recovery from Crisis Likely for Latin America." *World Bank,* May 13. http://web.worldbank.org/WBSITE/EXTERNAL/COUNTRIES/LACE XT/0,contentMDK:22178840~pagePK:146736~piPK:146830~theSitePK:258554,00 .html.

World Bank. 2009b. *Low Carbon, High Growth.* Washington, DC: World Bank.

World Bank. 2010. "Globalized, Resilient, Dynamic: The New Face of Latin America and the Caribbean." Office of the Chief Economist for the Latin America and the Caribbean Region, Washington, DC: World Bank.

World Bank. 2012a. "Agriculture Exports from Latin America and the Caribbean." Washington, DC: World Bank.

World Bank. 2012b. "Inclusive Green Growth in Latin America and the Caribbean." Washington, DC: World Bank.

World Bank. 2013. *World Development Indicators 2013*. Washington, DC: World Bank.

World Bank. 2014. "Brazil Overview." *World Bank*. http://www.worldbank.org/en/country/brazil/overview.

"World People's Climate Change Summit Ends." 2010. *Friends of the Earth International*. http://www.foei.org/en/blog/world-peoples-climate-change-summit-ends.

World People's Conference on Climate Change and the Rights of Mother Earth. 2010. "Call." *PWCCC*, January 15. http://pwccc.wordpress.com/2010/01/15/call/#more-12.

World Resources Institute (WRI). 2012. *CAIT (Climate Analysis Indicators Tool) Version 9.0*. Washington, DC: WRI.

World Resources Institute (WRI). 2014. Climate Analysis Indicators Tool (CAIT) 2.0.

World Resources Institute (WRI). n.d. "Intended Nationally Determined Contributions. http://www.wri.org/indc-definition.

World Wildlife Fund (WWF). 2013. "Peru towards COP 20: Ministry of the Environment and WWF Sign a Foint Commitment." *WWF*, November 11. http://wwf.panda.org/?212237/perutowardscop20ministryoftheenvironmentandwwfsignajoin tcommitment.

Ximenes, Antonio. 2008. "El ministro Carlos Minc tiene el plan nacional sobre el cambio climático en Poznan na Polonia." *Fundación Amazonas Sustentable*, December 11. http://fas-amazonas.org/2008/12/ministro-carlos-minc-apresenta-plano-nacional-de-mudancas-climaticas-do-brasil-em-poznan-na-polonia/?lang=es.

Yale School of Forestry and Environmental Sciences. 2013. "Environmental Policy Index." http://epi.yale.edu/the-metric/2014-epi-discussed-costa-ricas-media.

"Yasunidos buscará respuesta de la CIDH a dos solicitudes." 2014. *El Universo*, December 28. http://sitio.yasunidos.org/en/press/blog/28-prensa/blog-english/119-ethics-tribunal-ecuador-violated-rights-tribunal-marked-one-year-anniversary-of-decision-to-drill-yasuni.html.

Yeo, Sophie. 2014a. "Climate Activists Divided over Fossil Fuel Phase Out." *RTCC: Responding to Climate Change*, November 7. http://www.rtcc.org/2014/11/07/climate-activists-divided-over-fossil-fuel-phase-out.

Yeo, Sophie. 2014b. "Peru UN Climate Talks Chair Admits Time Running Out for Deal." *RTCC: Responding to Climate Change*, June 9. http://www.rtcc.org/2014/06/09/peru-un-climate-talks-chair-admits-time-running-out-for-deal.

Zahran, Sammy, Eunyi Kim, Xi Chen, and Mark Lubell. 2007. "Ecological Development and Global Climate Change: A Cross-National Study of Kyoto Protocol Ratification." *Society and Natural Resources* 20: 37–55.

Index

Politics, Science, and the Environment

Peter M. Haas and Sheila Jasanoff, editors